PLURALISM AND INEQUALITY IN QUEBEC

PLURALISM AND INEQUALITY IN QUEBEC

Leslie S. Laczko

University of Toronto Press
Toronto

PLURALISM AND INEQUALITY IN QUEBEC
Copyright © 1995 by Leslie S. Laczko

Published in Canada by University of Toronto Press Inc.
First published by St. Martin's Press.

Canadian Cataloging in Publication Data is available from the publisher.

ISBN 0-8020-0892-5 (hardcover)
ISBN 0-8020-7875-3 (paperback)

First Edition: December 1995
10   9   8   7   6   5   4   3   2   1

CONTENTS

LIST OF TABLES

PREFACE

The historian William McNeill (1986) has noted that the experience of polyethnicity, as well as the ambivalence that comes with having a larger and more powerful neighbor, has been a part of the lives of people in most human societies throughout recorded history. He was speaking of Canada as a whole, but the point is just as true of Quebec, and perhaps even more so. In this sense, the ongoing restructuring of power relationships within Quebec is of universal significance.

Sometime in late 1995, Quebec is due to hold its second referendum on political sovereignty in the last decade and a half. In the first referendum, held in 1980, a proposal to negotiate greater sovereignty for Quebec was defeated by a margin of 60 to 40 percent, with a narrower "no" margin of 52 to 48 percent among Francophone voters. Although the exact date and the wording of the referendum question are not yet known, the upcoming contest promises to be just as close as the earlier one, with a similar split along language lines. Once again, it appears likely that Francophone voters will be nearly evenly divided between the yes and no camps, with Quebec's various non-Francophone minorities overwhelmingly on the no side. In this context, this study of Quebec's changing internal cleavages is potentially valuable not only for what it reveals about the structure of Quebec society, but also for the lessons it might hold for other multilingual and polyethnic societies that are undergoing social change.

Funding for data collection and analysis for this study was provided to the author by the Quebec government's Conseil de la langue française and by the University of Ottawa's Faculty of Graduate Studies and Research. Most of the data analyzed in this work were initially gathered through the auspices of the Social Sciences and Humanities Research Council of Canada and its predecessors, the Canadian Unity Information Office, and the Canadian federal government's Multiculturalism and Citizenship Department. I would like to thank the latter two agencies for making their data sets available for further analysis, and the taxpayers of Canada who ultimately made all of these surveys possible.

Thanks are also due to the staff members of several government departments, libraries, and other organizations in Ottawa, Montreal, and Quebec City who provided help in locating useful information. As is customary in works that involve secondary analyses of survey data, it should be mentioned that neither the original sponsoring agencies nor the survey firms that carried out the fieldwork are responsible for the interpretations that are put forth here.

Students in my courses in both French and English at the University of Ottawa have stimulated my thinking over the years. The university is a microcosm of Canada's linguistic duality, and I am pleased to acknowledge that my outlook has been shaped by this special bilingual milieu.

For their efficient assistance with the manuscript and tables, my thanks to Francine D'Amour, Ginette Rozon, Paulette Arsenault and Martine Sarazin.

My thanks also to Simon Winder of St. Martin's Press, for the invitation and opportunity to publish this research for both a Canadian and international audience, as well as to the other members of the press's staff.

This book combines research done at different periods in recent years. Most of the empirical analyses reported in part II were first presented as part of a doctoral dissertation over a decade ago. I am indebted to Maurice Pinard for his guiding role at that stage, and for making the 1970 and 1977 data sets available for further analysis.

In addition, several colleagues and former teachers took the time to provide valuable feedback and much-appreciated encouragement. I would like to thank all of them, and especially Raymond Breton, Hubert Guindon, Arlie Hochschild, and R. A. Schermerhorn.

Critical readings of the penultimate version of the manuscript were generously provided by Nicole Bousquet and Raymond Murphy. I am grateful for their suggestions, and regret not being able to follow all of them. Responsibility for all errors and weaknesses remains entirely my own.

The spirit of nationality becomes intensified by restraint, for it is only under threatened deprivation that its value is fully appreciated. Air is indispensable, and yet only those who have gasped for want of it, really appreciate its supreme value. Nationality has been as free as air to English-speaking Canadians, and that is why they have seldom stopped to consider what it means to them and what its deprivation means to others.

—William Henry Moore (1919)

. . . the method of variation, however complex the results flowing from it, is the basic method of science. The main hindrance to the advance of sociology is that it has been insufficiently used. Practical, ideological, and aesthetic orientations have focussed attention elsewhere. But what advances have occurred have come largely from its use. . . . Careful measurement is less important than making the attempt at comparative analysis.

—Randall Collins (1975)

. . . the province of case studies is not to judge conclusively between competing versions of explanation, but to illuminate their contingent and partial character.

—Donald Horowitz (1980)

INTRODUCTION

The historical relationship between French and English Canada has been an uneasy and complicated one. Notwithstanding the complexity of the relationship, the level of conflict between the two linguistic communities has varied greatly from decade to decade over the past two hundred years. Furthermore, however intense communal conflict in Quebec, the heartland of French Canada, may appear to have been in recent years, it is clearly less severe than that which has beset a great many other plural societies in recent times.

An understanding of contemporary Quebec, then, can best be gained by viewing the workings of modern Quebec society as one case among many, as one element of a larger set of societies in which similar arrangements exist and/or have existed. In other words, intense conflict between communal segments is a possibility in all plural societies—that is, societies divided into separate cultural segments each with its own set of institutions. How can one account for the incidence of communal conflict? Its intensity? Its distribution in time and space?

These questions can be approached from two opposite directions. On the one hand, one can attempt to identify factors that are conflict producing. On the other hand, one can direct one's attention toward factors that might reduce the probability of conflict. The public policy implications of these two approaches are aptly expressed by an early American political theorist who wrote: "There are two methods of curing the mischiefs of faction: the one, by removing its causes; the other, by controlling its effects" (*The Federalist* [ca. 1788] 1966:2). This study of contemporary Quebec will draw on both of these approaches—the first explicitly, the second more implicitly.

CANADA'S PLURALISM IN WORLD PERSPECTIVE

The contemporary world system contains many more ethnic and linguistic groupings than it does independent states. Most states are to some extent polyethnic, and homogeneous states are relatively rare. Some states have more internal ethnic and linguistic diversity or pluralism than others. Which are they? If we take the world's existing states as our units of analysis, the overall relationship between national development and degree of pluralism is an inverse one. The more-developed states tend to have less internal pluralism, while the less-developed states have much more of it. Most of the world's highly plural societies are in the less-developed parts of the world (Haug 1967). In particular, the more-developed countries of the world are the ones that are the most likely to be linguistically homogeneous (Pool 1969; Fishman 1968).

In general terms, the overall inverse relationship between development and pluralism, whereby higher levels of socioeconomic development are associated with lower levels of pluralism, is consonant with the broad predictions of the modernization perspective in its many guises. In this view, the more developed countries of the world have less internal pluralism because the forces of industrialization, modern communications, the outward expansion of the modern state from center to internal peripheries, as well as the passage of time have all combined to reduce cultural and linguistic diversity within state boundaries throughout the developed world.

Canada occupies an exceptional position in this overall inverse relationship. Not only is Canada's level of pluralism very high, it is extremely high once one takes the country's level of development into account. Canada, then, has a level of ethnic and linguistic pluralism that is much higher than that which would be expected, given its very high level of social and economic development. This pattern is revealed if quantitative cross-national indicators are used to examine the relationship. Figure 1.1 shows the regression scatterplot of the overall inverse relationship between cultural pluralism (as measured by the index of "ethno-linguistic fractionalization" of the *Atlas Narodov Mira*) and socioeconomic development (as measured by GNP per capita).[1] As I have argued in more detail elsewhere, it is clear from Figure 1.1 that Belgium, Switzerland, Canada, and the United States all display a higher than expected degree of pluralism, and that Canada is in fact the most extreme outlier of them all (Laczko 1994).

Canada's pluralism is even higher than that of the other exceptional cases because it is simultaneously the setting for more types of pluralism than the other cases are. Canada combines the dynamics of overarching linguistic segmented pluralism, which it shares with Switzerland and Belgium, with the dynamics of aboriginal peoples and continual immigration, which it shares with the United States and other new world societies. Put differently, Canada combines a European-style, highly segmented

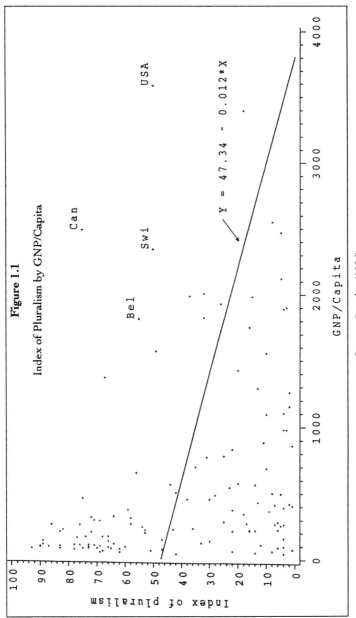

Figure 1.1

Index of Pluralism by GNP/Capita

Source: Laczko (1994)

linguistic pluralism pattern with a new world, settler society "aboriginals and immigrants" pattern. This book is about how these different types of pluralism come together in Quebec.

QUEBEC AS A SETTING

Canada's high level of pluralism is in a sense disproportionately concentrated in Quebec, which contains about one-fourth of Canada's population. Indeed, Quebec is at the heart of Canada's high level of pluralism, which has its origins in Quebec. French speakers constitute about one-fourth of Canada's population, and they are concentrated in Quebec. Quebec is in a sense a mini-Canada with its French-English proportions reversed, since over 80 percent of Quebec's population has been French-speaking throughout this century. In the relatively decentralized Canadian federal political system, Quebec has been called a quasi state that is the western world's most powerful subnational government (Dion 1992). The high level of development has tied French and English Canada together in a complex industrial economy, and a long history of federalism and parliamentary democracy has wed them in a common political culture. The uneven nature of the development process in Quebec also initially reinforced the privileged position of Quebec's English-speaking minority. This in turn fueled the rise of modern Québécois nationalism and an independence movement that is now stronger than ever.

Since the 1960s, the rise of a modern state-based Québécois nationalism has substantially transformed the historical pattern of the relationship between Quebec's French-speaking majority and its English-speaking minority. A growing number of French Canadians have come to define themselves as Québécois, a term which denotes their new majority status as members of a distinct French-speaking society. Long-standing inequalities between Francophones and Anglophones have been almost totally eliminated, and a new era of Francophone dominance has been established in most areas of social life. On most socioeconomic indicators, historic French-English inequalities have evened out.

In the political arena, Francophones, especially since the election of the Parti Québécois in 1976, have come to assert their majority status, and Francophone institutions have taken over many tasks, such as the integration of immigrants, formerly carried out by English-language institutions. At the same time, Anglophones have had to adjust to a new minority status with much reduced influence. In addition, Quebec's various aboriginal and immigrant communities have been under pressure to increase their use of the French language and to redefine themselves as Quebec minorities, distinct from their brethren in the rest of Canada. For the past two decades, almost every area of public life in Quebec has been affected by the competition between Québécois nationalism, which views Québec as well on its way toward the goal of independent statehood, and the federal vision of Quebec as a central part of a bilingual Canada.

Whatever the outcome of Canada's current and ongoing constitutional crisis, it is unlikely that the status quo will be maintained. The particular tenor of modern Québécois nationalism cannot be understood without looking at the past, and specifically at the uneven way the development process shaped the evolution of the French- and English-language communities and their institutions. It is the particular pattern of segmentation and inequality between French- and English-language communities that is currently being restructured in Quebec, and this book, with the help of theoretical thinking about the development process and its impact on intergroup relations, attempts to locate this restructuring in the light of broader world trends.

This is a book about Quebec society as a whole and not just about French Canadians, who have historically been an ethnic minority within Canada but a majority within Quebec. The focus is on the relationship between Quebec's French-speaking majority and its non-French-speaking minorities, how it is perceived and structured, and how it has been changing over the past two decades. The work has both empirical and theoretical aims and is directed at a general sociological audience.

On one level, this book, which is based mainly on public opinion survey data covering the period from 1970 to the 1990s, is about the way beliefs and perceptions are distributed within Quebec society. The empirical goal of this study is to investigate systematically the Quebec population's beliefs and perceptions about some key issues concerning relations between the Francophone (French-speaking) and Anglophone (English-speaking) communities in Quebec. Detailed analyses of survey data on intercommunal relations are still as rare in Quebec as they are in most other segmented societies. Consequently, it is hoped that the descriptive account of the belief system of Quebec society that is presented in this study will in itself be of some utility to the social science community.

It is especially important to examine beliefs, attitudes, and perceptions because they provide clues to latent and potential conflict. Although ethnic conflicts have often involved untold levels of violence and bloodshed, there can be little doubt that Canada's linguistic cleavage has evolved in a relatively peaceful manner. In broad comparative terms, then, the

Canadian experiment must be viewed as a great success. Still, as many early and more recent observers have remarked, deep resentments are present and are rarely far from the surface. This study will examine some of the structural sources of latent conflict that have been operating in Quebec society.

KEY ISSUES

The maintenance of a distinct French-language society in North America has been a central concern and dominant theme throughout French Canada's history. In recent decades, however, the goal of Quebec nationalists has moved far beyond mere survival, to encompass the creation of a modern French-language society with its own full range of institutions and to eliminate the long-standing inequalities between the Francophone majority and the Anglophone minority. In this work I present a series of secondary analyses of survey questions bearing on these two issues. The data are drawn from a number of surveys carried out since 1970. I investigate the Quebec population's orientations toward cultural pluralism and its perceptions of communal inequalities between French and English.

Regarding the normative dimension of contentious issues, Coser has pointed out that "legitimacy is a crucial intervening variable without which it is impossible to predict whether feelings of hostility arising out of an unequal distribution of privileges and rights actually lead to conflict" (Coser 1956:37).

In other words, the population's *perceptions* and *evaluations* of the degree of cultural pluralism and of the degree of inequality between communal groups can be viewed as an important intervening variable, linking the objective degree of cultural pluralism and inequality between cultural segments with the probability of conflict between them. Therefore, knowledge of the perceptual structure will improve the accuracy of our prediction of the probability of communal conflict, however limited and incomplete the initial grounds for such a prediction might be.[2]

THEORETICAL OBJECTIVES

In addition to the empirical goals, and just as important, the study is guided by theoretical interests. Perceptions and beliefs never exist in a vacuum. They are rooted in social structures, and these structures are themselves the product of historical and developmental forces. The central concern of this study is to examine the relationship between the development process, cultural and structural pluralism, group inequalities, and group conflict.[3]

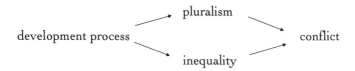

How does the social and economic development process shape the degree of cultural and structural pluralism in a given society? The degree of group inequality? How is the process modified by historical and contextual factors? How do changes in these dimensions change the probability of ethnic conflict? As we shall see, different theoretical perspectives make different predictions about how these dimensions tie together.

Despite the renewed interest, in most parts of the world, in ethnic and communal conflict, little work has been done in systematically evaluating the relative utility of different theoretical approaches. A major exception is Hechter's (1975) important longitudinal study of the evolution of the relationship between the Celtic minorities and the English majority in the United Kingdom, which was explicitly designed as a test of the functionalist and internal colonialism perspectives on ethnic change. As critics of Hechter's work have pointed out, one of its main limitations was that it provided no direct evidence for the central thesis linking internal colonialism and reactive ethnic protest. What was missing was some evidence about how actors actually perceived their situation.

The theoretical aim of this study is similar to Hechter's. The study tries to address some of the same theoretical questions by using public opinion survey data gathered over the last few decades in Quebec. By linking macrosociological development processes to micro-level attitudes and perceptions, this work provides us with precisely the kind of information that was missing in Hechter's study. It is hoped that the study will cast light on certain distinctive features of Quebec society. At the same time, it should also add to our general understanding of the processes at work in intergroup relations in other societies.

The methodological strategy adopted here is that of treating the internal workings of Quebec society as a black box that needs to be examined. We know that the inverse relationship between development and degree of pluralism within states is consonant with the predictions of long-dominant perspectives on national development, but that Canada is an important positive outlier in this overall pattern. The development process has indeed exerted downward pressure on Canada's internal ethnic and linguistic pluralism, but, at the same time, special features of the Canadian context have kept the level of pluralism high, even as the society has become highly developed. This makes Quebec an important case to examine in detail. It is a context in which we can observe close up the tug-of-war, as it were, between developmental pressures that reduce ethnic and linguistic diversity, and other features of the society that keep the level higher than it otherwise would be. An in-depth look at the workings of Quebec society will tell us more about the general developmentalist perspective, as well as about the Quebec case.

This approach is analogous to that adopted by Rueschemeyer, Stephens, and Stephens (1992) in their work on capitalist development and democracy. They begin with the finding that in analyzing cross-sectional data, there is a direct positive relationship between economic development and democracy, in keeping with the predictions of the modernization perspective. At the same time, these authors note that, if one examines changes over time within quite a number of countries, capitalist development hardly seems to lead to more democracy. To investigate the apparent anomaly between the results of the cross-sectional data and the results of longitudinal case studies, specific cases around the world are then analyzed as black boxes within which the relationship between development and democracy is scrutinized in detail.

COVERAGE

This work deals with the period from 1970 to the early 1990s. The 1960s was an eventful decade in Quebec. It was marked by the first wave of administrative reforms carried out by the Quebec government to change the traditional structures of Quebec society. Subsequent decades were marked by further waves of state intervention. In one form or another, almost all of them were aimed at correcting the historical inequalities between Quebec's Anglophone minority and its Francophone majority, which were the result of an uneven development process, and at transforming many traditional institutions into the state-based institutions of a modern society. Against the backdrop of these structural changes, we shall examine how individual Quebecers perceive cultural differences and group inequalities, and how the changing macro-level power relationship is reflected in perceptions at the micro level. This is our central focus, rather than the content of the legislative measures or even the institutional changes themselves.

A word about the book's coverage of social change is in order. The past few decades have been marked by a number of important political events, including the October Crisis in 1970, the election of the Parti québécois in 1976, the 1980 Referendum on Sovereignty, the patriation of the constitution from Westminster in 1982, the failure of the Meech Lake Accord in 1990, and the defeat of the Charlottetown Accord by referendum in October 1992. These developments have been and continue to be analyzed extensively by other scholars, and I will not be providing a detailed narrative account of these important political milestones. Our interest is more specifically focused on the impact that the changing political climate and state policies have had on the changing majority-minority relationship. This is a book about Quebec's internal stratification system, how and why it has been evolving and how Quebecers' micro-level perceptions and experiences can be understood as part of a much bigger picture.

WHAT FOLLOWS

The study is organized into three parts, followed by the conclusion. A background to modern Quebec history and a guide to the theoretical debate are provided in part I. An in-depth study of the belief system of Quebec society in 1970, after the decade of the Quiet Revolution, is the topic of part II. This portrait focuses on two key issues in the French-English relationship: cultural differences and group inequalities. Then, in part III, changes in the structure of perceptions from 1970 through the 1990s are examined.

This work is a case study, but one that is designed and executed in such a way as to facilitate comparisons of Quebec with other segmented and polyethnic societies. As Smelser (1976) has pointed out, the comparative method can be viewed as an application of the general scientific strategy of controlling and examining variations. This book attempts to interpret several sources of variation within a common framework. The two broad theoretical perspectives considered, the functionalist perspective and the communal competition perspective, both make predictions about changes in the pattern of intergroup relations in the course of industrialization and modernization. Their differing predictions will be culled from the literature, and contrasts between the two broad perspectives will be examined (chapter 2). The predictions will then be assessed by examining (1) variations in perceptions among various subgroups within Quebec society, using cross-sectional data (chapters 3-6), (2) variations in perceptions over time using trend data (chapter 7), (3) variations between the structure of perceptions of pluralism and inequality and the structure of perceptions of other cleavages (chapter 8), and (4) variations between the Quebec case and other settings (chapter 9).

Chapter 1 sketches the background to contemporary intergroup relations in Quebec, and describes the origins of the special set of institutional arrangements so aptly conveyed by the title of Hugh MacLennan's novel *Two Solitudes*. The industrialization of Quebec, led as it was by English-Canadian and American interests, affected Quebec's French and English communities in different ways, and this uneven development pattern initially reinforced the institutional separation and English domination of the economy that has long been a central grievance of Québécois nationalism. However, since the 1970s, through a new combination of state and market forces, this old order has been very substantially broken down. Chapter 1 provides an overview of the objective conditions of Quebec's stratification system, and of how these conditions have been changing.

Chapter 2 sets forth the debate between the functionalist and communal competition perspectives and shows how they lead to rather different expectations about intergroup relations in the course of a society's social and economic development. In particular, I try to pinpoint differences in the way these two perspectives conceive of the degree of cultural pluralism, the degree of group inequality, and the consequences of these for intergroup conflict.

Part II, which is divided into chapters 3 through 6, examines the structure of the Quebec population's belief system, using cross-sectional data from the 1970 Quebec Social Movements Study (appendix A).

In chapter 3 the empirical investigation of orientations toward cultural pluralism in Quebec begins. Definitions of the main dimensions of cultural pluralism are given, and the available measures of each are presented. Then, hypotheses derived from the functionalist and communal competition perspectives are put to the test. This is done by examining the shape of the distribution of orientations and also by examining the role of language group membership.

Chapter 4 investigates the way stratification variables *within* each linguistic community shape the structure of orientations toward cultural pluralism. The findings are assessed in light of competing hypotheses derived from the two perspectives.

Chapter 5 examines the structure of perceptions of French-English inequalities in Quebec. Measures of perceptions of communal inequalities in several areas are introduced, and their distribution in Quebec society is presented. Here again, competing hypotheses are put to the test.

Chapter 6 deals with the relationship between cultural pluralism and group inequality. The nature of this relationship is yet another area in which the two theoretical perspectives lead to different expectations, and these are evaluated by examining the linkages between *perceptions* of the two dimensions.

Part III, which is divided into chapters 7 through 9, examines different aspects of Quebec's evolving pluralism.

Chapter 7 focuses on changes in perceptions over time in recent Quebec history. The overall power relationship between French and English has shifted substantially in recent decades, and this chapter assesses the ways in which this is, and is not, reflected in the perceptual structure.

Chapter 8 explores the changing relationship between Quebec's overarching linguistic communities and its aboriginal and immigrant communities.

Chapter 9 looks at Quebec's restructuring in comparative perspective. No detailed comparisons are carried out, but a number of summary comparative observations are put forth, in view of facilitating future systematic research.

Finally, the conclusion sets forth some lessons that can be learned from the Quebec case, and discusses possible future trends.

A NOTE ON TERMINOLOGY AND DATA SETS

The terminology commonly used to denote ethnic and linguistic groups in Quebec and Canada has been in flux over the past few decades, and the changes are suggestive of the underlying dynamics. In Quebec, until the early 1970s, it was common to refer to French Canadians and English Canadians. In the 1970s, use of these terms gave way to the now-widespread use of Francophones and Anglophones, which clearly puts more emphasis on language rather than ethnic origin. A little later, in elite public discourse, the new terms "cultural communities" and "Allophones" appeared as new labels for those of other ethnic and linguistic backgrounds. The actual usage of these terms is, of course, fraught with ambiguity, but the changes themselves are an important clue in our story. This shift in vocabulary, which has its parallels in many polyethnic societies undergoing social change, is important to keep in mind when we reach parts II and III: each of the various data sets that are analyzed here is a product of its own time and place and uses the cultural categories and vocabulary of the period. The data sets are described in appendix A.

Part I

HISTORICAL AND
THEORETICAL BACKGROUND

INTRODUCTION TO PART I

I have mentioned that Canada's level of ethnic and linguistic pluralism is exceptionally high, compared to that of other developed societies. Compared to the United States, for example, which is an outlier in its own right, Canada has a higher proportion of native peoples and more legal types of native people, more French-English dualism (both French and English are official languages, and two types of legal systems are used, common law in most of the country and the civil code in Quebec), a higher proportion of immigrants and more symbolic recognition of immigrant ethnicity, more powerful provincial governments, and a historically greater public recognition of religion. As I have argued elsewhere, this higher level of pluralism in Canada can be traced to the Canadian state's development alongside its larger and more powerful neighbor to the south (Laczko 1994). We shall be returning to this link between a state's external environment and its degree of internal ethnic and linguistic pluralism in our concluding chapter.

Canada's high level of pluralism is concentrated in Quebec and has its roots in Quebec history. Chapter 1 provides an overview of how Quebec's historical development has led to a complex pattern of pluralism shaped by the interaction of aboriginal peoples, the French and English European-origin majority groups, as well as later immigrants. The chapter sets forth the historical context of the way Quebec's Francophone majority and Anglophone minority evolved as distinct collectivities sharing the same territory. Many changes in the intergroup relationship have taken place since 1960, and the basic parameters of Quebec's wide-ranging program aimed at reducing the historic inequalities between Francophones and Anglophones are outlined.

How can one account for the overall inverse relationship between development and pluralism? As I have mentioned, the long-dominant perspective on the development of modern societies holds that for a number of reasons, economic, technological, and political factors, as well as the passage of time, will, in the long run, combine to reduce the level of diversity and pluralism to be found within states. Chapter 2 sets out the theoretical debate between this functionalist perspective and the communal competition perspective.

1

Contemporary Quebec: The Setting

Quebec's complex ethnic and linguistic pluralism stems from the history of its aboriginal peoples and their contacts with the early French settlers, the subsequent contact of both the native peoples and the Canadians with the British, and the later ongoing interaction of all three groups with later waves of immigrants. This particular historical sequence has created three distinct axes of intergroup relations in Quebec, and indeed in all of Canada. They are (1) the relationship between aboriginal peoples and the larger society, (2) the relationship between the French and English segments of the larger society, and (3) the relationship of other immigrants and the descendants of those immigrants to the larger society. Quebec's history of double European colonization, not unlike that of South Africa, has left two groups or sets of groups with a strong sense of indigenousness, the aboriginals and the French, and two unequal European-origin segments, French and British, in the dominant larger society. Thus French Canadians in Quebec were to become simultaneously an indigenous subordinate group and a demographic majority with a wide if incomplete range of institutions.

BEGINNINGS

Ever since the territory was first "settled" by Europeans, Quebec has had a French majority, and a large majority of all French Canadians have always lived in Quebec.[1] With the Treaty of Paris in 1763, the political status of Quebec shifted from that of an overseas possession of France to that of an overseas possession of Britain. The British crown's initial goal was to transform New France into a British-style society, with British institutions, with a view toward the possible eventual absorption of the French. It planned to do this through the familiar colonial strategy of promoting British settlement. The policy was soon abandoned, however, due to the cohesiveness of the French Canadians, on the one hand, and to the geopolitical realities of the American Revolution, on the other.

Although the American Revolution is often described as the founding of a new nation out of the 13 colonies, it can also be understood as the *failure* of the new American government to establish control over *all* the British colonies in North America. Why did the French Canadian population, only recently conquered by Britain, not join the revolt of the 13 southern colonies? It has been argued that it was because of a real possibility that the French Canadian population might do so that the British crown was prompted to guarantee full autonomy and official status to the French language, French civil law, and the Catholic religion in the Quebec Act of 1774, passed just before the American Revolution. The British crown became the "protector" of the French language, the French civil code, and the Catholic Church (Neatby 1972). Quebec's newly strengthened seigneurial and clerical elites were thus not tempted by the prospect of becoming the fourteenth colony in the new American republic (McRoberts 1988:46). These arrangements are at the origin of Quebec and Canada's linguistic dualism and of the historically important role played by the Catholic Church.

After the American Revolution, "the influx of Anglophone Loyalists," McRoberts notes, ". . . changed Quebec once and for all from a homogeneous French-Canadian society to one with a prosperous and vocal English minority" (1988:46). Faced with the new arrangements, most of New France's political and economic elite returned to France, and those who remained were soon outnumbered. As a result, the British in short order took control of the economy and the political apparatus. This marked the origin of Quebec's ethnic and linguistic division of labor. The English minority, reinforced by many waves of immigration, beginning in the 1800s, first from the British Isles and later from farther afield, was to maintain its privileged position for two centuries.

The Act of Confederation of 1867, nearly a century after the American Revolution, joined the four British North American colonies into the Dominion of Canada. The bargain struck between the four colonies and this new overarching state was at once a formula of accommodation between French and English elites, each of which had a regional organizational base and a formula for bringing existing colonial governments into a larger unit. That the provinces of Quebec, Ontario, New Brunswick, and Nova Scotia antedate the federal government by over a century is an important historical reason for the continued relative importance of provincial governments in Canada. Their importance is appreciable, even when compared to that of provincial governments in other decentralized federal systems.

For much of the first century of coexistence, contacts between French and English were kept to a minimum. The French majority was overwhelmingly rural, and the British group, which was much more urban, was concentrated in Montreal, which was becoming the most important metropolis in all of Canada. The industrialization of Quebec in the twentieth century generalized the experience of contact between the two groups in the work world. In Guindon's account,

> Anglo-Saxon industry moved into a society faced with an acute population surplus, a distinctive political and religious elite, and a developing set of institutions anchored in the rural parish. This society, politically stable, economically conservative, and technically unskilled, provided ideal conditions for investing Anglo-Saxon capitalists. They could invest their capital, open industries, and be supplied with an abundant source of unskilled labor seeking employment. The managerial and technical levels were filled, *with no protest* [emphasis added], by the incoming group, who also brought along their own set of institutions servicing their own nationals. (Guindon 1988:56)

Why no protest? One reason is that from Confederation up until the 1960s, French and British elites operated according to an unwritten understanding that Francophones would run the provincial political system and Anglophones would continue to dominate the economy while maintaining full autonomous control over English-language institutions (Levine 1990:30). These basic rules of the game were to be seriously challenged in the 1960s, and permanently changed in succeeding decades.

QUEBEC IN 1960

The industrialization of Quebec produced a society characterized by sets of parallel but unequal institutions. The educational level of Francophones was considerably below that of Anglophones. A French-Canadian business class certainly existed, yet "the fact remained that in the 1950s Quebec's economy was characterized by a predominance of non-French capital and ownership in large corporations. Even in the late 1960s only twenty-six of the 165 enterprises in the province with an annual production worth over $10 million were owned by French Canadians" (McRoberts 1988:71). On the whole, French firms tended to be smaller and more oriented toward the local Quebec market.

Until the 1960s, Francophones were underrepresented in the most modern sectors of the economy, in managerial and professional occupations, and among high income earners. One Royal Commission on Bilingualism and Biculturalism study of incomes in the 1960s revealed that those of French origin ranked tenth on a list of twelve ethnic origin categories, barely ahead of Italians and Native Indians (Gagnon 1969:235). This type of ethnic stratification, although found here in an industrial economy in a wealthy country, bears a more-than-passing resemblance to a broader pattern found in a great many colonial settings around the world.

> Overall, the disparity between backward and advanced groups was that created between indigenous and immigrant groups. . . . Descendants of immigrants and colonial immigrants swelled the ranks of advanced groups; protected peoples ended up backward. (Horowitz 1985:158, 160)

Analyses suggested that 60 percent of the income disparity between Montrealers of French and English origin could not be accounted for by differences in age and education and was due to a preference of Anglophone employers for English-Canadian candidates.[2]

In this old order of Quebec, which existed until the 1960s, English was the dominant language of business and advancement. Bilingualism was widespread, of course, but Francophones in Montreal (over 60 percent of the population), were much more bilingual than Anglophones, because they had to be. The bilingualism rate of Anglophones was low, and in interactions between members of the two groups English tended to be used more than French, often even reflecting a sort of "colonial protocol" whereby the presence of a single English-speaker in a group would dictate that the language used was to be English. The traditional linguistic rules of the game in the old order reflected the long-standing balance of power resulting from a laissez-faire attitude according to which

Francophones were free to develop their own institutions and speak their own language, and Anglophones were free to do the same. Such a situation, embodied and legitimated by a policy of official bilingualism, soon came to be denounced as permanently favoring English and Anglophones at the expense of the advancement of French and of Francophones.

THE 1960S: QUEBEC'S QUIET REVOLUTION

The term Quiet Revolution has come to be applied to two related phenomena that took place in the 1960s in Quebec, namely a set of administrative reforms carried out by the Quebec state and a period of cultural effervescence and revival during which many French Canadians experienced a violent reaction against the Catholic *survivance* ideology developed by the traditional clerical and political elite. The traditional nationalist ideology of surviving as a Catholic, French-speaking, predominantly rural people with a special agrarian vocation no longer corresponded to the needs of an urban industrial population. A new nationalist ideology developed, aimed at transforming Quebec into a modern, secular, French-speaking society. This new ideology involved a shift from the long-held view of French Canadians as a minority in the Canadian context to a new majority identity centered in Quebec. The active goal of cultural *épanouissement* (development) came to replace the defensive, past-oriented survival strategies of the traditional elites. Disaffection with the church became widespread, and Quebecers were soon to go from being the most devout Catholics in Canada to having church attendance rates below those of Catholics elsewhere in Canada (Bibby 1987:20), just as the Quebec birthrate, long the highest in Canada, soon dropped to be the lowest.

In the 1960s, a new middle class whose power base was in the provincial government became the main backer of a range of state initiatives aimed at bringing about a *rattrapage* (catching up) of Francophone institutions with Anglophone institutions and, more generally, of Quebec with the rest of the industrialized world. Quebec's educational system, which had been under the jurisdiction of church authorities, was taken over by the provincial government and was vastly expanded and modernized. The Quebec civil service grew to take over the management of health and welfare functions that had previously been in church and private hands. A number of state-owned enterprises were created, all with the express goal of increasing Francophone control over the economy, and of using the Quebec state as a bulwark or counterweight that would compensate for the historic weakness of the "national bourgeoisie." Hydro-

Quebec, the public electrical utility, became a special symbol of the new nation-building role of the Quebec state. All in all, the prevailing ideology of the 1960s was to transform Quebec into a "normal" society, where Francophone Quebecers would be *maîtres chez nous* (masters in our own house). The provincial state was to be the *moteur principal* of this process. These two shifts—the cultural shift away from traditional Catholic survival ideology, and the new focus on the state—both contributed to making language the most important marker and symbol of the emerging new identity.

THE 1970S: LANGUAGE POLICY

It has been noticed that although the French and English languages have coexisted in Quebec and Canada for over two centuries, language legislation was very infrequent until the late 1960s. In 1969, the federal government, led by Prime Minister Pierre Trudeau, enacted the Official Languages Act, which declared French and English to have equal status as the official languages of Canada. This policy was in keeping with Mr. Trudeau's aim of strengthening the Francophone and Quebec presence in the federal government and *not* granting any special status or powers to the Quebec government. It was a key part of his strategy of combatting Quebec state-building nationalists. Almost ever since it was passed, the act has been widely criticized in Quebec for not doing enough for the French language in Quebec. By consecrating the official equality of French and English, the federal policy was seen as condoning the perpetuation of the arrangements that had allowed Anglophone Quebecers to maintain their dominant position in Quebec, and to remain insulated from the Francophone majority. In the same year, the Quebec government passed its own language bill, and two further bills were to become law over the next seven years.

Bill 101, which became known as the Charter of the French Language, was enacted in 1977, following the election of the Parti Québécois in 1976. It proclaimed an end to the two-century-old policy of a bilingual Quebec. In opposition to the federal policy, it declared the goal of making Quebec an essentially French-language society: French was to be the normal language of activity in all walks of life. The legislation contained measures to reduce the status and control the growth of the Anglophone community and its institutions, beginning with the demotion of English from the status of official language. A central goal was to end the Anglophone community's position as a *minorité majoritaire* (a minority that acts like a majority). Its specific goals were to promote a Francophone presence in management jobs, to make French the main language of work, and to allow French-language schools to assume the task of educating and integrating new immigrants, something that had been disproportionately done by English-language schools for over half a century. The thrust of the educational provisions was to make French the "default" or natural language of schooling for all children, with English schooling reserved for those who qualified for an exemption. In practice, this meant that Francophones and new immigrants had to attend French schools, and over 90 percent of all public school enrollments were soon to be in French schools.

Several explanatory factors have been advanced to account for the wave of language legislation in the 1970s in Quebec. The anglicization of French minorities outside of Quebec, the declining birthrate among Francophones in Quebec, the continued domination of the English language in the private sector in Montreal, as well as the continuing trend of new immigrants appearing to prefer English schooling for their children, all contributed to the increased pressure on the government to act (D'Anglejean 1984; Laporte 1984; Rocher 1992). For all of these reasons, language has been a central political and social issue in Quebec since the early 1970s, and the differing language policies of the Quebec and federal governments have been a key element in the ongoing power struggle between the governments in Quebec and Ottawa.

QUEBEC IN THE 1980S AND 1990S

The dynamics can be better understood if we look at table 1.1, which compares Quebec with its wealthier and more powerful neighbor and longtime rival, Ontario. As the two largest and most powerful provinces in the Canadian federation, Quebec and Ontario together account for over 60 percent of Canada's population.

Quebec's Francophone majority measured by home language (82.5 percent) is larger than the percentage of its population reporting French ethnic origins (80 percent). In a more striking fashion, Ontario's Anglophone majority (86 percent) is much larger than the percentage of its population reporting British origins (53 percent). In Ontario, the percentage of the population who speak French at home (3.9 percent) is less than half the percentage of the population reporting French ethnic origins (8 percent), and the percentage of the population who speak other languages at home (10.1 percent) is only one-fourth of the percentage of the population reporting other ethnic origins (40 percent). In Ontario and in the

TABLE 1.1

POPULATION, INCOME, ETHNIC ORIGINS, AND LANGUAGE,
QUEBEC, ONTARIO, ALL OF CANADA, 1981

	Population (000s)	Per capita income index	Ethnic origins			Home language (%)		
			British	French	Other	English	French	Other
Quebec	6,369	92.5	8	80	12	12.7	82.5	4.8
Ontario	8,534	107.5	53	8	40	86.0	3.9	10.1
Canada	24,083	100.0	40	27	33	68.2	24.6	7.2

Source: Adapted from Leslie (1989:49)

other English-majority provinces, English has expanded far beyond its original British base group. In Quebec, English-speakers (12.7 percent) outnumber those of British origin (8 percent), indicating the dominant-language role that English has enjoyed for much of Quebec's history. Quebec is special in that both French and English have gained by absorbing speakers of other languages over time. The Anglophone community, however, because of its past head start and other factors, is already much more multiethnic than the Francophone community. Because of their shared dual-majority role (see Anctil 1984), neither French nor English has been able to capture the market in Quebec. The aim of the new policies can be understood as attempting to make French as hegemonic in Quebec as English has become in other provinces. One consequence and symptom of this dual-majority context is that the "language/origins ratio" for "other" language speakers (Allophones) in Quebec is much higher (4.8 : 12) than in Ontario (10.1 : 40) or in Canada as a whole (7.2 : 33). The retention of immigrant third languages is higher in Quebec than elsewhere in Canada, partly because of the presence of two competing dominant languages. I should add that, in similar fashion, the retention of aboriginal languages is higher in Quebec than elsewhere in Canada.

Table 1.2 illustrates another aspect of the population dynamics of recent decades. While the overwhelming majority of the Quebec population continues to be Quebec-born, there is a slow decline in the proportion of the Quebec population born elsewhere in Canada (which is linked to the relative decline of Montreal as a head-office center and to Anglophone out-migration from Quebec in the 1970s), and a corresponding increase in the proportion born outside Canada.

TABLE 1.2

QUEBEC POPULATION,
BY PLACE OF BIRTH, 1951–1986

Year	Born in Quebec (1)	Born elsewhere in Canada (2)	Born outside Canada (3)	Born outside Quebec (2 + 3)
1951	90.3	5.3	4.3	9.6
1961	88.4	4.2	7.4	11.6
1971	88.0	5.8	6.2	12.0
1981	88.0	3.6	8.2	12.0
1986	87.7	4.0	8.2	12.3

Source: Langlois et al. (1990:585)

Looking Ahead

Many of the indicators mentioned above show some interesting and substantial changes over the past three decades. French has become the main public language in Quebec, although English is still widely used in Montreal. Since the early 1970s, the bilingualism rate of Anglophones has more than doubled. Immigrants attend French schools. Francophone educational levels have increased, although non-Francophones are still overrepresented at the postsecondary level. Francophone-owned firms now provide 60 percent of all jobs, up from 47 percent in 1961 and 55 percent in 1978. Francophones accounted for 58 percent of all top managers in 1988, up from 31 percent in 1959. By 1985, Francophones' share of total income was nearly 80 percent, very close to their proportion in the population. The income gap between Francophones and Anglophones has narrowed, and Francophone bilinguals now earn more than Anglophone bilinguals. Once education is taken into account, Francophones had higher incomes than Anglophones in both 1980 and 1985.[3]

These, then, are the broad parameters of Quebec's state-sponsored ethnic and linguistic restructuring over the past few decades. In broad sequence, the language debates of the 1970s, the immigrant integration debates of the 1980s, and finally, the renewed attention to aboriginal issues since 1990 have highlighted the whole period. This sets the stage for a detailed look at how the Quebec population's perceptions are structured.

Our empirical analyses will begin with the overarching linguistic cleavage, then move on to examine how it has been changing, and how the new dynamics bear on immigrant integration and the aboriginal nations within Quebec. Before turning to the data (in part II), we need to review some theoretical issues.

2

Theoretical Background

Years ago, Everett C. Hughes, in his classic study *French Canada in Transition* ([1943] 1963), described the impact of industrialization on French-English relations in a small industrial community in the Eastern Townships of Quebec. What Hughes found was the kind of division of labor referred to in the previous chapter. The town's industrial structure was dominated by a few externally controlled large firms. It was manned at the upper and middle levels by migrant English-speaking personnel, and local French Canadians held the vast majority of jobs below the foreman level. Outside the workplace, the two groups went about life for the most part within linguistically separate and self-sufficient institutions. Hughes discussed the dilemma faced by the Francophone middle classes. They were being supplanted or, more accurately, sidestepped in their leadership role in the community:

> For such are the trends one finds in the cities and economies where industry is run by an outside itinerant managerial and technological elite. The local business and professional people and landholders adapt themselves to the new state of things; the little people of town and surrounding territory come up by degrees in both the industries and the local businesses and services. The process is the same whether the itinerant innovators are of the same ethnic background and religion as the local people, as in the American South or even in small cities in the North; whether, as in the Rhineland, the innovators are of the same language but different religion (Protestant) from the local people (Catholic), or whether, as in Quebec, the innovators

are strangers in religion, language, and national identity. (Hughes
[1943] 1963:xiii)

Hughes raised an important question: was the Quebec experience
indeed part of a more general pattern? His answer was affirmative. In
claiming that "the process is the same," Hughes was putting forth a
convergence argument regarding the impact of industrialization on
intergroup relations. He hoped that his analysis would "suggest comparisons with other regions where industrialization and urbanization
are complicated—as they generally are—by ethnic differences" ([1943]
1963:x). Such systematic comparisons have not been much pursued, and
will only be hinted at in this research. Like Hughes's study, this research
focuses on a single society. Unlike Hughes's study, this book is aimed
at assessing the relative utility of two broad theoretical perspectives, the
key assumptions and predictions of which have often been left implicit
and buried in the ethnographic literature. It is hoped that this systematic
test of opposing perspectives on intergroup relations in divided societies
undergoing social change will not only cast light on the Quebec case,
but also give a clearer picture of some general processes at work in
polyethnic societies. Hopefully, this formal assessment of competing
theoretical approaches will facilitate the needed systematic comparative
research in the future.

Wallace Clement (1977:32) has noted that ". . . Canada lends itself
for comparison to probably a wider range of nations than does any other
single country." This is probably no less true even if one wants to narrow
one's range and focus one's comparisons on the country's linguistic and
ethnic group relations. And students and observers of Canadian society
whose special interest is the evolution of the relationship between French
and English Canada are faced with no shortage of comparative prisms
through which both remote history and recent developments can be
assessed. Should Canada be seen as the setting of two of Louis Hartz's
new society fragment cultures (Hartz 1964)? Should the evolution of
Quebec over the last half century be seen as a process of "decolonization"?
Are Francophones in Canada in a position similar to that of the historic
"national minorities" of Central Europe? Similarly, are Francophones in
Quebec a "national majority"? Or should we restrict our comparisons to
other industrialized multilingual states, such as Belgium, Finland, and
Switzerland? What insights can be gleaned from looking at other feder-
ations, confederations, and "consociational democracies"? Such a list of
potentially useful comparative reference points could, of course, be easily

extended. The above examples are mentioned here only to make the further point that each comparative context suggests, either implicity or explicity, its own relevant theoretical and conceptual apparatus. Thus, observers of Quebec society have used quite a range of images in their studies: Protestant ethic, ethnic class, vertical mosaic, plural society, internal colonialism, and triple dependency are a few of the phrases that come to mind.

This multitude of theoretical approaches has not, however, so far been translated into systematic research designed with the goal of assessing and evaluating the relative utility of competing perspectives. The remainder of this chapter will set forth the two broad theoretical perspectives that will be used to inform our data analyses.

If we return for a moment to the conceptual framework set forth in the introduction, we can note that the various dimensions of that framework were presented, but nothing was said about how they might be related to one another. As it turns out, the functionalist perspective and the communal competition perspective offer rather different ways of looking at cultural pluralism, at group inequalities, at the links between the two, and at the links between pluralism and inequality, on the one hand, and communal conflict, on the other.

It was also mentioned that Hechter's study (1975) is one of the few recent works on intergroup relations to be explicitly designed as a test of competing theoretical perspectives. Hechter's presentation of his theoretical debate is a good starting point for our own. His study aims at testing what he refers to as the "diffusion model of national development," which includes a more specific "functional theory of ethnic change," against an "internal colonial model of national development," which includes a more specific "reactive theory of ethnic change."

These two models and sets of theories are derived from, and representative of, the broad traditions in sociological theory that are often referred to, respectively, as functionalist theory and conflict theory (see Zeitlin 1973; Turner 1974). The formulation of the competing perspectives to be evaluated in this study is similar, but not identical to that advanced in Hechter's study. There are two basic differences between Hechter's formulation of his theoretical debate and the one put forth here. The first is that the debate between the functionalist perspective and the communal competition perspective, as we conceive it in this study, is by and large broader in scope than the debate set forth by Hechter. Our conception of what is meant by the functionalist perspective and the communal competition perspective includes a broader range of authors and is, in general, more all-encompassing than the debate set forth by Hechter, and by others (Nielsen 1980; Olzak 1982).

The second difference between Hechter's theoretical debate and the one put forth here is closely related to the first. This is that while Hechter's study focused on the relationship between a culturally distinct dominant (core) region and subordinate (peripheral) regions within the United Kingdom, our study focuses on the relationship between dominant and subordinate communal groups within one geographical area, namely Quebec. As critics of Hechter's study have pointed out, his theoretical discussion of ethnic stratification patterns ("the cultural division of labor") need not be wedded to a model of regional inequality to be useful and valuable (see McRoberts 1979; Verdery 1979). The view adopted in this study is that our theoretical debate can be fruitfully compared with Hechter's once this basic difference in study design is noted.

After all of these introductory remarks have been made, what do the two theoretical perspectives have to say? Let us consider them in turn, beginning with the functionalist perspective.

The Functionalist Perspective

As already mentioned, Hechter's formulation of the functionalist perspective presents a theory of ethnic change that is imbedded in a larger diffusion model of national development. This view draws on the work of the classical social theorists, several variants of modern structural functionalism, and modern communications theory.

The basic elements of this perspective can be outlined as follows. This part of our presentation is similar, though not identical, to Hechter's because, as already mentioned, our study design is not formulated in terms of relationships between regions, but in terms of relationships between dominant and subordinate communal groups within the same region or territory. According to the functionalist perspective, the processes of industrialization and of the expansion of national state structures can both be conceived of as emanating outward from a certain center or core area and eventually extending into one or more peripheral areas. As a consequence, the social structure of the dominant group, as well as its more modern and "industrial" culture and customs, will eventually diffuse into peripheral areas. I might add that where the dominant and subordinate cultural groups share one territory, the prediction is that the social structure and culture of the dominant group will eventually diffuse down into the subordinate group:

Since the cultural forms of the periphery were evolved in isolation from the rest of the world, contact with modernizing core regions will transform these cultural forms by updating them, as it were. For a time, it has been argued, the massive social dislocation associated with industrialization and the expansion of core-periphery interaction may heighten the sense of cultural separateness in the periphery. This is because individuals and groups in the periphery are, at first, likely to cling to their customary social patterns as a refuge from the chaos of rapid social change. This is an understandable reaction of dismay in the face of an uncertain future. (Hechter 1975:8)

This perspective, which has also been labelled the developmentalist perspective or the nation-building perspective (see Ragin 1977), yields several predictions:

But such "traditional" behavior will tend to decline as the new routine of industrial life becomes perceived as more and more satisfactory in promoting the general welfare, and as initial regional differences become muted following industrialization. In the long run, the core and peripheral regions will tend to become culturally homogeneous because the economic, cultural, and political foundations for separate ethnic identification disappear. Many attributes of the regions themselves will converge following industrialization. In the third, and final, stage of national development, regional wealth should equilibrate; cultural differences should cease to be meaningful; and political processes will occur within a framework of national parties, with luck, in a democratic setting, thereby insuring representation to all significant groups. (Hechter 1975:8)

In terms of the dimensions of the conceptual framework set forth in the introduction, several key predictions are given, however summarily, in the paragraph just quoted. The first of these is that the degree of cultural pluralism within a give state will decrease with the processes of industrialization and modernization and with the expansion of a centralized state authority over an area or territory. Among most authors working in this tradition, the unspoken assumption about the process by which this occurs is that the dominant language and culture will come to be diffused among peripheral and subordinate cultural groups. The eventual consequence will be that the language and culture of the peripheral and subordinate groups will recede in importance, leaving the language and culture of the dominant group all the more dominant throughout the society, because of its adoption, to greater or lesser degrees, by the peripheral and subordinate groups. Implicit in this assumption is the further point that both components of the pluralism dimension, namely cultural differences and social separation, ought to decrease over time.

A second key prediction of the functionalist perspective that is given in the paragraph quoted above concerns the fate of inequalities between ethnic and communal groups. Such inequalities, it is predicted, will eventually be reduced, so that core and peripheral (initially culturally distinct) regions and (initially) dominant and subordinate groups will, in fact, become more equal. Thus, group inequalities ought to be reduced as a consequence of the workings of the development process, if only in the latter stages of the process.

A third key prediction of the functionalist perspective that is apparent in the above quote is that because of the predicted decline in the degree of cultural pluralism and of group inequalities over time, the conflict potential of these dimensions will be reduced as well. By and large, the prediction is that ethnic and communal conflict is likely to occur in the early stages of industrialization and modernization, while the uprooting and unsettling aspects of the processes of social change are still getting sorted out, as it were.

A corollary of this view is that if and when communal conflict *does* occur in the later stages of industrialization, it is likely to be not very intense or protracted—or perhaps to be a sort of minor latter-stage dysfunction in the operation of a modernized society and polity—due to the presence of lags, atavistic elements in the system, the incomplete diffusion of key elements of modernity, and the like.

The processes held to be responsible for these predicted trends are those that are developed in the various strands of structural-functionalism in the social sciences. The general forces of modernization involve a shift from ascribed to achieved criteria and from particularistic to universalistic value orientations. Ethnic attachments, viewed in this perspective as by definition ascribed, are necessarily bound to decline in importance over time. This decline will be almost naturally accompanied by a decline in ethnic inequalities, leaving at most inequalities between individuals instead of between groups. The Marxist variant of this view argues that ethnic attachments and ethnic inequalities will decline over time, leaving *class* characteristics more prominent, by virtue of their becoming unmasked and less complicated by ethnic factors.

This kind of prediction, derived from a general reading of Parson's early work (1951), is often buttressed and supplemented by references to the work of less abstract theorists who attempted, mainly in the 1950s and 1960s, to spell out the mechanisms at work in bringing about these results as part of the modernization process. Among these one could mention the work of acculturation theorists such as Redfield, Linton, and Herskovits (1936), and the work of social communications theorists such as Deutsch (1953), as well as Smelser's application of the concept of structural differentiation to the study of social change (1964), and, especially, the work of Kerr and his colleagues (1960). Kerr and his colleagues, whose work has been labeled a kind of "technological functionalism," attempted to specify certain relatively invariant concomitants and consequences of what is termed the "logic of industrialization," or the "logic of industrialism."

A general, if often only implicit, part of this logic is that industrialization is bound to reduce the importance and significance of ethnic factors in the long run. As we have seen, this means a gradual decline in ethnic and cultural diversity, and a decline in group inequalities. These two trends lead to a decline in the social significance of ethnic diversity, which in turn decreases the probability of ethnic conflict.

The specific mechanisms by which industrialism is held to bring about these changes have been summarized by Blumer (1965) in his cogent critique of the technological functionalist position concerning the effects of industrialization on race relations. We shall return to Blumer's critique shortly, but for the moment let us simply list the basic elements that Blumer identifies as key mechanisms in the functionalist argument.

The mechanisms at work flow from the following "needs" or "requirements" of an industrial system of production (Blumer 1965:53):

- the commitment to a rational and secular outlook
- the replacement of status relations by contractual relations
- the introduction of a number of *impersonal* markets into social life, the most important of which is the labor market
- the physical mobility of the components of industrialism, especially that of personnel
- social mobility
- an "in-built dynamic context which presses to keep the five foregoing characteristics in play."

To these several strands of thought that are more or less directly inspired by functionalist thinking, I should like to add two further lines of contemporary sociological theorizing that share many of the same predictions, even if they are more difficult to classify as emanating from the same functionalist fountainhead.

The first important body of work that shares the same general predictions as the functionalist perspective is the large body of American theory and research on intergroup relations that can be categorized as the Chicago School tradition. The work of Hughes that I have already referred to represents the first major application of this research tradition to the Canadian context. This tradition is not mentioned at all by Hechter, perhaps intentionally because it developed out of research on urban immigrant ethnic groups rather than on the kinds of regionally concentrated cultural minorities that have undergone some sort of internal colonization process.

Much of the early work in the Chicago School tradition, focusing as it did on the adjustment problems of urban migrants, many of whom were relatively recent immigrants from rural Europe, was descriptive in character. Out of this large body of descriptive work, Robert E. Park more or less inductively arrived at his well-known race relations cycle hypothesis, first put forth in 1926 (see Park 1950).

Based on his observations of a remarkable range of intergroup contexts around the world, Park's general idea was that

> In the relations of races there is a cycle of events which tends everywhere to repeat itself. . . . The race relations cycle which takes the form, to state it abstractly, of contacts, competition, accommodation, and eventual assimilation, is apparently progressive and irreversible. Customs regulations, immigration restrictions and racial barriers may slacken the tempo of the movement; may perhaps halt it altogether for a time; but cannot change its direction; cannot, at any rate, reverse it. (Park 1950:150)

For several decades, this "assimilationist" perspective on the end result of intergroup relations was the dominant perspective in American sociological studies of ethnic relations. An important reason for this was that the predictions of the Park cycle hypothesis were, to greater or lesser degrees, confirmed by the experiences of the successive waves of white European immigrants to the United States. Beyond this, however, it may be that the influence of the Park race relations cycle has been so pervasive because the basic predictions of the Park cycle hypothesis, namely the trends toward less cultural diversity, less group inequality, and less conflict, were consonant with those of the dominant theoretical approach of structural functionalism that we have been examining.

The same predictions flow from the influential nation-building perspective on the development of modern states, which was largely based on the history of the large western European states. According to this view, the process by which modern states are constructed follows a predictable pattern. The state-building process involves a series of stages by which the central authority progressively extends its control over other organizations and interest groups. The general prediction is that, in the early stages, the central state takes on other large organizations, for example the church, and eventually asserts complete sovereignty over them. Once the modern state successfully asserts its dominance over other large corporate actors to be found in its territory, it can proceed to incorporate subpopulations as *individual* members of the polity. Once the process of incorporating individuals is complete, the degree of cultural and structural pluralism cannot but decrease over time, according to this perspective (see Rokkan 1970).

The Communal Competition Perspective

In our presentation of the basic features of the functionalist perspective, I took the liberty of classifying quite a range of authors under the same umbrella. This was done for heuristic purposes, in order to emphasize the basic convergence in key predictions about the course of intergroup relations in societies undergoing social change.

Now that I am about to present the basic features of the communal competition perspective, we should note that the same comment is just as applicable here. The basic elements of the perspective were developed through studies of quite a range of societies in both the industrialized and the less-developed parts of the world. Consequently, we should not expect that all of the authors who have contributed to the development of the perspective should have identical views of the processes involved. Rather, these authors have in common a few key assumptions, and they display a certain convergence in their main predictions about the way intergroup relations are expected to evolve in societies undergoing social change.

Let us begin by noting that the very choice of the label "communal competition" for this broad perspective is itself somewhat arbitrary, and this label is not the only one that could have been chosen. It is used because an essential contrast between the two perspectives is their relative emphasis on individual and group competition.

As in the previous section, we can begin our exposition by referring to Hechter's work. In Hechter's study, the alternate model that is tested against the functionalist model is referred to as an internal colonial model of national development, which incorporates, as one of its central components, a reactive theory of ethnic change.

The internal colonial model is our first important strand within the communal competition perspective. Although the internal colonial model of national development has historically been applied to regionally distinct groups, it can still be usefully applied to the relations between communal groups within a given territory. Blauner (1972), for example, applied the concept of internal colonialism to the situation of Blacks, Chicanos, and other American minorities whose group existence in the United States is not the result of (relatively) voluntary migrations.

The internal colonialism model holds that

> . . . the spatially uneven wave of modernization over state territory creates relatively advanced and less advanced groups. As a consequence of this initial fortuitous advantage, there is crystallization of the unequal distribution of resources between the two groups. The superordinate group, or core, seeks to stabilize and monopolize its advantages through policies aiming at the institutionalization of the existing stratification system. It attempts to regulate the allocation of social roles such that those roles commonly defined as having high prestige are reserved for its members. Conversely, individuals from the less advanced group are denied access to these roles. This stratification system, which may be termed a cultural division of labor, contributes to the development of distinctive ethnic identifications in the two groups. Actors come to categorize themselves and others according to the range of roles each may be expected to play. They are aided in this categorization by the presence of visible signs, or cultural markers, which are seen to categorize both groups. (Hechter 1975:9)

A likely consequence of this pattern is that the subordinate group will respond to its exclusion and "reactively assert its own culture as equal or superior to that of the relatively advantaged core" or dominant group (Hechter 1975:10). This possibility constitutes the "reactive theory of ethnic change" that is imbedded in Hechter's internal colonial model.

The internal colonial model, and the communal competition perspective more generally, lead to some predictions that are at variance with those of the functionalist perspective. The first of these concerns the consequences of the process of industrialization on the degree of cultural diversity and pluralism over time. According to the communal competition perspective, there is no assumption or expectation that the subordinate culture will eventually fade away and be replaced or supplanted by the "more modern" culture of the dominant group. The prediction, then, is that the degree of cultural pluralism will not necessarily decrease with industrialization and modernization.

In fact, some authors who espouse this perspective, including Hechter, suggest that cultural differences might even increase, since the subordinate group is likely to reassert itself reactively against the dominant group. This prediction is a part of the communal competition perspective that I am putting forth here. According to Hechter's reactive theory, however, such trends towards greater subordinate group solidarity are seen as necessarily resulting from the subordinate group's disadvantaged status, and from this source only.

> The persistence of objective cultural distinctiveness in the periphery *must* [emphasis added] itself be the function of the maintenance of an unequal distribution of resources between core and peripheral groups. (Hechter 1975:37)

My own view is that such trends can result whenever communal groups with their own sets of institutions are in competition. A group's subordinate position may well amplify its members' loyalty and attachment to their culture, but a subordinate position is not a necessary condition for such attachments to be maintained in contexts of communal competition. These variants of the communal competition perspective will be discussed in more detail in later chapters. The important distinction between the functionalist perspective and the communal competition perspective on this point is that the former predicts that the degree of cultural diversity and pluralism will decrease over time, while the latter predicts that the degree of cultural diversity and pluralism will either remain stable or increase, but will not necessarily decrease.

A second important prediction of the communal competition perspective concerns the fate of group inequalities in the course of economic development. According to this perspective, the basic prediction is that group inequalities are not viewed as necessarily declining over time as a result of the workings of the processes of industrialization and modernization. Rather, inequalities are likely to persist, and in some contexts they might even increase.

Hechter is ambiguous on the exact version of this prediction that he prefers: at some points he refers to the "crystallization" and simple maintenance of inequalities over time and at other times to their being increased by industrialization. For example, the following suggests that inequalities between groups are simply maintained:

> The uneven wave of industrialization over territorial space creates relatively advanced and less advanced groups, and therefore acute cleavages of interest arise between these groups. As a consequence of this initial fortuitous advantage there is a crystallization of the unequal distribution of resources and power between the two groups. (Hechter 1975:39)

Elsewhere in the study, however, Hechter states that:

> The internal colonial model posits altogether different consequences resulting from heightened core-periphery interaction. According to this model, structural inequalities between the regions should *increase* [emphasis added], as the periphery develops in a dependent mode. (Hechter 1975:344)

I prefer the broad version of the prediction. According to this formulation of the communal competition perspective, economic development does not necessarily reduce communal inequalities, but it is not held to necessarily increase them either. Despite these differences in the exact predictions of the communal competition perspective, the important distinction is between the predictions of the functionalist perspective and the predictions of the communal competition perspective. According to the former, communal inequalities should decrease. According to the latter, communal inequalities should either remain constant over time because of the crystallization of the social structure, or they should increase.

A third prediction of the communal competition perspective bears directly on the dimension of communal conflict. Given that cultural diversity and pluralism and group inequalities are not viewed as necessarily declining, it is not assumed that the possibility of communal conflict is a transitory phenomenon limited to the early stages of industrialization and due to an incomplete access to modern values and social structures. Rather, the communal competition perspective suggests that given the cultural and structural pluralism, and given the communal inequalities (when they exist), the probability is high that tension and conflict of any kind is likely to display communal overtones and can easily become communal conflict.

Now that these basic predictions of the communal competition perspective have been listed, let us round out our review of strands and currents within this tradition. In addition to the internal colonialism theory, another intellectual source of the communal competition perspective is the work of plural society theorists. The most extensive macrosociological historical and comparative development of this tradition can be found in the work of Van den Berghe (1973). Van den Berghe traces the origins of the plural society concept to the simultaneous but relatively independent work of social scientists in three different parts of the world: that of Aguirre Beltran (1957) on the legacy of the Spanish conquest in the Western Hemisphere, that of Balandier (1965) on the colonial situation in Africa, and that of Furnivall (1948) and Boeke (1953) on plural societies in the Asian context. These scholars were confronted with societies in which ethnic differences were not only salient, but often constituted the central attribute and principal source of cleavage in the society. Furnivall's plural society was one in which

> Each group holds by its own religion, its own culture and language, its own ideas and ways. As individuals they meet, but only in the market place, in buying and selling. There is a plural society, with different sections of the community living side by side, but separately, within the same political unit. Even in the economic sphere there is a division of labour along racial lines. (Furnivall 1948:304)

Van den Berghe's work was one of the first to go beyond definitional debates on the nature of a "plural society": he considered the *degree* of pluralism as a variable attribute of a wide range of societies. Several of the highly plural societies of the developed world have been analyzed as consociational democracies (see McRae 1973; Lijphart 1977). At the theoretical level, the macrosociological overview attempted by Schermerhorn (1978) remains the most comprehensive synthesis of the field, and we shall return to it in some detail when I formulate the specific hypotheses to be tested in this study.

An interesting point needs to be mentioned in connection with Nagel and Olzak's presentation of the competition model (1982). In their view, it is the development process that is ultimately responsible for the increase in ethnic mobilization and conflict in both old and new states. This brings us exactly 180 degrees from the predictions of the functionalist perspective, namely that the development process will eventually lead to a decrease in ethnic conflict. As Connor has observed, "there is a danger of countering the assumption that the processes of modernization lead to cultural assimilation with an opposing iron law of political disintegration which contends that modernization results, of necessity, in increasing demands for ethnic separation" (1977:244). Clearly research needs to be done in order to specify the conditions under which the two perspectives are more or less useful. The predictions of the two perspectives are summarized in figure 2.1.

Figure 2.1

FUNCTIONALIST PERSPECTIVE

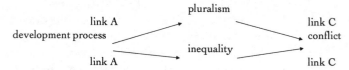

COMMUNAL COMPETITION PERSPECTIVE

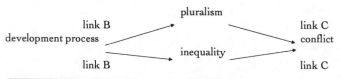

linkages:
A: The development process reduces both pluralism and inequality.
B: The development process does not necessarily reduce, may maintain, or may increase pluralism and inequality.
C: Implicitly, the greater the degree of pluralism and group inequality, the greater the probability of conflict.

A number of other strands in the literature represent further developments, offshoots, and applications of what I have termed the communal competition perspective. Two theoretical accounts of the process of communal competition are provided by Melson and Wolpe (1970) and by Horowitz (1985). It is interesting that Horowitz's massive study on ethnic conflict, which deals mainly with third world contexts, contains a number of examples from Quebec history. Also, the works of Parkin (1979) and Murphy (1988), which extend the Weberian notion of group closure to the study of ethnic stratification, are important attempts to link some of the mechanisms at work in processes of communal competition to a larger body of classical sociological theory.

A relatively autonomous intellectual tradition that has much in common with the communal competition perspective is the sociological study of nationalist movements. To Gellner (1964) and Smith (1971), nationalist movements, more often than not, involve competition between different cultural fractions of the middle class and elite strata of society. To these authors, the *exclusion* (cultural and linguistic) that is experienced by elites of subordinate communal groups is one key factor in explaining the social composition of these movements. Another key factor is the opportunities provided for the same groups by the creation of bureaucratic organizations linked to new and/or expanding state structures.

SUMMARY

This completes our overview of the various strands within the functionalist and communal competition perspectives. The work of specific authors will be dealt with in more detail when we proceed to test the hypotheses that flow from the general predictions that have been reviewed here. As we shall see, a central contrast between the two perspectives is their relative emphasis on competition between individuals as opposed to competition between groups (Banton 1983). Now that these opposing sets of predictions have been set out, let us turn to the task of evaluating them with the data at hand on Quebec society.

Part II

Perceptions of Cultural Pluralism and Inequality: Quebec's Internal Cleavages in 1970

INTRODUCTION TO PART II

Our empirical analyses begin with a detailed examination of data gathered in 1970, after the first decade of the Quiet Revolution, which had been an eventful decade in Quebec. In 1970, hopes were high in many quarters that the process of Francophones becoming "masters in their own house" would continue apace. The aim of Quebec's new middle class and state elites was to have Francophones, the demographic majority in Quebec, become *majoritaires* not only in numbers but in economic power, status position, and psychology as well. The nationalist goal of building a modern French-language society sat uneasily, however, with the still-dominant position of English in the work world in Montreal. Some demographic projections in the late 1960s had suggested that with the dropping birthrate and with immigrants continuing to favor English, Francophones might lose their majority status in Montreal at some point—if not in the year 2000, then later. To many observers at the time, the future of a dynamic French-language society was seen as very problematic if the demographic balance in Montreal itself were to ever shift toward English. These concerns about a possible eventual *minorisation* were to lead to a decade of heated public debate on the language issue. In 1970, the historically dominant position of the English language in Montreal, long taken as a given because of the continental context, was coming under increasing attack. The vision of Montreal as a dual-language city with a full range of parallel institutions was increasingly being challenged by the nationalist vision of a French-language city that contained an English-language minority.[1]

The next four chapters focus on perceptions of cultural pluralism and communal inequalities at the time. The chapters are written using the ethnographic present tense. The methodological strategy here is to hold time constant for this detailed portrait. The portrait will then serve as a baseline for comparison when we directly examine changes over time in part III.

3

Orientations toward Cultural Pluralism

In the previous chapters, we saw that cultural pluralism can be seen as a variable attribute of a society. The degree of cultural pluralism can vary from state to state, and it can also vary over time within a given state or geopolitical area (see Laczko 1994). The definition of pluralism can be broken down into two components: the degree of cultural diversity or heterogeneity (including both objective differences and subjective or perceived differences), and the degree of social and institutional separation or segmentation. The degree of cultural pluralism in a given society at a given point in time can be determined by empirical observation.

In this and the following chapter, we shall be concerned with the structural underpinnings of the subjective side of cultural pluralism. Our principal aim is *not* to analyze the objective degree of cultural pluralism between Francophones and Anglophones in Quebec, nor is it to analyze the patterns of institutional separation and segmentation between the two communities, although these arrangements have been undergoing change, as we have already seen.

The object of this chapter is to (1) present some measures of subjective orientations toward cultural pluralism, (2) describe how these measures are distributed in the Quebec population, (3) describe how the Francophone and Anglophone linguistic communities differ in their outlooks on these measures, and (4) attempt a tentative explanation of the patterns observed in view of the debate between our two opposing theoretical perspectives.

Dualism In Quebec

As mentioned earlier, the focus of this part of the study is on the relationship between the Francophone and Anglophone linguistic collectivities. It is this linguistic dualism that is referred to in our ensuing uses of the term "pluralism." The Francophone-Anglophone distinction is the principal axis of cultural differentiation in Quebec society, so much so that all other types of cultural diversity and differentiation in Quebec are simply impossible to understand without taking into account how the groups in question fit into the overarching linguistic cleavage. Members of aboriginal groups and other ethnic groups are all members, to some extent, of either the Francophone or Anglophone linguistic community, by technical necessity if not by choice. For this reason, the French-English cleavage is the focus of our attention here.

Quebec society has historically been characterized by a high degree of institutional parallelism (Breton 1978a).[2] Educational and religious institutions, social associations, and the media are sharply divided along linguistic lines. The French and English language communities could each be said to have a high degree of institutional completeness, with the significant exception of the work world that brings them together. This institutional pluralism is accompanied by widespread residential segregation. Three-fourths of Quebec's Anglophones live in the metropolitan Montreal area. Both in Montreal and elsewhere in the province, Francophones and Anglophones tend to cluster in separate neighborhoods. This is true not only objectively but also subjectively, in the sense that people perceive themselves as residing in "English neighborhoods" or "French neighborhoods." In 1970, it could still be said that most members of each community could go about their lives without much necessity of participating in the other group's institutions. A good example of this can be found in the educational system in Quebec, which for most of Quebec's history consisted of two autonomous sets of institutions, one Protestant and one Catholic. While the Protestant system was almost entirely English speaking until the 1970s, the Catholic system was divided into a majority French-language sector and a relatively autonomous minority English-language sector. These parallel institutions allowed students to go from kindergarten through college and university without very much contact with the institutions of the other linguistic community. This type of structural pluralism between Francophones and Anglophones has been a permanent feature of Quebec society. We shall be examining the ways it has been changing in part III.

These, then, are the institutional and structural dimensions of pluralism in Quebec in 1970. What can be said about the other component of pluralism, the cultural dimension? As I have already noted, it refers to any sort of cultural difference between groups.

Cultural differences between groups do not always follow or coincide with whatever structural or institutional divisions might exist. Cultural diversity or pluralism, then, is analytically separable from structural pluralism. Nonetheless, the two are often quite closely related empirically. As Schermerhorn has noted, ". . . culture and social structure are virtual Siamese twins, with each implicated in the other" (Schermerhorn 1978:124).

This close empirical relationship between the cultural and structural dimensions of pluralism can become problematic if one has the idea that the two dimensions ought to be separable empirically as well as analytically. For while structural pluralism and institutional duplication are readily observable and measurable, cultural differences are much more slippery. For example, one can easily observe that the Montreal Board of Trade and the Chambre de Commerce de Montréal, which were separate and parallel organizations for most of their history, eventually merged under Francophone leadership in the 1990s. But to say what the *cultural* differences between Francophones and Anglophones are is a much tougher task.

The difference between the French and English languages is the first and most obvious observable difference. Beyond this, however, researchers must tread with great care: "ways of being" and "mentalities" are notoriously difficult to observe and measure. These difficulties notwithstanding, the question of the extent of cultural difference between segments of a plural society is an important one and should be asked. Let us now examine this issue more closely.

ORIENTATIONS TOWARD CULTURAL PLURALISM: DIMENSIONS AND INDICATORS

Important as the question is, I shall not attempt in this study to measure objective cultural differences between Francophones and Anglophones directly. Rather, we shall examine indirect evidence bearing on the population's assessments and evaluations of the degree of cultural pluralism between Francophones and Anglophones in Quebec.

In this study, our interest is in the social bases of variations in subjective perceptions of cultural differences, or in other words, in the structural underpinnings of feelings and perceptions of group distinctiveness. These *subjective* orientations toward cultural pluralism are not necessarily closely linked to the magnitude of whatever *objective* differences may exist, as I have already mentioned.

Referring to the link between the subjective and the objective, Hechter goes so far as to say that ". . . the actual extent of cultural difference between two groups is *irrelevant* [emphasis added] to the emotional impact of the ethnic tie which unites the individuals within each of them" (1976:1164). Although the use of terms such as "irrelevant" really overstates the case, the important point is that subjective orientations toward cultural pluralism are not a direct function of the objective differences.

For example, the overall perception of group distinctiveness between Protestants and Catholics in Northern Ireland may be very high, perhaps even higher than in other contexts in which the objective differences between communal segments are greater. Nonetheless, the degree of objective cultural difference is hardly irrelevant. One could argue that, *ceteris paribus,* if the objective differences between Protestants and Catholics in Northern Ireland were greater than they are, the subjective feeling of group distinctiveness would be even greater as well.

Two kinds of orientations toward cultural pluralism will be investigated here. The first consists of perceptions and assessments of the degree of cultural pluralism between Francophones and Anglophones. The second consists of normative evaluations of the degree of cultural pluralism. The former refers to what is; the latter refers to what ought to be (Schermerhorn 1978:122).

We shall use as dependent variables in this analysis two measures designed to tap *subjective assessments* of the cultural dimension, and two measures bearing on *normative evaluations* of the cultural dimension. The exact wording of the questions is as follows:

(1) *Subjective assessments of the cultural dimension*

(P1: Q2-65) Do you think that in their mentality and ways of living French Canadians and English Canadians are very different, fairly different, quite similar, or very similar?

(P2: Q2-76) To what extent do you think that the culture and ways of life of French Canadians are in danger of disappearing: are they in great danger, in a little danger, or in no danger of disappearing?

(2) *Normative evaluations of the cultural dimension*

(P3: Q2-33) Do you think French Canadians should try and maintain their ways of living, or that they should become more like the other Canadians?

(P4: Q2-35) Which would you say it is most important for a people to maintain: its language and culture or its standard of living?

What do these four measures have in common? Before discussing their validity, let us focus on their level of measurement. If we follow the lead suggested by Schermerhorn, we can see that each of these measures is characterized by an underlying ordinality. Schermerhorn, building on Wirth's (1945) well-known typology of minority groups' reactions to their disadvantaged position, puts forth the paired concepts of *centripetal* and *centrifugal* tendencies.

These concepts refer to both the cultural and the structural dimensions of pluralism. In Schermerhorn's words,

> Centripetal tendencies refer both to cultural trends such as acceptance of common values, styles of life, etc., as well as structural features like increased participation in a common set of groups, associations, and institutions.

> Conversely, centrifugal tendencies among subordinate groups are those that foster separation from the dominant group or from societal bonds in one respect or another. Culturally this most frequently means retention and preservation of the group's distinctive traditions in spheres like language, religion, recreation, etc., together with the particularistic values associated with them: Wirth's cultural pluralism. But in order to protect these values, structural requirements are needed, so there are demands for endogamy, separate associations, and even at times a restricted range of occupations. *In toto* trends like these may be only mildly centrifugal, calling for autonomy, separation, or federation: if they are more extreme, secessionist policy may clamor for a complete rupture with the larger social system. (Schermerhorn 1978:82)

In short, centripetal tendencies refer to increased sharing between groups, either of values or ways of doing things (the cultural dimension) or of institutions and organizations (the structural dimension). Centrifugal tendencies, on the other hand, are those that foster either greater cultural differences or institutional separation between groups. Thus, centripetal and centrifugal tendencies represent trends toward lower and higher degrees of pluralism between groups.

If we now examine our four dependent variable measures in light of these paired concepts, we can see that the possible responses to each question range from a very centrifugal response to a very centripetal response. Let us consider the first pair of measures, those bearing on the population's assessments of the degree of cultural pluralism. Here, those who respond that the two cultures are very different and that French Canadian culture is in great danger are giving the most *centrifugal* response. Those who answer that the two cultures are very similar and that French Canadian culture is in no danger are giving the most *centripetal* response.

Similar observations can be made about the second pair of measures, those dealing with normative evaluations. Respondents who reply that French Canadians should maintain their ways of living and that it is more important for a people to maintain its language and culture than its standard of living are giving a *centrifugal* response. Those who answer that French Canadians should become more like non-French Canadians and that it is more important for a people to maintain its standard of living than its language and culture are giving a *centripetal* response.

How valid are these measures? Let us begin by assessing each in terms of the simple and straightforward criterion of face validity. Each measure does tap an orientation toward cultural pluralism. The first measure, about the degree of perceived difference between the two cultures, is clear and straightforward.

The second measure, dealing with the extent to which French Canadian culture is threatened, is more problematic. Here, the question measures perceived cultural differences only indirectly. It is a good measure of perceived assessments of cultural pluralism only to the extent that one can assume that those who see the two cultures as different will be more likely to see French Canadian culture as threatened, and vice versa. We shall see shortly that this assumption is confirmed by the positive relationship between these two measures.

The third measure, which deals with the normative issue of whether French Canadians should maintain their ways of living or become more like other Canadians, also bears directly on the issue, but it, too, is problematic. The problem with this measure is that "maintaining their ways of living" can be interpreted in at least two different ways. It can be interpreted as remaining traditional and nonmodern or as retaining the French language, French culture, and so forth. This ambiguity will be kept in mind as the analysis proceeds.

The fourth measure, which deals with the relative importance of a people's standard of living on the one hand, and its language and culture on the other, is also straightforward and presents no apparent ambiguities, especially since answers to the effect that "both are equally important" were accepted.

Another form of validation that we can perform is an *inter-item validity check*. Table 3.1 gives information on how the four measures are related to one another. All but one of the intercorrelations are positive. This means that on the whole, a centrifugal orientation on one measure is associated with a centrifugal orientation on the others. This confirms our initial judgment (about *face validity*) that each of the four measures does indeed tap orientations toward cultural pluralism.

The one correlation that is near zero is that between the first and third measures. This single nonpositive coefficient indicates that the subjective assessment of the French and English cultures as very different or fairly different from each other is not associated with the normative view that French Canadians should maintain their ways of living. This is probably due to the ambiguities that I have already mentioned that are inherent in the latter question. Despite this, this measure does behave similarly to the other measures throughout the analysis, as we shall see. For this reason, it has been retained, and not discarded, despite its limitations.

The overall positive *direction* or sign of the correlations notwithstanding, it should be noted that their *magnitude* is not very strong. This speaks against combining the four variables to form a single composite measure.

It should also be noted that the two measures of subjective assessments of the degree of pluralism, P1 and P2, are more strongly related to each other ($r = .18$) than either one of them is to the two measures of normative evaluations. Similarly, the two measures of the normative dimension, P3 and P4, are more highly correlated with each other ($r = .15$) than either one of them is with the two measures of assessments and perceptions. This pattern (of inter-item validity) confirms our initial judgment (about face validity) that each pair of questions taps a different dimension of cultural pluralism.

TABLE 3.1

INTERCORRELATIONS OF MEASURES OF ORIENTATIONS
TOWARD CULTURAL PLURALISM

	P1: (Q2-65) (French and English different?)	P2: (Q2-76) (Threat to French culture?)	P3: (Q2-33) (Maintain ways?)	P4: Q2-35) (Language and culture or . . . ?)
P1	1.00	.18	-.01	.11
P2		1.00	.10	.10
P3			1.00	.15
P4				1.00

All entries are Pearson correlation coefficients. (N = 6,073-6,114).
Respondents who gave no answer have been excluded.
The variables have been trichotomized and coded as follows:
  (1 = centripetal; 3; 5 = centrifugal).

	1 (centripetal responses)	3	5 (centrifugal responses)
P1	quite similar, very similar	don't know, qualified answer	very different, fairly different
P2	in no danger	don't know, qualified answer	in great danger in little danger
P3	become more like other Canadians	don't know, qualified answer, both	maintain their ways
P4	standard of living	don't know, qualified answer, both equally important	language and culture

THEORETICAL QUESTIONS AND HYPOTHESES

As we saw in the previous chapter, the functionalist and communal
competition perspectives both make predictions about the degree of cultural diversity or pluralism; about group inequalities; about the incidence
of intergroup conflict; about the way these dimensions change over time
in the course of industrialization and modernization; and also about the
way the degree of pluralism, the degree of group inequality, and the
incidence of conflict are related to one another.

With respect to changes in the degree of cultural diversity and the extent of group differences over time, the two perspectives offer predictions that are to some extent antithetical. The functionalist perspective predicts that intergroup cultural diversity will, in general, decrease over time as a result of the process of industrialization and capitalist development. Karl Marx, who, along with most of the other classical social theorists, held some variant of this view, put it this way: "National distinctions and contrasts are already tending to disappear more and more as the bourgeoisie develops, as free trade becomes more general, as the world market grows in size and importance, as manufacturing processes and the resulting conditions of life become more uniform" (Marx [1868] 1962:64).

This view, which Hechter (1975) has labelled the functionalist theory of ethnic change, has appeared and reappeared in a remarkable number of guises in the literature, as we saw in the preceding chapter. The long-range decrease in cultural diversity predicted by the functionalist perspective is held to have important consequences, the chief of which is that as ethnic identities become less salient, ethnic conflict will become less likely to occur and will be less intense when it does occur.

According to the communal competition perspective, on the other hand, there is no necessary expectation that cultural diversity will decrease, although some authors, notably Hannan (1979), fully agree with the functionalist prediction on this point. The communal competition perspective argues that regardless of the actual degree of diversity, group competition may well be likely to increase perceptions of cultural difference and to exacerbate feelings of group distinctiveness. A consequence of these heightened feelings of group distinctiveness, according to this perspective, is that the probability of communal conflict will be increased.

Let us now consider the way in which these two perspectives can inform the analysis of our data on Quebec. The two broad theoretical perspectives, the functionalist perspective and the communal competition perspective, give rise to different expectations about what the pattern of orientations toward cultural pluralism will look like in a given polyethnic society at any one point in time. Their opposing expectations will be assessed in this and the following chapter.

We should mention that the survey materials at hand bear on only one point in time and space and therefore an empirical evaluation of these opposing predictions does not constitute a definitive test of these two broad perspectives. For a definitive test, data on changes around the world and over time would be necessary. What we shall be doing in this and the following chapters is carrying out a series of partial and indirect tests of the two competing perspectives by using cross-sectional data.

The strategy being put to use here is similar to that set forth by Fischer and his colleagues (1977). They attempt to test a historical argument, the "decline of community" thesis, by using survey data bearing on a single society at single points in time. The key element of such a strategy is to be able to formulate hypotheses about cross-sectional variations that are consonant with the predictions of the historical arguments in question.

For the purposes of this chapter, hypotheses can be derived from the two broad perspectives regarding (1) the central or modal tendency of the distribution of orientations, and (2) the role of language group membership in shaping orientations, or what we shall call more simply the communal effect.

The object of these hypotheses is to attempt to link the macrosociological theories of ethnic change that we have been discussing with the conceptualization of orientations toward cultural pluralism that we have derived from Schermerhorn. Let us begin with the hypotheses bearing on the central tendency of the distribution of orientations.

The Distribution of Orientations

The first pair of hypotheses has to do with the overall direction of the distribution of orientations toward cultural pluralism. The functionalist perspective predicts that cultural diversity and group differences will decrease over time in the course of a society's industrialization and modernization. As a consequence, we should expect, *ceteris paribus*, that at a given point in time, the distribution of each of our four measures of orientations toward cultural pluralism should have its central tendency in the *centripetal* direction. According to the communal competition perspective, on the other hand, as we saw in the previous chapter, there is no expectation that the extent of cultural diversity or group differences will necessarily decline over time as a result of the processes of industrialization and modernization. On the contrary, this perspective points to the possibility that a likely consequence of the modernization of a segmented society is the maintaining, or even increasing of feelings of group awareness and perceptions of group differences. As a consequence, we should expect, *ceteris paribus*, that the central tendency of the distribution of our measures of orientations toward cultural pluralism should be in the centrifugal direction.

The univariate distribution is important to consider, because it is a key intervening variable in both perspectives. The distribution of orientations provides a link between the actual degree of diversity, on the one hand, and the probability of communal conflict, on the other. The more the central tendency is skewed in a centripetal direction, the lower the probability of conflict. The more the central tendency is skewed in a centrifugal direction, the higher the probability of conflict.

This assumption, which is shared by authors in both perspectives, may be misleading, however. As Schermerhorn has noted, it may be a mistake to assume that centrifugal orientations will lead to more conflict, and centripetal orientations to less conflict (Schermerhorn 1978:82). Schermerhorn argues that the degree of agreement or disagreement between dominant and subordinate groups is as important as the central tendency itself. If the dominant and subordinate groups both agree, there will be a lower likelihood of conflict than if they disagree. This will hold true whether the central tendency of the distribution of orientations is toward the centrifugal or toward the centripetal direction.

For this reason, we need to examine whether the dominant and subordinate groups agree or disagree in their orientations toward cultural pluralism. Let us now turn to a pair of hypotheses bearing on this question.

The Communal Effect

The second set of competing hypotheses concerns the impact of communal membership on orientations toward cultural pluralism. In particular, the two perspectives lead us to expect the communal effect to be in opposite directions. According to the functionalist perspective, the expectation is that subordinate ethnic and communal groups will, in the long run, become less distinct from, and even merge with, the dominant communal group in the society. As a consequence, one might expect subordinate communal groups to be less centrifugal (or no more centrifugal) than dominant communal groups.

To the extent that the dominant communal group has succeeded in imposing its cultural standards on the society's principal institutions, in particular in the labor market and in the workplace, one can expect that members of the subordinate group will tend to downplay the importance of cultural differences at least as much as, if not more than, members of the dominant group. This is likely to occur because members of the subordinate group will see their own culture and its continued distinctive-

ness as a liability or a handicap and the acquisition of the dominant culture as an asset (see Breton 1978b). Thus, according to the functionalist perspective, we can expect Francophones in Quebec to display orientations toward cultural pluralism that are less centrifugal (or, at most, as centrifugal) as those of Anglophones, both with respect to their subjective assessments of differences and with respect to the normative dimension of whether the differences should be maintained or reduced.

According to the communal competition perspective, on the other hand, the degree of cultural diversity between communal groups is not seen as necessarily diminishing. Subordinate group members are likely to view their communal group and its culture and language as being in competition with the dominant group and *its* culture and language. Since the subordinate group is likely to be viewed as the weaker partner in the competition (by definition of what constitutes a subordinate group), members of the subordinate group may well view their culture and language as being threatened or encroached upon by the dominant culture and language. As a consequence, one might expect members of the subordinate communal group to display orientations toward cultural pluralism that are more centrifugal than those of members of the dominant communal group.

This will be so because to the extent that the culture and language of the dominant communal group (for example Anglophones in Quebec) have become dominant throughout the society's institutions, possession of the dominant culture and language becomes a resource that is quite unequally distributed throughout the society. For example, while mastery of the dominant language may be the type of requirement that applies equally to all members of the society (in the sense of the "formal equality" of dominant group institutions discussed by Bourdieu and Passeron [1970], Collins [1975], and Murphy [1981]), it is a requirement that is much more easily met by members of the dominant communal group than by members of the subordinate group. As a consequence, participation in the society's dominant institutions, to the extent that they do reflect the culture and language of the dominant communal group, imposes constraints and costs on members of the subordinate communal group that are not imposed on members of the dominant communal group. The upshot of such a situation is that members of the subordinate communal group are likely to be more aware of cultural differences between the two groups, if only because they cannot afford to be as ignorant of them as members of the dominant group can.

Members of the subordinate group are more likely to see their culture as threatened. Also, they are more likely to advocate the maintenance and retention of whatever differences are perceived to exist (in the normative dimension), because the subordinate group culture and language are viewed as a collective resource and tool that should be protected and strengthened. According to the communal competition perspective, the costs and handicaps that subordinate communal group members face vis-à-vis the dominant culture are most typically counteracted by efforts at strengthening the subordinate group's language and culture in order to improve its competitive position. Implicit in this perspective is the assumption that the immediate, or at least the long-term, rewards offered by taking action to improve the collective position of the subordinate group's language and culture are sufficient in magnitude to outweigh the costs and handicaps that individual members of the subordinate group face in daily life because of the dominant position in the society of the dominant communal group's language and culture. For all of these reasons, the communal competition perspective would predict that, *ceteris paribus*, Francophones in Quebec will be more centrifugal in their orientations toward cultural pluralism than Anglophones.

THE DISTRIBUTION OF ORIENTATIONS AND THE ROLE OF COMMUNAL MEMBERSHIP

Let us now assess these two pairs of hypotheses with the help of table 3.2. The table presents information on the population's subjective assessments of the extent of French-English dualism in Quebec, as well as its normative evaluations of whether cultural differences ought to be maintained or reduced. The first panel presents the distributions of the two indicators of the population's subjective assessments of the cultural aspects of dualism, and the second panel gives the distributions of the two indicators of the normative evaluations of dualism.[2]

What overall pattern is revealed by the data? Each of the measures of orientations toward cultural pluralism used here is distributed in similar fashion throughout the Quebec population. None of the measures is extremely skewed in its distribution, but each measure nonetheless shows that the central tendency is for responses to be mildly clustered around the first two response categories of each question.

If we examine the overall distributions given in the right-hand columns, we can see that there is a slight tendency for responses to the first three measures to be clustered toward the centrifugal side of the continua. The

TABLE 3.2

ORIENTATIONS TOWARD CULTURAL PLURALISM,
BY LANGUAGE GROUP

	Francophones	Anglophones	Total Quebec
(P1: Q2-65)			
Do you think that in their mentality and ways of living French Canadians and English Canadians are very different, fairly different, quite similar, or very similar?			
very different	21%	15%	20%
fairly different	37	25	35
qualified answer (that depends, etc.)	1	4	2
quite similar	30	38	32
very similar	4	13	5
don't know	6	5	6
	100%	100%	100%
	(5,215)	(885)	(6,100)
(P2: Q2-76)			
To what extent do you think that the culture and way of life of French Canadians are in danger of disappearing: are they in great danger, in a little danger, or in no danger of disappearing?			
in great danger	22%	9%	20%
in a little danger	43	24	40
qualified answer (that depends, etc.)	2	4	2
in no danger	30	54	34
don't know	3	8	4
	100%	100%	100%
	(5,227)	(887)	(6,614)

fourth measure, in which respondents are asked to choose, in a sense, between the value of one's language and culture and the value of one's standard of living, is the only one that is not skewed in a centrifugal direction.

On the whole, the population's overall assessments of the degree of cultural pluralism as well as its overall evaluations of whether cultural pluralism should be maintained are distributed fairly evenly across the full range of "most centrifugal" to "most centripetal" responses, but there is a

TABLE 3.2
Continued

	Francophones	Anglophones	Total Quebec
(P3: Q2-33)			
Do you think French Canadians should try and maintain their ways of living, or that they should become more like the other Canadians?			
maintain their ways	53%	33%	50%
both	10	16	11
qualified answer (that depends, etc.)	4	10	5
become more like the others	30	36	31
don't know	3	5	3
	100%	100%	100%
	(5,207)	(882)	(6,089)
(P4: Q2-35)			
Which would you say it is most important for a people to maintain: its language and culture or its standard of living?			
its language and culture	28%	9%	25%
both are equally important	42	38	41
qualified answer (that depends, etc.)	1	3	1
its standard of living	29	48	31
don't know	1	2	1
	100%	100%	100%
	(5,223)	(884)	(6,107)

Respondents who gave no answer have been excluded. Percentage totals may deviate from 100% because of rounding errors.

A weighting factor has been applied throughout the analysis. All reported case bases (Ns) are weighted. A real total of 1,982 respondents corresponds to a weighted total of 6,116 respondents.

slight tendency toward more centrifugal responses. The results of these univariate distributions, then, can be interpreted as supportive of both the functionalist and communal competition perspectives, although the predictions of the latter appear to be slightly more supported than the predictions of the former.

What about the role of communal divisions in shaping orientations toward cultural pluralism? It is clear from table 3.2 that according to every one of our measures, the responses of Francophones differ from those of Anglophones. Thus, Francophones are the ones who are more likely to assess the cultural differences between the two communities as being large, and also the more likely to perceive French-Canadian culture as being threatened.

From the third panel of the table, we can see that not only are Francophones more likely to advance this sort of assessment of the degree of cultural pluralism, they are also more likely to support the normative ideal that the cultural differences between the two communities should be maintained. Francophones are also much more likely than Anglophones to hold the view that a people should maintain its language and culture, even if it has to choose between its language and culture and its standard of living.

On every one of these measures, then, Francophones espouse orientations toward cultural pluralism that are much more centrifugal than those of Anglophones. On each measure, the strong communal effect is in the direction predicted by the communal competition perspective.

SUMMARY AND DISCUSSION

This chapter has presented evidence concerning orientations toward cultural pluralism in Quebec. Let us now systematically review the principal findings and discuss each of them briefly in terms of the light they cast on the debate between the functionalist and communal competition perspectives.

The Distribution of Orientations

Our first pair of competing hypotheses had to do with the central tendency of the univariate distributions of orientations. For three of the four measures of orientations toward cultural pluralism, we found that the central tendency is slightly toward the centrifugal side of the continuum. This is more consonant with the predictions of the communal competition perspective than with those of the functionalist perspective. However, we should consider the degree of confirmation of these competing hypotheses itself as a variable that assumes different values over time and space. If one considers the range of polyethnic settings over time and space in which this pair of competing hypotheses about the central tendency of the distribution of orientations could be applied, it becomes clear that there are a large number of settings where the functionalist perspective would be more supported than it is in Quebec, and also a large number of other settings where the communal competition perspective would be even more supported than it is in Quebec.

For example, while comparable survey data concerning other segmented societies are rare, we can hazard the following impressionistic comparison. On the one hand, the mildly centrifugal pattern displayed here is probably much more centrifugal than what one would find among the majority of immigrant ethnic groups in North America, if one thinks of the relationship of the immigrant ethnic group to its larger host society. On the other hand, this mildly centrifugal pattern is probably much less centrifugal than that which exists in many societies characterized by an even higher degree of structural pluralism or in societies in which communal identities are much more polarized. For example, Mason has noted that ". . . Catholics and Protestants in Northern Ireland; Hindus and Muslims in the Punjab; nobles and serfs in Russia—all have felt themselves to be essentially different from each other" (Mason 1970:162). Compared to such contexts, the pattern we have observed in Quebec can be termed rather mildly centrifugal.

The Existence of a Communal Effect

By every one of our measures of orientations toward cultural pluralism, Francophones are more centrifugal and less centripetal in their outlook than Anglophones. Schermerhorn (1978:chapter 2) notes that intergroup arenas are often characterized by incongruencies between communal groups over group goals and aspirations and that these disagreements are a potential source of conflict. This holds true whether or not the central tendency of the distribution of orientations is toward the centrifugal or toward the centripetal direction. Here we found that there are persistent differences between Francophones and Anglophones in their subjective assessments of the extent of cultural pluralism and also in their normative evaluations of whether group differences ought to be maintained. This confirms the hypothesis that we derived from the communal competition perspective.

Another way of appreciating this communal effect is to compare the distributions in the two language groups. Taken by themselves, the responses of Francophones are skewed in a centrifugal direction; this corresponds to the predictions of the communal competition perspective. The responses of Anglophones, on the other hand, taken by themselves, are more evenly distributed across the range of responses and tend to be skewed in a centripetal direction. This corresponds to the predictions of the functionalist perspective. This juxtaposition illustrates the point made by Schermerhorn (1978), and even more graphically by Horton (1966) that it can be *theoretically* misleading to examine the outlook of either a subordinate or a dominant group in isolation (see also Juteau-Lee 1981).

We should note that this pair of competing hypotheses bearing on the direction of the communal effect was formulated for cases, like that of Quebec, in which there is a history of inequality between the communal groups in question. In cases in which the communal groups are equal or nearly equal in resources, both the functionalist perspective and the communal competition perspective would predict that we should not expect very large differences between communal groups in their orientations toward cultural pluralism. This would hold true whether the overall central tendency is in a centrifugal or a centripetal direction. What this implies is that if the Francophone and Anglophone communities, and the French and English languages, were *in every way* equally powerful in Quebec and Canada, Francophones would not necessarily be more convinced than Anglophones that the two cultures are different, that French Canadian culture is in danger, that the differences that do exist ought to be maintained, and that a people's language and culture ought to be given priority over its standard of living.

The absolute and relative size of the groups involved is important here as a component of the groups' relative resources. It is, of course, possible for groups to feel threatened because of their numerical minority status, independent of their current socioeconomic position. Under such conditions, one might expect the minority to display more centrifugal orientations than the majority even if the two groups are relatively equal in other socioeconomic dimensions. This perception of minority status has long been a component of French Canadian nationalism, as has the perception of subordinate group status, which will be investigated further in the following chapters.

Orientations toward Cultural Pluralism: The Role of the Stratification System

We have just seen that members of Quebec's historically dominant and subordinate communal groups react quite differently when asked to give their views on the issue of cultural pluralism. Our next task is to examine the way the stratification system within each linguistic community shapes the structure of orientations toward cultural pluralism. In this chapter, I shall discuss this issue and deal with the way stratification variables combine with language group membership to influence the structure of orientations. The body of the chapter consists of three sections, each of which is devoted to a different aspect of the stratification system.

In addition to the long-standing power differences *between* the Francophone and Anglophone communities in Quebec, the effects of which we examined in the preceding chapter, there are, of course, important class differences to be found *within* each linguistic community.

The class structure of each language group contains a full range of educational and occupational categories, although Anglophones have, on the average, been more privileged through most of Quebec's history. Consequently, the first section of this chapter will investigate the role of educational and occupational differences in shaping orientations toward cultural pluralism.

In addition to the vertical stratification dimensions that exist within each language group, each community is differentiated horizontally as well. Each language group is composed of members who have different ethnic origins and different degrees of lifetime exposure to Quebec society. The role of these two demographic features of the stratification system — ethnic origin and degree of exposure — will be examined in the second section of the chapter.

The third section will take a closer look at the sources of highly centrifugal orientations among privileged members of the Francophone community, by taking into account the role of certain structural aspects of the workplace.

STRATIFICATION EFFECTS:
THE ROLE OF EDUCATION AND OCCUPATION

What bearing do socioeconomic differences have on orientations toward cultural pluralism? Let us begin by trying to spell out what the two competing perspectives have to say about the role of class membership and socioeconomic status in shaping a person's outlook. In this section, our hypotheses concern, for the most part, class differences within the historically subordinate group, although class differences within the dominant group will not be completely ignored in the analysis and discussion that is to follow.

The role of class differences *within* ethnic and communal groups has received little systematic attention by authors working in the functionalist perspective. This is true of the abstract functionalists such as Parsons (1951; 1965), for whom ethnic factors are seen as ascribed and hence as receding in importance as a consequence of the processes of social and economic development. It is also true of the major Chicago School theorists (Wirth 1964; Park 1950), for whom ethnic ties are seen as more or less temporary and as especially likely to be weakened by upward mobility, either in the current or in subsequent generations. The same could be said of the technological functionalists, such as Kerr et al. (1960), who predict that ethnic attachments will decline because of the "logic of industrialism" and its meritocratic emphasis on rationality and achievement, the operation of which would leave less and less room for particularistic and ascribed group identities.

Although the question of class differences within groups has been given only tangential attention in these various strands in the literature, it is still possible to derive predictions that are implicit in the works in this tradition.

According to the functionalist perspective, it is the more-privileged (higher socioeconomic status, middle-class) members of subordinate communal groups who have the most skills and resources—for example educational credentials—necessary for advancement in the larger society. As a consequence, one could expect that the more-privileged members of subordinate communal groups would be more inclined and motivated than their less-privileged brethren to shed their subordinate group culture. In other words, in this perspective it is the more-privileged members of the subordinate communal group who will be most likely to downplay cultural differences, and the least likely to insist on the importance of maintaining them.

Another reason that this should be so is that since the more-privileged or middle-class members of subordinate communal groups are likely to be the most integrated into (and on the most equal terms with) the larger society, they may well be less aware of cultural differences between the communal groups simply because they themselves, by virtue of their educational credentials and linguistic skills, for example, are not all that different from their counterparts in the dominant communal group. For similar reasons, one might expect the more-privileged members of the subordinate group to be the least inclined to want to maintain whatever cultural differences exist or are perceived to exist. For all of these reasons, the functionalist perspective would lead us to expect the more-privileged, middle-class Francophones in Quebec to be less centrifugal in their orientations toward cultural pluralism than their less-privileged brethren.

According to the communal competition perspective, class differences in orientations toward cultural pluralism are determined by the level at which the greatest volume of intercommunal competition actually occurs. According to Bonacich's split-labor market theory (1972), ethnic antagonism is the result of competition among two culturally different segments of the working class. According to this formulation, one would expect the working-class members of the competing dominant and subordinate communal groups to hold more centrifugal orientations than their middle-class brethren, simply because it is the working-class members of each communal group who are most in competition with each other. Other theorists, most notably theorists of nationalism (see Smith 1971), emphasize the importance of competition at the middle-class level, among members of white-collar occupations. These formulations would lead us to expect that the more-privileged or middle-class members of competing communal groups will display more centrifugal orientations than their less-privileged or working-class brethren.

Of these two variants of the communal competition perspective, the second is more applicable to the study of French-English relations in Quebec. This is so because the main arena of French-English occupational competition in Quebec is located at the white collar level. The main reason there is relatively less competition between Francophones and Anglophones at the blue-collar level is that Francophones have a near-monopoly on all blue-collar jobs in Quebec. Furthermore, where this is not the case, as in certain service industries and in the clothing and garment industries, it is because Francophones have passed through these occupations in large numbers in the past, but are now finding and taking over better-paying jobs, leaving more, if not most, of the low-paying work to immigrants.

As a consequence, we might expect more centrifugal orientations among the white collar groups and middle classes in Quebec. Let us focus on the Francophone communal group and attempt to specify some of the mechanisms linking the volume of competition at this level with the espousal of centrifugal orientations toward cultural pluralism. Gellner (1964) has argued, in his theory of nationalism, that the paramount feature of the culture of an industrial society is its emphasis on *literacy*, and that this cannot be operational other than through the medium of a particular *language*. In other words, the "culture of industrial society" that functionalist theorists speak of cannot exist in a universalistic vacuum. As we have already seen, according to the communal competition perspective, to the extent that the language and culture of the dominant communal group is the dominant language and culture throughout the society's institutions, members of the subordinate group face costs and handicaps that are not shared by members of the dominant group. What we now need to add to this is that it is precisely in the middle class and in white collar occupations that literacy and the use of language is so important. Thus, in this formulation, we should expect the middle class and white collar workers of the subordinate communal group to display more centrifugal orientations than their working-class or blue-collar brethren.

Let us now turn to the data. As a first step in examining how an individual's location in the stratification system shapes that individual's outlook, we can consider the impact of educational and occupational divisions on the structure of orientations toward cultural pluralism. The effects of formal education on each of our measures of orientations are shown in table 4.1.

TABLE 4.1

ORIENTATIONS TOWARD CULTURAL PLURALISM,
BY EDUCATION AND LANGUAGE GROUP

Education	Francophones			Anglophones		
	L	M	H	L	M	H
	(% giving a centrifugal response)					
A.						
P1: (French and English different or similar?)	54[a] (3,800)	65 (983)	73 (431)	38 (460)	39 (240)	48 (185)
P2: (Threat to French culture?)	63 (3,814)	69 (983)	70 (429)	26 (462)	38 (240)	48 (185)
B.						
P3: (Maintain ways or become more like others?)	52 (3,807)	58 (972)	52 (427)	24 (457)	45 (240)	40 (185)
P4: (Importance of language and culture or standard of living?)	26 (3,810)	32 (983)	34 (429)	9 (459)	9 (240)	13 (185)

[a]Read: "Of the 3,800 Francophones with a low education, 54 percent gave a centrifugal response."

The dependent variables are coded as in table 3.1. Responses coded as "centrifugal" are the following:

P1: very different, fairly different
P2: in great danger, in little danger
P3: maintain their ways
P4: language and culture

The independent variable is trichotomized as follows:

	Low	Medium	High
Education	≤11 years	12-14 years	≥15 years

Respondents who gave no answer have been excluded.

A weighting factor has been applied throughout the analysis. All reported case bases (Ns) are weighted. A real total of 1,982 respondents corresponds to a weighted total of 6,116 respondents.

The first striking feature of the table is that despite the very apparent impact of educational divisions within each linguistic community on individual outlooks, the communal effect that we have already discussed still makes its presence felt very strongly. In both panels of the table (A and B, which present the measures of assessments and evaluations of cultural pluralism in sequence), the effect of communal membership is so visible that whatever measure we consider, the most centrifugal subset of Anglophones is still considerably less centrifugal in its outlook than the least centrifugal subgroup of Francophones.

This persistent communal difference notwithstanding, there are very noticeable differences in outlook within each linguistic community. It is clear that the more educated respondents espouse more centrifugal views than those who are less educated. This holds true in both linguistic categories.

This general pattern is accompanied by some less clear-cut details. In most cases the effect of educational status is monotonic: the higher one's educational level, the more centrifugal one's orientations toward cultural pluralism. The significant exception to this is the curvilinear pattern displayed in the third measure, which asks whether French Canadians should maintain their ways of living or become like other Canadians.

On this question, the most centrifugal orientations are held not by the most educated but by those with a medium (12 to 14 years) level of education. This exceptional curvilinear pattern, observed in both linguistic communities, is probably due to the ambiguity inherent in the wording of the measure, a problem discussed in the previous chapter. French Canadians "maintaining their ways" may well be interpreted as remaining traditional, remaining unmodern, and so forth. If this question is interpreted in this way by the most educated segments of the population, the curvilinear pattern is accounted for.

Let us now turn to the effects of occupational differences, as shown in table 4.2.

Here again, the strong communal effect is striking: the most centrifugal subsets of Anglophones are comparable to the least centrifugal subsets of Francophones in their outlook.

Beyond this, the effect of occupational status is less clear-cut than the effect of education that we have just examined. All in all, though, it is apparent that members of the three white-collar categories (professional and technical, managers and proprietors, and sales and clerical) hold more centrifugal views than blue-collar workers and farmers.

We can conclude from this first glance at the data that the results are in line with the predictions of the communal competition perspective, and, more specifically, with the prediction that it is those in white-collar occupations who will display the most centrifugal orientations.

TABLE 4.2

ORIENTATIONS TOWARD CULTURAL PLURALISM,
BY OCCUPATION AND LANGUAGE GROUP

Occupation	Francophones					Anglophones				
	PT	MP	SC	W	F	PT	MP	SC	W	F
	(% centrifugal)									
P1: (French and English different or similar?)	71[a]	60	63	55	44	40	35	46	39	-b
P2: (Threat to French Canadian culture?)	72	57	61	65	72	40	44	38	23	—
P3: (Should F.C. maintain ways or . . . ?)	61	50	58	51	58	38	38	39	25	—
P4: (Language and culture/ standard of living?)	36	29	24	29	16	15	4	8	8	—
	N (range)									
	(649)	(627)	(724)	(2,780)	(363)	(235)	(144)	(168)	(291)	(16)
	(654)	(631)	(730)	(2,791)	(369)	(240)	(144)	(168)	(294)	(16)

Occupation (see appendix B) is divided into the following categories:
PT: professional and technical   SC: sales and clerical   F: farmers
MP: managers and proprietors   W: blue collar (skilled, semiskilled, unskilled)

[a]Read: "71 percent of the Francophones in professional and technical occupations (of whom there are between 649 and 654, depending on the item), gave a centrifugal response."

TABLE 4.3

ORIENTATIONS TOWARD CULTURAL PLURALISM, BY EDUCATION AND OCCUPATION, BY LANGUAGE GROUP

	Education	Francophones					Anglophones				
		PT	MP	SC	W	F	PT	MP	SC	W	F
		(% centrifugal)									
P1: (French and English different or similar?)	low	68 (168)	60 (371)	61 (429)	53 (2464)	40 (332)	25 (52)	19 (48)	43 (95)	42 (234)	-[b]
	high	72[a] (485)	60 (256)	65 (301)	67 (323)	84 (31)	45 (188)	43 (96)	49 (73)	27 (60)	-
P2: (Threat to French Canadian culture?)	low	54 (168)	52 (375)	61 (429)	64 (2468)	70 (338)	19 (52)	33 (48)	39 (95)	22 (234)	-
	high	78 (483)	63 (256)	62 (301)	67 (323)	90 (31)	46 (188)	49 (96)	36 (73)	27 (60)	-
P3: (Should F.C. maintain ways or . . . ?)	low	71 (167)	50 (375)	57 (429)	50 (2468)	58 (338)	19 (47)	29 (48)	38 (95)	21 (234)	-
	high	57 (481)	50 (256)	59 (295)	58 (318)	55 (31)	43 (188)	42 (96)	41 (73)	42 (60)	-
P4: (Language and culture/ standard of living?)	low	28 (168)	25 (375)	23 (429)	29 (2464)	14 (339)	14 (52)	0 (48)	12 (95)	10 (231)	-
	high	39 (483)	34 (256)	25 (301)	31 (323)	45 (31)	16 (188)	6 (96)	3 (73)	3 (60)	-

Occupation is divided into the following categories:

PT: professional and technical   SC: sales and clerical   F: farmers
MP: managers and proprietors   W: blue collar (skilled, semiskilled, unskilled)

Education is coded as follows: (low: 11 years or less; high: 12 years or more)

[a]Read: "Of the 485 highly educated Francophones in professional and technical occupations, 72% gave a centrifugal response."

[b]There are too few Anglophone farmers in the sample to compute reliable percentages.

Let us now try to examine these effects of stratification variables in more detail. We can begin by asking why it is that the impact of educational status appears to be stronger than that of occupational status. A further question has to do with the combined effect of educational and occupational status. Do these two stratification dimensions each have an independent influence on orientations toward cultural pluralism, or is one dimension a much more important source of variation than the other?

To answer these two questions, we can examine the joint impact of education and occupation on the dependent variables.

We can see from table 4.3 that neither educational nor occupational differences in outlook are spurious: each of the stratification dimensions exerts an independent effect on each of the dependent variables.

The overall picture that emerges is that the higher-status Francophones, especially those in professional and technical occupations, are at one extreme, and the lower-status Anglophones are at the other. Thus, it is clear from the first panel of the table that it is the most privileged Francophones who are most likely to advance the assessment that French and English Canadians are different and that French Canadian culture is in danger. Similarly, professional and technical Francophones are the most likely to espouse the normative ideal that French-English differences ought to be maintained, just as they are the most likely to insist on the priority of a people's maintaining its language and culture over its standard of living.

Conversely, there is a tendency for the less-privileged Anglophones to be the least likely to judge the two cultures as being very different from one another, and the least likely to view French Canadian culture as being in any danger. Also, it is the less-privileged Anglophones who are the least likely to value and to want to maintain whatever cultural differences they perceive between the two communities.

Within this overall pattern, further important details are made clear by examination of the joint effects of education and occupation. The impact of occupational differences appears to be much stronger in the Francophone community than in the Anglophone community.

A particularly noteworthy occupational difference in the Francophone community is the difference between the professional and technical group, on the one hand, and the managers and proprietors, on the other. Members of the professional and technical category are consistently more centrifugal in their views than managers and proprietors are, even when education is controlled for. This significant divergence of views within the

Francophone middle class is an issue that we shall return to in more detail in a later section of this chapter.

Another significant detail revealed by table 4.3 is that the effects of educational differences appear to be much stronger in the Anglophone community than in the Francophone community.

Now that I have given these basic descriptive details of the way language group membership, education, and occupation combine to shape orientations toward cultural pluralism in Quebec, let us try to fill out the explanation already suggested by our results so far. If the evidence is consistent with the broad predictions of the communal competition perspective, our next step is to spell out some of the mechanisms that are responsible for the overall pattern summarized in table 4.3.

This closer look at the impact of the stratification system will be developed in the next two sections. I should mention that the arguments advanced as partial explanations contain two threads that are quite interwoven and often hard to separate. These two threads might be labeled interests and exposure. It will be argued that an individual's orientations toward cultural pluralism can be viewed as a (complex) function of that individual's interests, on the one hand, and that individual's differential exposure to social milieus, on the other hand.

We shall proceed by extending the overall results of table 4.3 in two directions. In the next section, we shall examine the impact of ethnic origin and degree of exposure to Quebec society. These two demographic variables are correlated with education and are similar to education in that they reflect differences in types of knowledge about, and experience of, Quebec society. This second section will thus be a sort of takeoff from the educational effect just observed.

The third section will take a closer look at who within the Francophone community has the most centrifugal orientations. It will thus be a sort of takeoff from the occupational effect just observed, and will focus on the structural bases of divergent interests within the Francophone community.

THE ROLE OF ETHNIC ORIGIN
AND DEMOGRAPHIC EXPOSURE

Sociologists have long been interested in the mechanisms by which common life-experiences and a common heritage influence people's outlooks. This immediately raises the question that Karl Deutsch has formulated, "When is a 'common' heritage common?" (Deutsch 1953:19).

Our choice of the two further independent variables to be examined in this section, namely ethnic origin and demographic exposure, is motivated by Deutsch's general discussion of the social bases of nationality (Deutsch 1953). Variables such as these are central components of Deutsch's long-influential social communications theory of nationality and national consciousness.

Let us begin with a consideration of the ethnic composition of the Francophone and Anglophone linguistic collectivities in Quebec. Ethnic origin is clearly an important source of potential differences in outlook for several reasons. First of all, those of non-French and non-English origin constituted roughly 10 percent of the Quebec population in 1970 (and 10.2 percent of this sample). As a statistical aggregate, the set of those of non-French and non-English origin includes a wide range of origin groups that vary markedly in their size, history of group formation in Canada, and, most important, in their institutional completeness.

Furthermore, among a set of people who share a particular ethnic origin, there is usually much variation in the extent to which individuals identify with the group and participate in group activities. The existence of minority ethnic communities means, by definition, that at least some members of various origin groups have patterns of living that *might* make them less knowledgeable about the mainstream of social and political life in Quebec.

Table 4.4 presents information about the joint effect of education, ethnic origin, and language group on each of our dependent variables.

From the case bases shown between parentheses at the bottom of the table, it is evident that the Francophone community is much more homogeneous than the Anglophone community: 94 percent of the Francophones in the sample are of French origin, while only 60 percent of the Anglophones are of English origin. As mentioned in chapter 1, this particularly asymmetric distribution is but another example and consequence of the past uneven development pattern followed by the two language groups. Less than 1 percent of the Francophone sample (38 weighted cases) is of English origin, and the number of Anglophones who are of French origin (16 weighted cases) is even lower, though their proportion (2 percent of the Anglophone community) is higher. The small minority of Francophones who are of English origin and Anglophones who are of French origin have been omitted from the table because given the number of variables involved, the majority of case bases are too small to compute percentages.

TABLE 4.4

ORIENTATIONS TOWARD CULTURAL PLURALISM, BY EDUCATION AND ETHNIC ORIGIN, BY LANGUAGE GROUP

	Francophones						Anglophones					
Ethnic origin	French			Other			English			Other		
Education	L	M	H	L	M	H	L	M	H	L	M	H
A.						(% centrifugal)						
P1: (French and English different or similar?)	55	65	74	52	58	69	39	31	44	34	49	59
P2: (Threat to French Canadian culture?)	64	70	72	31	51	53	27	41	54	23	29	31
P3: (Should F.C. maintain ways or . . . ?)	54	60	54	19	30	35	26	41	40	20	47	38
P4: (Language & culture/ standard of living?)	26	33	34	21	32	34	8	12	9	10	3	21
B.						(% "don't know")						
P1: (French and English different or similar?)	7	1	2	14	21	7	5	5	2	8	3	13
P2: (Threat to French Canadian culture?)	3	1	1	27	2	7	6	5	3	18	6	7
P3: (Should F.C. maintain ways or . . . ?)	4	0	0	12	2	0	5	4	2	11	0	7
P4: (Language & culture/ standard of living?)	1	0	0	10	0	0	0	3	0	3	0	7
						N (range)						
	(3,588)	(907)	(367)	(172)	(53)	(54)	(266)	(136)	(120)	(179)	(90)	(61)
	(3,602)	(918)	(369)	(176)	(53)	(58)	(271)	(136)	(120)	(181)	(90)	(61)

The first striking feature of the table (panel A) is that the strong communal effect by which Francophones are much more centrifugal in their orientations than Anglophones is still evident. It is also clear from panel A that the strong positive effect of educational status on centrifugal attitudes holds true within each ethnolinguistic subset of the population. As seen earlier, this educational effect is monotonic, with few exceptions. What can be said about the effects of ethnic origin? The table clearly points to the heterogeneity in outlook of the set of people who are of non-French and non-English origins. Those who are Francophones (which means here those who answered the questionnaire in French) by and large hold views similar to those of the Francophone majority of French origin on the first and fourth dependent variables, which deal with subjective assessments of whether French and English Canadians are different or similar and with the relative importance of a people's language and culture as opposed to its standard of living. Those of other origins are, however, less likely than other Francophones to perceive French Canadian culture as being threatened and less likely to hold the normative view that whatever differences between the two cultures exist should be maintained.

As for the differences within the Anglophone community between those of English origin and those of other origins, we cannot conclude from panel A of the table that there are no differences according to origin, but we can conclude that they are not large or systematic. Regardless of whether we consider these intracommunal ethnic differences as large or small, it is clear that those of other origins are closer in outlook to their linguistic brethren in their respective linguistic communities than they are to members of the other language community.

All of this suggests that (1) the role of ethnic factors is complex, and it would be fruitful, in further research, to examine other factors that might further explain these ethnic effects; and/but (2) the role of ethnic origin appears to be clearly less important than the overriding effect of communal membership. The latter finding is of importance in our assessment of the relative utility of the functionalist and communal competition perspectives, and more will be said about it later.

Where ethnic origin does appear to have a direct and non-spurious impact is in the way it is related to the transmission of information about Quebec society and history. One indicator of a lack of knowledge and awareness of Quebec society and history is the propensity to give "don't know" as an answer to questions about intercommunal relations such as the ones we are analyzing here.

As can be seen from panel B of table 4.4, those of non-French and non-English origins are more likely than members of the two "charter" origin groups to give "don't know" responses to each of the dependent variable measures. This ethnic effect is especially strong among those who have the least formal education. Although it is the least-educated of all origins who are most likely to give "don't know" responses, the tendency is much more pronounced among the least-educated of those of other (non-French, non-English) origins.

We should also note that the proportion of "don't know" answers is higher for the first two measures, which deal with the populations's subjective assessments of cultural pluralism, than for the last two which deal with normative evaluations. In other words, there is more indecision and uncertainty in the population regarding what the differences are between French and English and the degree to which French Canadian culture is actually threatened than there is on the issue of the extent to which cultural differences, to whatever extent they might be perceived to exist, *ought* to be maintained.

A final comment is in order about panel B. While the highest proportions of "don't know" responses are indeed to be found among the less-educated of other (non-French, non-English) origins, the positive effect of education on the proportion of "don't know" responses is not monotonic among those of other origins who are in the Anglophone community. These "don't know" responses among the more-educated respondents suggest the utility of examining another background variable that might help explain what has just been observed.

What is it, then, that makes Anglophones more likely to say "don't know" than Francophones, those of other (non-French, non-English) origins more likely to say so than those of English origin, and those of French origin least likely of all? One possibility that we shall now examine is a demographic factor suggested by the above rank orderings. One quantity that Francophones as a group have more of than Anglophones, and that Quebecers of French origin have most of and those of other (non-French, non-English) origins have least of, is what can be called a cumulative lifetime exposure to Quebec society.

This suggests that it might be useful to take into account in some way the respondents' backgrounds in terms of their overall past exposure to the Quebec milieu. As John Porter (1965:33) once put it, few parts of the world have so resembled a demographic railway station as the non-French parts of Canada over the past century. The high rates of in- and out-migration have been as characteristic of the non-French population of Quebec as of the population of other parts of Canada, and highly educated professional, technical, and managerial personnel have long been an important component of the population migrating into Quebec, whether from other parts of Canada or from elsewhere.

A simple, crude demographic variable that is included in this study is a question asking respondents if they have ever lived or worked outside the province of Quebec. The distribution of this variable within ethnolinguistic categories is shown in table 4.5. This variable clearly measures the respondents' lifetime exposure to Quebec society. It is dichotomized by considering those who have never lived or worked outside of Quebec, in other words those who have spent 100 percent of their lives in Quebec, as having a "high" degree of exposure, and those who have spent anything less than 100 percent of their lives in Quebec as having a "low" degree of exposure. It is clear from panel A that Francophones have a much higher cumulative lifetime exposure to Quebec than Anglophones do and that those of French origin have the highest degree of exposure, followed by those of English origin, with those of other origins having the lowest degree of exposure.

Panel B of the table reveals that cumulative exposure to Quebec society is negatively associated with education in both linguistic communities. The

TABLE 4.5

LIFETIME EXPOSURE TO QUEBEC SOCIETY, BY ETHNIC ORIGIN,
EDUCATION, AND LANGUAGE GROUP

		Francophones			Anglophones	
			(% high exposure)[a]			
A.	Ethnic origin					
	French	English	Other	French	English	Other
	82	45	24	–	53	20
	(4,880)	(38)	(288)	(16)	(525)	(332)
B.	Education[b]					
	Low	Medium	High	Low	Medium	High
	80	80	60	48	31	32
	(3,808)	(980)	(431)	(462)	(240)	(183)

[a]This is the percentage of respondents who replied "no" to the following question:
"Have you ever lived or worked outside the province of Quebec?"

[b]Education is coded as in table 4.1.

less educated show the greatest cumulative exposure to Quebec society. The shape of the relationship is different, however, in the two linguistic communities. Among Francophones, it is those with a high level of education who are more likely than the rest of their brethren to have lived or worked outside of Quebec.

It is likely that a good proportion of the Francophones who have lived or worked outside of Quebec went outside Quebec to pursue their college or university-level studies and then returned. Among Anglophones, it is also those with a high level of education who are more likely than the rest of their brethren to have lived or worked outside Quebec.

Let us now examine the joint effect of education and exposure to Quebec society on the structure of orientations. This is done in table 4.6.

It is clear that both education and lifetime exposure to Quebec society contribute, each independently of the other, to centrifugal orientations. This is true in both linguistic communities. These two factors also contribute independently to reducing the proportion of "don't know" answers in both linguistic communities. This holds true even though the two factors are negatively related to each other. In each community, the overall pattern is that the lower one's education and/or level of exposure to Quebec society, the less likely one is to hold centrifugal views and the more likely one is to give a "don't know" answer.

We might note that the curvilinear relationship observed earlier in the chapter, between formal education and the third dependent variable, appears here as well. This is explained by the ambiguity inherent in the way the idea of French Canadians "maintaining their ways" can be interpreted. It is possible that the most educated do not give the most centrifugal response of "maintaining ways" because this is taken to mean an espousal of traditional ways, a refusal of modernity, and so forth.

An interesting feature of the multivariate relationship shown in table 4.6 is the slight interaction effect between exposure and education among Francophones. While the overall pattern of those with a higher lifetime exposure to Quebec society displaying more centrifugal views holds in most educational categories, a clear reversal is noticeable among the most educated group of Francophones. In this group, it is those who have lived or worked (or studied, as suggested earlier) outside of Quebec who are the most centrifugal in their views. This may be due to other factors that are specific to highly educated Francophones, a group to which we shall turn our attention in the next section.

In this section, we have examined the ways in which orientations toward cultural pluralism are shaped by ethnic origin and demographic

TABLE 4.6

ORIENTATIONS TOWARD CULTURAL PLURALISM, BY EDUCATION, LIFETIME EXPOSURE TO QUEBEC SOCIETY, AND LANGUAGE GROUP

	Francophones						Anglophones					
Education	L		M		H		L		M		H	
Lifetime Exposure	Lo	Hi	Lo	Hi	Lo	Hi	Lo	Hi	Lo	Hi	Lo	Hi
A.					(% centrifugal)							
P1: (French and English different?)	56	54	56	67	75	72	35	40	37	44	38	49
P2: (Threat to French Canadian culture?)	55	64	56	73	73	68	31	20	36	42	43	59
P3: (Should F.C. maintain ways?)	41	54	62	57	53	51	25	23	48	39	36	49
P4: (Language & culture/ standard of living?)	24	27	30	33	35	34	6	11	7	11	11	17
B.					(% "don't know")							
P1: (French and English different?)	6	8	6	1	2	3	9	2	6	0	6	3
P2: (Threat to French Canadian culture?)	7	3	0	2	2	1	13	7	6	3	3	5
P3: (Should F.C. maintain ways?)	7	3	2	1	0	0	10	7	1	4	3	5
P4: (Language & culture/ standard of living?)	4	1	0	0	0	0	4	0	1	3	3	0
					N (range)							
	(747)	(3,043)	(197)	(772)	(170)	(257)	(239)	(215)	(166)	(74)	(124)	(59)
	(751)	(3,057)	(203)	(777)	(174)	(257)	(242)	(220)	(166)	(74)	(124)	(59)

exposure. This look at these two horizontal dimensions of Quebec society has provided a specification of the way these two further sources of differentiation combine with educational status and language group membership in shaping orientations toward cultural pluralism.

In a sense, we have just presented a partial answer to Deutsch's question mentioned at the beginning of this section. I have specified that ethnic heritage is less important in shaping outlooks than is a common membership in one or the other of the two overarching linguistic communities in Quebec. We have also shown that living in Quebec all of one's life is a source of more centrifugal orientations and that this effect operates in *both* linguistic communities.

These findings will be discussed further at the end of the chapter. Let us turn for the moment to a more detailed look at some structural sources of highly centrifugal orientations within the Francophone community.

WHO HAS THE MOST-CENTRIFUGAL VIEWS? A CLOSER LOOK

We have already seen that, consonant with the general predictions of the communal competition perspective, the most-centrifugal orientations toward cultural pluralism in Quebec are to be found among the more privileged members of the Francophone community. Beyond this, the literature provides us with further leads as to which subsets of the Francophone middle classes should be expected to display the most-centrifugal orientations.

One strand in the literature on nationalist movements emphasizes the role of the intelligentsia as carriers and developers of nationalist sentiment and ideology (see Gellner 1964; Smith 1971). While definitions of "intelligentsia" vary considerably, the term is often used in a broad sense to denote highly educated members of the middle class, as for example in Taylor's (1965) discussion of the social bases of contemporary Québécois nationalism. In this sense, our results concerning the independent effects of education in shaping centrifugal outlooks can be seen as a confirmation, if only a weak one, of this general hypothesis. On this general point, this source of support for Quebec nationalism has its parallels in the many smaller European nationalist movements surveyed by Hroch in his comparative study (1985).

Another related but distinct strand in the literature focuses not so much on the educated middle classes in general as on those who work in more or less intellectual occupations. According to this view, nationalist concerns are likely to be stronger among those in professional and technical occupations, for example, than among managers and proprietors. The mechanism assumed to be at work here is the one referred to earlier in our discussion of the communal competition perspective. As Gellner (1964) and others have argued, nationalist sentiment arises because members of subordinate communal groups are handicapped by having to function in a (dominant) foreign language not their own.

As an extension of this logic, I have already suggested (and seen) that within the Francophone community in Quebec, the most-centrifugal orientations are found among those in white-collar occupations. A further extension would suggest that within the white-collar category, those in professional and technical occupations should be expected to be more centrifugal in their orientations than managers and proprietors, since professional and technical occupations involve more manipulation of symbols and language. A similar argument is put forth by Fournier (1977) and Niosi (1980), who argue that nationalist sentiment is likely to be strongest among those whose work is most tied to the use of the French language.

Also, since professional and technical occupations are likely to involve a broader range of intellectual activity, those in such occupations should be more sensitized to the overall predicament of their communal group by virtue of this broadening effect of intellectual sophistication. This prediction is also confirmed by our results presented in table 4.2. Those in professional and technical occupations are consistently more likely to espouse centrifugal orientations than those who are managers and proprietors, and in fact they are more likely to than those in all other occupational groups.

Another strand in the literature focuses attention on the importance of public bureaucracies as generating milieus for nationalist ideology and sentiment. For example, in an article published in 1978, A. D. Smith gives much greater weight to the diffusion of bureaucracy as a factor in the diffusion of nationalism than he did in his earlier work (1971). The mechanism involved here is basically that a bureaucratic apparatus is a minimum requirement for a state structure to exist, and this makes state bureaucracies, real or potential, the natural battleground for communal competition. The existence of a state bureaucratic apparatus accounts for the widespread appeal of nationalism because it affords an arena in which those who are excluded from or disadvantaged in the dominant language and culture's occupational structure can pursue careers without structural barriers to advancement.

Another aspect of this line of thinking is that a state bureaucratic apparatus is often the focus of nationalist struggles because it is a mechanism or weapon by which the language and culture of "the excluded," in Gellner's (1964) terms, can be transformed from handicaps and liabilities into valuable assets and resources. In Smith's (1978) view, state bureaucracies are especially likely to be the focus of competition between communal groups for the further reason that the operation of a bureaucracy always involves some fusion of ascribed and achieved criteria for advancement, with the former often masquerading as the latter. Mastery of the dominant language of work in an organization, for example, becomes a skill that anyone can acquire, but those for whom the dominant language is a first language often happen to be more skilled than others. Public bureaucracies, then, are special because of the great legitimacy that accrues to the language and culture that become dominant within them.

This emphasis on the language issue in public bureaucracies is also central in the work of Horowitz (1971) on communal competition in the new states of the Third World. To Horowitz, communal conflict in the numerous segmented societies of the Third World regularly takes the form of language conflict over public service positions. This pattern occurs repeatedly because

> . . . language, like government service, is an issue that ties careerism to political status and elite to mass. The dualistic character of the language issue needs to be stressed. Without careerist incentives, there would be much less leadership for linguistic causes. Without the symbolic value of the issue, there would only be careerism behind it. It is the coalescence of these different goals . . . that guarantees the explosiveness of the issue. (Horowitz 1971:177)

Although they were developed independently, the ideas of Gellner, Smith and Horowitz have much in common with those of Bourdieu (1970) and Collins (1975) on the use of cultural symbols in intergroup competition. If schools, for example, transmit the culture of the privileged classes of society, under the guise of transmitting "knowledge," then those from less-privileged backgrounds face a handicap. In this way, the school, despite the "formal equality" with which it treats all its students, reproduces, in Bourdieu's terms, the inequalities between social classes in society (see the discussion in Murphy 1979).

Similarly, to the extent that a communal group succeeds in imposing its language and culture on a work organization, *its* language becomes *the* working language. And although all members of the society may be "free" to learn and use the organizations's language of work, those for whom it is a first language have an advantage over others. Language, then, functions in a way similar to educational credentials. Both are "formally equal," and theoretically open to be equally acquired by all. In practice, however, their acquisition is much easier for some members of society than for others.

An emphasis on the ways in which communal and cultural interest groups attempt to control state bureaucracies is also found in the literature on elites in developing societies. To authors such as Kraus, Maxwell, and Vanneman (1979) and Skocpol (1979), "modernizing elites" in dependent societies often take as their base of operation the state apparatus. An hypothesis that can be derived from this research is that the common unifying vested interest in the state bureaucracy might often have the effect of overriding and muting divergences of outlook between class fractions within the state elite.

In analyses of Quebec society, emphasis on public bureaucracies appears in the work of Guindon (1964, 1968, 1978), who speaks of the "new middle class" of French Canada as having its base in the public sector. This is also the key defining element of what Milner (1978) describes as the "state middle class." To Albert Breton (1964), Quebec's "new middle class" is located in both the private and public sectors, but is led to promote an expansion of the provincial state apparatus as a way of providing an outlet for its economic aspirations and interests.

To Guindon, the principal factor behind contemporary Québécois nationalism is the blocked occupational mobility of the Francophone new middle class. In his earlier analyses (1964, 1968), Guindon emphasizes the exclusion of Francophones from the middle and upper levels of the private sector, and also mentions the barriers to advancement faced by Francophones within the *federal* bureaucracies operating in Quebec. In his subsequent work (1978), which is basically a commentary on the events of the 1970s, attention is also given to the ceiling effect on the rapid expansion of the *provincial* public service that took place in the 1960s and early 1970s. Guindon, Milner, and Albert Breton do not dwell much on possible differences in outlook between occupational groups within the public sector.

All of these strands in the literature have in common the general view that competition between communal groups often centers on control of organizations, and, more particularly, state bureaucracies. Language and culture, according to this general view, are resources like any other and are likely to be used as such in competitive struggles. Organizations that are controlled by a communal group, or within which the language and

TABLE 4.7

ORIENTATIONS TOWARD CULTURAL PLURALISM,
BY EMPLOYMENT SECTOR
(FRANCOPHONES ONLY)

		Private	Public (Federal)	Public (Provincial and municipal)
		(% centrifugal)		
P1:	(French and English different or similar?)	54	66	63
P2:	(Threat to French Canadian culture?)	63	60	73
P3:	(Should F.C. maintain ways or . . . ?)	52	54	56
P4:	(Language & culture/ standard of living?)	27	29	33
		N (range)		
		(4,126)	(119)	(697)
		(4,138)	(119)	(712)

culture of a communal group are dominant, are likely to serve as institutional bases of operation in the process of communal competition.

Let us now turn to the data. As can be seen from table 4.7, the minority of Francophones who work in the public sector do indeed display more centrifugal orientations toward cultural pluralism, both in their subjective assessments of the differences that exist between French and English and in their normative evaluations of whether differences should be maintained.

It is also clear that within the public sector, there is a tendency for those employed in provincial and municipal administrations to hold more centrifugal views than those employed in federal bureaucracies. In fact, those in the federal public service display contradictory tendencies: on one measure, they are even more centrifugal than those in the provincial public service; on another measure, they are even less centrifugal than those in the private sector.

The ambiguous (and apparently ambivalent) pattern displayed by Francophones in the federal public service brings us back to the question of what it is about the public sector that makes its members hold more centrifugal orientations. The previously mentioned hypothesis about blocked mobility (in the private sector) as a source of centrifugal orientations will be examined later on in the context of our assessment of the "reactive ethnicity" hypothesis.

Another hypothesis that could be advanced is that the *security* provided by employment in the public sector allows Francophones employed in that sector to be more affirmative about their language and culture than Francophones employed in the private sector. Given the differences in outlook between those employed in the federal public service and those employed in the provincial administration, it is unlikely that employment in the public sector as such provides any cushion against risk.

Rather, the key mechanism in providing security against risk is probably the relative dominance of the French language and culture in the work organization. Employment in sectors that are controlled by Francophones or in which a large majority of the workforce is French-speaking affords Francophone workers a greater opportunity to affirm their belief in cultural differences and, conversely, allows them to carry few if any penalties for doing so. It also provides no incentives for individuals to want to minimize assessments and evaluations of cultural differences. Furthermore, to the extent that Francophones *are* dominant in certain organizations, for example the provincial public service bureaucracies, these organizations are likely to become operational bases from which members of the subordinate communal group might attempt to implement the goal of further strengthening the group's institutions (see Breton 1979).

In segmented societies in which the communal groups are unequal in power and resources, the subordinate group's *most complete* institutions are likely to constitute a power base for the elite of the subordinate group. These elites may be especially concerned with equalizing the power relationship between its institutions and the competing communal group's institutions. Such a strategy may well lead those who are employed in Francophone-controlled institutions to espouse highly centrifugal orientations toward cultural pluralism.

What I have just suggested is that it is Francophone dominance or control of work organizations that is the source of the more centrifugal orientations displayed by those employed in the provincial and municipal public bureaucracies. Work organizations in which Francophones are in some sense and to some extent dominant are not, of course, restricted to the public sector. We should note that only 20 percent of the respondents in our sample are employed in the public sector.

For this reason, we need to examine the joint effect of an individual's employment sector and a measure of Francophone control of the work organization on that individual's orientations toward cultural pluralism. In the Quebec Social Movements Study being analyzed here, the best available measure of Francophone control of the work organization is a question about the ethnic origin of the organization's top management. This multivariate relationship is shown in table 4.8.

Several important findings are revealed in table 4.8. First of all, the ambiguous position of those in the federal public service is still visible and is difficult to interpret given the relatively low (weighted) case base shown at the bottom of the second column of the table.

If we compare the private sector to the provincial (and municipal) public sector, it is clear that employment in the provincial (and municipal) public sector results in more centrifugal orientations mainly when the organization's top management is French Canadian. There is, then, a slight interaction effect between communal control of the workplace and its public sector status. The most centrifugal views are held by those in the provincial (and municipal) public sector who have French Canadian superiors. In the private sector, on the other hand, there is little systematic difference in outlook between those whose top superiors are French Canadians and others.

What this suggests is that the private sector is not only much larger, but also more heterogeneous than the public sector. Further characteristics of private sector work organizations (size, industrial sector, market structure, and so forth) need to be investigated to test for possible interactions with the measure of organizational control that we have just examined. These specifications would take us too far afield to be pursued here. What we shall do, however, is examine the joint effects of occupation and employment sector, as well as the joint effects of occupation and ethnic origin of top management, on the structure of orientations. These further multivariate analyses will hopefully allow us to specify in greater detail the mechanisms involved in the several hypotheses discussed so far in this section.

Table 4.9 presents the joint effects of employment sector and occupation on each of the dependent variables. Here, I have excluded federal public employees because their low case bases would not permit separate analyses within each occupational category and because their ambiguous outlooks caution against combining them with those in provincial and municipal public service bureaucracies.

There is clearly a slight interaction effect between the two independent variables: the effect of employment in the (provincial and municipal) public sector is not equally strong in all occupations. The effect is almost

TABLE 4.8

ORIENTATIONS TOWARD CULTURAL PLURALISM, BY EMPLOYMENT SECTOR
AND ETHNIC ORIGIN OF TOP MANAGEMENT (FRANCOPHONES ONLY)

Top management[a]	French Canadian			Other		
Employment sector	Private	Public federal	Public provincial[b]	Private	Public federal	Public provincial[b]
	(% centrifugal)					
P1:						
(French and English different or similar?)	56	78	62	60	61	63
P2:						
(Threat to French Canadian culture?)	62	53	76	63	55	52
P3:						
(Should F.C. maintain ways or . . . ?)	53	50	55	50	54	65
P4:						
(Language & culture/standard of living?)	26	33	34	28	30	19
	N (range)					
	(2,205)	(36)	(591)	(1,611)	(67)	(69)
	(2,211)	(36)	(606)	(1,620)	(67)	(71)

[a]Based on responses to the question: "Are the members of the top level management of this organization French Canadians, English Canadians, Canadians of some other origin, or non-Canadians?" (Check several responses if necessary.)

[b]Includes municipal and local administrations.

negligible among blue-collar workers and is not clear-cut among sales and clerical workers.

Where the impact of public sector employment on centrifugal orientations is consistent and noticeable is in the two upper white-collar groups, and in these two groups only. If one compares these two sets of occupations, it is

TABLE 4.9

ORIENTATIONS TOWARD CULTURAL PLURALISM, BY OCCUPATION
AND EMPLOYMENT SECTOR (FRANCOPHONES ONLY)

Occupation	Professional and technical		Managers and proprietors		Sales and clerical		Workers		Farmers
Employment sector	Private	Public[a]	Private	Public[a]	Private	Public[a]	Private	Public[a]	Private
	(% centrifugal)								
P1: (French and English different or similar?)	69	72	59	81	64	54	56	52	44
P2: (Threat to French Canadian culture?)	65	78	56	84	61	72	64	64	72
P3: (Should F.C. maintain ways or . . . ?)	58	62	48	59	57	60	51	47	58
P4: (Language and culture/ standard of living?)	34	39	28	38	21	32	29	26	17
	N (range)								
	(266)	(315)	(563)	(32)	(551)	(103)	(2,373)	(239)	(361)
	(268)	(319)	(567)	(32)	(557)	(103)	(2,377)	(250)	(367)

[a]Federal public employees are excluded because of low case bases.

among managers and proprietors that the public/private distinction has the greater impact. Put differently, the lesser centrifugal orientations associated with the private sector are more visible among managers than among those in professional and technical occupations. We should note, however. that this pattern is based on the responses of a very small number of public sector managers (32 weighted cases).

Another way to interpret this relationship is to note that the occupational effect (managers and proprietors versus professional and technical staff) is stronger and more clear-cut in the private sector than in the public sector. What this shows is that a highly centrifugal orientation is associated with either being in a professional or technical occupation or holding *any* upper-level job in the public service. The effect of public sector employment among managers can be seen as much stronger than that prevailing among the professional and technical group simply because the latter already hold more–highly centrifugal views. The minority of managers who are in the public service display a pattern of views that definitely sets them off from their private sector colleagues. We cannot say, however, that they adopt views that are identical to those of their public service brethren in professional and technical occupations.

How should this pattern be interpreted theoretically? As mentioned earlier, several "new middle class" theorists have emphasized the role of all upper-level white-collar groups in the (provincial) public sector as the most consistent supporters and promoters of contemporary Québécois nationalism. Other authors have emphasized the different orientations that can be expected of professional and technical personnel, especially when they are compared to their managerial counterparts.

These findings suggest that *both* of these perspectives are useful, and they show that occupation and employment sector cannot be considered independently, given the strong interaction effect between the two factors. The specification of the joint effect of occupation and employment sector confirms the hypothesis that we derived from the work of Kraus, Maxwell, and Vanneman (1979) to the effect that membership in the state apparatus might moderate divergences in outlook between elite fractions, in this case professional and technical staff on the one hand, and managers on the other.[1]

Further useful information can be gleaned from examining the joint effect of occupation and ethnic origin of top management, as given in table 4.10.

Here, we find an even stronger interaction effect: the impact of having French Canadian bosses is negative among sales and clerical workers, and ambiguous among blue-collar workers. Espousing a more-centrifugal outlook as a result of having French Canadian superiors appears to occur

TABLE 4.10

ORIENTATIONS TOWARD CULTURAL PLURALISM,
BY OCCUPATION AND ETHNIC ORIGIN OF TOP MANAGEMENT (FRANCOPHONES ONLY)

Occupation	Professional Technical		Managers Proprietors		Sales Clerical		Workers		Farmers	
Top Management	FC	Other	FC	Other	FC	Other	FC	Other	FC	Other
					(% centrifugal)					
P1: (French and English different or similar?)	71	72	64	52	59	70	53	57	45	–
P2: (Threat to French Canadian culture?)	77	63	60	48	59	62	63	65	72	–
P3: (Should F.C. maintain ways or ...?)	62	55	52	48	49	68	52	46	62	–
P4: (Language & culture/ standard of living?)	39	32	30	25	21	27	30	27	19	–
					N (range)					
	(435)	(171)	(433)	(162)	(397)	(290)	(1,404)	(1,163)	(304)	(9)
	(439)	(173)	(433)	(162)	(403)	(290)	(1,415)	(1,167)	(304)	(9)

consistently only among members of the two upper-level white-collar categories. Both managers and proprietors and professional and technical staff are responsive (in a more centrifugal direction) to the presence of French Canadian superiors.

This pattern among members of the two upper-level white-collar groups is clearly different from that observed among sales and clerical and blue-collar workers. The contrast is most visible if we note that among the sales and clerical category, a strong effect in exactly the opposite direction is visible. In this lower-level white-collar category, Francophones who have non–French Canadian employers are consistently more centrifugal in their orientations than are those whose employers are French Canadian.

How can this complex pattern be explained? One possible interpretation flows from the idea that control of a work organization by a communal group can have rather different consequences for members of different occupational categories *within* the communal group. These differences between occupational categories may be related to the way the occupations are inserted into the labor market.

Upper-level white-collar Francophones in Francophone- controlled organizations espouse more-centrifugal orientations than do their counterparts in non-Francophone organizations. This can be seen as the result of two sets of factors: the benefits that accrue to Francophones who do display more centrifugal orientations in Francophone-controlled organizations, and the costs that Francophones in non-Francophone organizations might face if they were to display centrifugal orientations.

Professional, technical, and managerial personnel are typically expected to internalize the general goals of the employing organization. Commitment to the goals of the organization is a necessary, if not sufficient, condition for promotion and advancement for upper-level personnel. Given these attributes of upper-level white-collar occupations, upper-level white-collar Francophones who work in Anglophone organizations are likely to feel that they should downplay their language and culture and dampen whatever opinions they might have about their language and culture's threatened position, their language and culture's distinctiveness, the desirability of maintaining differences, and so forth.

Upper-level Francophones in Francophone organizations, on the other hand, are likely to feel that they are *expected* to display more-centrifugal orientations, as a sign of their commitment to the organization. Francophone-controlled organizations are likely to be viewed as institutions of the communal group as a whole. Commitment to the organization, then, is likely to be manifested, and recognized by others, by the same cultural "signals" and symbols as a general commitment to the communal group.

Lower-level white-collar sales and clerical workers face a different situation. Their positions require less commitment to the goals of the organization. When advancement is possible, it is more a function of having their performance at specific tasks judged to be satisfactory by superiors than a function of their overall commitment to the organization. While it is true that sales and clerical workers can easily be replaced, it is also true, *ceteris paribus*, that they can find new employers. Thus there is generally the possibility of a certain amount of (at least horizontal) mobility at the lower white-collar levels in industrial societies.

A consequence of this is that Francophones who hold sales and clerical positions with Anglophone (or rather, non-Francophone) employers can feel quite free to espouse centrifugal views should they feel moved to do so. To the extent that their Anglophone employers might find this objectionable, possible reprisals are less likely to have the effect of harming these employees' overall chances for advancement.

It should be remembered that at the lower white-collar level Francophones were not seriously underrepresented in the occupational structure of Quebec in 1970. It was at the upper levels that Francophones were (still) underrepresented, and it is at the upper levels that advancement is most likely to involve what E. C. Hughes ([1943] 1963) has called "a vote of confidence" on the part of top management.

We should add to this that, even in 1970, Francophones working in Anglophone organizations were sooner or later exposed to a whole range of subtle and potentially annoying features of the unequal relationship between the two language communities in Quebec. Chief among these were the lower level of bilingualism of Anglophones and the relative dominance of the English language in quite a range of interaction contexts.

The day-to-day operation of the system was such that potentially grievance-producing events were bound to occur with some regularity. Such potentially grievance-producing events might or might not lead to the adoption of a more-centrifugal orientation toward cultural pluralism. Whatever the impact of contacts may be, the explanation that we have just advanced suggests why upper-level Francophones working in Anglophone organizations are more likely than their lower-level counterparts to suppress whatever grievances they might have.

Within this upper-level white-collar group, there are further noticeable differences. The effect of having French Canadian superiors and the occupational effect (professional and technical staff versus managers and proprietors) combine additively, and clearly neither effect is negligible. One can see from the four left-hand columns of table 4.10 that the most centrifugal views are held by professional and technical staff who have French Canadians as their top superiors. The least centrifugal views within the upper white-collar group are held by managers and proprietors whose top superiors are non–French Canadian.

This finding needs to be interpreted with the pattern shown by the previous tables kept in mind. Taken together, the data suggest that what is most responsible for the impact of public sector employment on the centrifugal outlooks of the upper-level white-collar group is not so much the concentration of Francophones as the existence of some sort of Francophone control of the organization. The data also suggest, though, that this particular relationship holds only among members of the upper-level white-collar group.

We can conclude from all of this, then, that it is Francophone control of the work organization that apparently signals an increase in the legitimacy, if not in the dominance, of the French language and culture at the workplace. This signal is most pertinent to the upper-level white-collar group, whose work is most tied to the use of language and whose occupational interests are consequently linked to the importance and dominance of their language at the workplace.

The upper-level white-collar group, and especially the professional and technical staff, are particularly sensitive to the dominant language of the workplace. As a consequence, these groups are especially likely to give high assessments of the degree of cultural distinctiveness between French and English and to attach a high value to the maintenance of these distinctions. They will be all the more likely to hold such centrifugal views if the norms of the workplace allow, require, or encourage them to do so, and/or if the norms of the workplace do not in any way handicap those who do.

What the whole pattern suggests is that in contexts of communal competition, it is the members of the elite of each communal group who are most sensitive to the fact that the competition takes the form of competition between organizations. We might add that in contexts of communal competition between unequal groups, as in the case of Quebec, the elites of the subordinate group might be even more inclined to hold this view than the elites of the dominant group. Consequently, upper-level white-collar members of the subordinate communal group will display rather different orientations depending on whether they are employed in Francophone-controlled or Anglophone-controlled organizations.

SUMMARY AND DISCUSSION

A large body of information on the impact of intracommunal stratification variables on the structure of orientations toward cultural pluralism within Quebec society in 1970 has been presented in this chapter. Let us now briefly review the principal findings and offer some further comments on them in view of the theoretical debate between the functionalist and communal competition perspectives.

Within each linguistic community, the more privileged, and especially the more educated, are more centrifugal in their orientations. Language-group membership and socioeconomic status exert strong and independent effects on the dependent variables. The more-privileged Francophones are the most centrifugal in their orientations, and the less-privileged Anglophones are the least centrifugal.

Within the less-centrifugal group, an important component of the less-centrifugal attitude is the lack of information about Quebec society and history. This lack of information is most widespread among the less educated and among those with a low cumulative lifetime exposure to Quebec society. Because of these factors, "don't know" answers are more frequent among Anglophones than among Francophones and among those of other (non-French, non-English) origins in each linguistic community.

While those of "other" ethnic origins are more likely to give "don't know" answers to the questions for each of our dependent variable measures, there is little evidence of clear-cut and discernible "other ethnic" effect in the structure of centrifugal orientations. Whatever "other ethnic" effects are visible are not systematic and are less pronounced than the overriding impact of communal group membership. This finding suggests a specification of the relative utility and applicability of the functionalist and communal competition perspectives in linguistically segmented societies in which each linguistic community is composed of members of different ethnic origins.

The pattern observed here, although not clear-cut, suggests that ethnic origin (an ascribed characteristic) *as such* becomes less important as a source of differentiation in outlooks *within* each language community. This is consonant with the predictions of the functionalist perspective. The persistence of a strong communal effect, on the other hand, is consonant with the predictions of the communal competition perspective. This points to the necessity of distinguishing analytically between ethnic origin groups and language groups.

This examination of the sources of less-centrifugal and "don't know" opinions also points out that these sources, which include education and cumulative exposure to Quebec society, while especially relevant to an understanding of the reactions of Anglophones and those of other (non-French, non-English) origins, *do* operate in similar fashion in both linguistic communities.

Among those with the most-centrifugal orientations, namely the more-privileged and more-educated Francophones, it was found that education and occupation have independent effects. Within the upper-level white-collar group, those in professional and technical occupations hold systematically more centrifugal views than do managers and proprietors. Blue-collar workers are not especially centrifugal in their orientations.

Employment in the public sector, and especially in the Quebec provincial and municipal public service, is a further source of highly centrifugal views, as has been predicted by theorists of nationalism in general, and authors on contemporary Québécois nationalism in particular.

A further structural characteristic of work organizations — Francophone control of the work organization, measured here by the presence of French Canadian top superiors — was also found to be an important source of centrifugal views. This was found to be especially important in the public sector. This specifies one of the mechanisms involved in the public bureaucracies' role as generating milieus of centrifugal outlooks.

A further specification is that the impact of public sector employment on centrifugal orientations is noticeable only in the two upper-level white-collar occupational groups. Also, differences between professional and technical staff, on the one hand, and managers and proprietors, on the other, are not as strong in the public sector as they are in the private sector. This confirms the hypothesis that membership in the state apparatus imposes a certain uniformity of interests among white-collar fractions that are often otherwise divergent.

Francophone control of the workplace (measured by the presence of French Canadians among the top management) is more important than the mere presence of a French-speaking majority in signaling the relevance, legitimacy, and appropriateness of the French language and culture at the workplace. This accounts for the greater sensitivity of the white-collar groups to this feature of the workplace organization and provides a further specification of a mechanism involved in producing more-centrifugal views. This general picture of the stratification effect within the Francophone community can now be put in broader perspective by comparing our results with those of other recent Canadian studies.

In a recent study of three ethnic groups — Slavs, Italians, and Jews — in Toronto, it was found that the more-educated, Canadian-born members of these groups were the least oriented toward participating in and maintaining their respective ethnic communities (Weinfeld 1985). Another study found that there was a negative relationship between ethnic group identity and the experience of (upward) social mobility among Japanese Canadians in Toronto (Makabe 1979). These findings, which are consonant with the predictions of the functionalist perspective, suggest that, *ceteris paribus*, the functionalist perspective is more likely to be confirmed in this way when applied to immigrant ethnic communities and their relationship to their larger societies than when applied to communal groups in segmented societies.[2]

In the Canadian case, the Francophone and Anglophone communal segments are the outgrowth of the two initial "charter groups" (Porter 1965) formed by the British conquest of New France. Each of the charter ethnic groups has been so powerful that it has become more than just an "ethnic group." Each has extended its full range of institutions into those of an overarching linguistic community, which, as we have seen, is composed of members of various ethnic origins.

Stated more formally, the historical setting variable (and more specifically, whether the group in question was formed by voluntary migration or whether it is the result of annexation or conquest) may be an important macrosociological predictor of whether the functionalist or communal competition perspective is likely to be the more appropriate.

What is the significance of the historical setting variable? Theoretical works have attempted to spell out the differences between subordinate groups created through immigration and those created through conquest. Lieberson (1961) advances a framework that suggests that dominant-subordinate group relations in settings characterized by migrant superordination follow quite a different course from those in settings where the migrant group enters a subordinate position in the society. Schermerhorn (1978:chapter 4) argues that the degree of cultural and structural pluralism is likely to be greatest in intergroup contexts formed by conquest and annexation, and lowest in settings that are the result of voluntary migration. The empirical findings I have just reported can be interpreted as being consonant with the thrust of Schermerhorn's argument. Indeed, we have specified one important intervening variable that is part of the causal process involved in Schermerhorn's argument, that of the structure of orientations toward pluralism within different types of subordinate groups.

The data we have just examined highlight, in yet another way, the difference between Francophones in Quebec and most other North American minorities. The population of most parts of North America, with a few notable exceptions, is a product of successive waves of (relatively) voluntary migrations. Unlike most other North Americans, Francophone Quebecers, along with Spanish-speaking Americans in the Southwest, have a collective identity and group institutions that antedate their formal incorporation into the Canadian and American state structures. Myrdal, in his study of American race relations, noted that "the minority peoples of the United States are fighting for status in the larger society; the minorities of Europe are mainly fighting for independence from it" (Myrdal 1944:50). From this point of view, as in so many other ways, Quebec is a European enclave in North America.

I would like to conclude this part of the discussion by referring to yet another North American case study, namely Cuneo's (1976) investigation of support for political continentalism in Canada. Cuneo's dependent variable is a measure of the degree to which respondents agreed with a statement that "Canada and the United States should join together as one country." This is clearly related to our discussion, since political unification, or the merging of state structures, can be conceived of as a reduction in the degree of worldwide structural pluralism in political institutions, or in the terms used here, as a trend in the centripetal direction. Cuneo found that support for political continentalism (merging the two states) was higher among Francophones than among Anglophones, higher in Quebec and the Maritimes than in the other provinces, and, in general, strongest among the least-privileged segments of the Canadian population.

In his explanation, Cuneo draws on the center-periphery distinction popular in the development literature. Those whose structural location in Canadian society is in some way peripheral are more continentalist than those who are in the center. The least continentalist are the educated, the affluent, English-speakers, and residents of Ontario. Notice that the latter groups display the same pattern of centrifugal responses as was observed among educated Francophones in Quebec. This tells us that privileged English-speaking Canadians are more attached to the Canadian state (and probably, by extension, to separate Canadian institutions) and more interested in keeping these institutions separate from their U.S. counterparts than are the less privileged, just as educated Francophones in Quebec are more attached to separate French and English institutions, and more interested in keeping them separate than are the less educated.

In contrasting Cuneo's results with our own, it might at first glance appear paradoxical that Francophones display more centrifugal orientations than do Anglophones on the question of French-English dualism in Quebec, and more centripetal orientations than Anglophones on the issue of continentalism. To be sure, the studies are not strictly comparable, since Cuneo's analysis does not report the *joint* effects of language and education in Quebec. Thus we are unable to say whether educated Francophones in Quebec are more or less continentalist than other segments of the Quebec population. Nonetheless, these two different orientations on the part of Francophones can be understood as two aspects of the same issue. Francophones are less attached to the Canadian state structure than are Anglophones and are also more attached to the Quebec state than are Anglophones (see Pinard 1975). We also know that within Quebec, it is the most educated and privileged Francophones who feel the most distant from the federal government (Grabb 1979).

Francophone dissatisfaction with the federal state will naturally find expression in support of moves to change current political arrangements. What we have just seen, however, is that Francophone discontent can not only take the form of favoring increased decentralization of the federal system; it can also find expression in support for a merger of the Canadian and American state structures. All of these orientations can be seen as efforts on the part of Francophone Canadians to reduce the power of English-Canadian institutions. These orientations can also be seen as simply a reflection of the fact that for many Francophones, the Canada–United States boundary may be less relevant—the relevant boundary being that between Quebec/French Canada, on the one hand, and, the rest of the world on the other.[3] We shall be returning to these issues in chapter nine.

Cuneo's findings can be explained by the communal competition perspective. They also illustrate some parallel social bases of English Canadian and Québécois nationalism. Cuneo, in his explanation, builds on the work of S. D. Clark (1968) and others who have argued that the less-privileged social groups and regions of Canada, having no control over or interest in the bureaucratic organizations represented by the expanding Canadian state and its extensions, have historically been less attached to it. The more-privileged social groups and regions, on the other hand, because of the benefits they derive from the existence of a Canadian state that is distinct and separate from the United States, have been the main supporters of Canadian nationalism.

This is consonant with the predictions of theories of nationalism, which, as we have seen, emphasize middle class and elite competition as a source of nationalist sentiment and ideology.[4] Also present is the emphasis on *control of,* or *benefits from,* organizations, especially state organizations. From this perspective, the position of more-privileged Canadians vis-à-vis the Canadian state and the position of more-privileged Francophones vis-à-vis the Quebec state are identical.

What this comparison illustrates is that the *objective* cultural differences between competing (communal or national) elites need not necessarily be very great in order for assertions of distinctiveness to be proclaimed. This suggests that language differences, while certainly important as a potential barrier when they do exist, are not necessarily the only type of cultural difference around which groups can be mobilized. This supports the view of Smith (1971) who takes Gellner (1964) to task on precisely this point. Gellner insists on the linguistic nature of nationalist movements.

This highlights the ambiguous way language differences are conceived in the literature on communal conflict. In the work of Gellner (1964) and others, at times it is the technical and functional aspects of language as a necessary tool of communication that are emphasized, and at other times emphasis is not on the necessity of a given language as such, but on the broader notion of literacy and the shared symbols of an industrial society. Either way, the accent is on the "naturalness" and inevitability of language being a rallying point in competition between communal groups in segmented societies.

A different point of view can be deduced from the work of Weber (1978), Collins (1975), and Parkin (1979). These authors would imply that there is little or nothing that is "natural" or inevitable about language being a rallying point in communal conflict. In their view, language is one cultural trait among many that can be seized upon as a significant difference between communal groups.

This issue needs to be investigated more thoroughly. It is likely that some synthesis of the above positions can be arrived at. While language differences may not inherently be any more likely to be seized upon than other kinds of differences, it may nonetheless be possible to specify the conditions under which they are likely to be more salient than other kinds of differences.

One reason for the increasing emphasis on language in Quebec, Belgium, and elsewhere is that language is a (relatively) more achieved and less ascribed characteristic than ethnic origin, race, or religion. As a consequence, given the value system of advanced industrial societies, exclusion or selection on the basis of language skills is not only more "rational" but also more "legitimate" than exclusion or selection on the basis of other more-ascribed criteria. Selection on the basis of language proficiency, then, in industrial societies, can be seen as similar to selection on the basis of educational credentials: both are legitimate means of differentiating between competing candidates, however strongly language proficiency and educational credentials may be correlated with ascribed characteristics.

Observers (see, for example, Rocher 1973) have often referred to the Janus-like character of Francophone Quebec society: an intelligentsia oriented toward the French language and European culture, on the one hand, and the majority of the population under the more direct influence of the English language and North American cultural trends, on the other. In this section, I have tried to put this special feature of elite-mass relations in Quebec into a broader theoretical and comparative perspective by examining how elite-mass differences in orientations vary over several intergroup contexts.

Finally, what can be said about the theoretical debate, mentioned earlier, concerning the effects of the development process on the degree of cultural pluralism? Basically, this analysis has pointed to the importance of a key intervening variable—the distribution of centripetal versus centrifugal orientations among the population, and especially the extent and direction of mass-elite differences in this respect. A proposition that emerges from the preceding discussion is that, *ceteris paribus*, the sign of the bivariate relationship between centrifugal orientations and social privilege within a subordinate group is an important predictor variable. In contexts in which the sign is positive (in which elites are more "centrifugal" than the masses), the degree of cultural and structural pluralism is likely to be higher *over time* than in contexts in which the sign is negative (in which elites are more "centripetal" than the masses).

5

Perceptions of
Communal Inequalities

As we have already seen in chapter 1, although the Quiet Revolution spawned the first of several waves of measures aimed at reducing them, the inequalities between French and English were still appreciable in 1970. In this chapter, we shall investigate the mass belief system and the perceptual structure that were generated by the long-standing and wide-ranging inequalities between the two linguistic communities.[1] Over the years, quite a range of thoughtful literary and impressionistic evidence has been brought to bear on the subject, but little in the way of systematic empirical research has been done. We shall examine how French-English inequalities are perceived by different subgroups of the Quebec population in 1970 and compare our results to those of the only other large-scale investigation of the topic, which was carried out five years earlier. This will set the stage for our look forward in time in part 3 of this book.

The hypotheses that were derived from the two different theoretical perspectives will be presented in the context of the discussion that follows the presentation of the data. In parallel fashion to what we saw in chapter 3 regarding orientations toward cultural pluralism, we shall see that the two perspectives present contrasting predictions about how we should expect beliefs to be structured at any one point in time. The body of this chapter will thus successively (1) set forth the five dimensions along which inequalities between Francophones and Anglophones can be classified and analyzed, (2) present the distributions of the ten indicators of perceptions of French-English inequalities, along with their breakdown according to language group and social stratification variables, (3) briefly discuss these findings in the light of the debate between the functionalist and communal competition perspectives, and (4) compare the results with those of the earlier large-scale study by Roseborough and Breton (1971).

COMMUNAL INEQUALITIES: THE FIVE DIMENSIONS

We shall examine two broad dimensions of socioeconomic gaps between Francophones and Anglophones and two dimensions of power disparities. In addition, we shall examine a fifth dimension, that of status inequalities between the two linguistic communities. Two indicators of each dimension will be used.

The first dimension has to do with perceptions of socioeconomic gaps in wealth between the two linguistic communities. To examine this dimension, we analyze one question in which the respondents are asked to give a subjective assessment of the difference in wealth between French and English Canadians, and another question bearing on the respondents' normative evaluation of this inequality.

The second dimension deals with the socioeconomic gaps between the two linguistic communities in terms of access to jobs. To examine this dimension, the respondents' answers to two questions are analyzed. The first asks the respondent if French Canadians and English Canadians of equal competence have the same chance of getting job offers or promotions. This measure of perceptions of the relative advantage of the two language groups in access to employment is similar, though not identical, to the indicator of perceived economic advantage used in the Roseborough and Breton study. In addition to this measure of *perceptions* of the situation, a second question focuses on *experiences* in the work world. The second question asks if the respondent himself (or herself), or any member of his or her personal network has ever been treated in a discriminatory fashion in getting a job or a promotion.

The third dimension has to do with communal inequalities in the world of business and finance in Quebec. This type of power disparity between the two linguistic communities is measured by two questions. The first asks respondents to assess which of the two groups occupies the "most important place in the world of business and finance in Quebec." The second asks them to *evaluate* this state of affairs as normal or abnormal.

The fourth dimension focuses on power disparities in the realm of politics. Two questions are used as measures of this dimension. The first deals with the power of French Canadians in the federal government. Respondents are asked if the position of French Canadians in Ottawa is as important as it should be. The second question we use to analyze communal inequalities in politics is a more indirect one. It asks respondents to evaluate the extent to which the Quebec case is similar or dissimilar to a colonial situation. Unfortunately, no measure of the relative power of Francophones and Anglophones in the provincial government was available in 1970. This reflects the weight of past and still-prevailing power arrangements at the time. The provincial government and civil service were understood to be disproportionately Francophone controlled, and legitimately so, as a counterweight to the historical underrepresentation of Francophones in the private sector.

The fifth and final dimension of communal inequalities that we shall analyze deals more with communal differences in status than with socio-economic gaps or power disparities. The two questions used to measure this dimension have to do with perceived communal inequalities in the professions. The first asks whether the better doctors are French Canadian or English Canadian. The second question asks whether the greatest scientists are found among French Canadians or among English Canadians.

Taken together, the five dimensions of French-English inequalities that we examine in this chapter can be seen as spanning the familiar Weberian tripartite division of inequalities in class, status, and political power. We are now ready to take a closer look at each of our measures and to examine their distribution in each linguistic community.

THE STRATIFICATION SYSTEM AND THE STRUCTURE OF PERCEPTIONS: DESCRIPTION

In this section, we shall investigate the links between measures of socio-economic status and social privilege, on the one hand, and each of our measures of perceived French-English inequalities, on the other. In addition, as in chapter 4, we shall attempt to assess how stratification variables combine with language group membership in shaping the structure of perceptions.

Wealth

Let us begin with our first dimension, that of perceptions of communal inequalities in wealth. Table 5.1 shows the joint effects of education and

TABLE 5.1

PERCEPTIONS OF COMMUNAL INEQUALITIES IN WEALTH, BY EDUCATION AND OCCUPATION, BY LANGUAGE GROUP

Occupation	Francophones					Anglophones			
	PT	MP	SC	W	F	MP	SC	W	F
A. Education									
					(% "English")				
Which group is wealthier? low	68	66	56	57	54	31	40	36	—
high	78[a]	68	73	71	81	52	49	37	—
					(% "should be reduced")				
Is this acceptable? low	43	53	62	50	65	53	50	42	—
high	69	70	68	66	96	68	39	29	—
B.					(% "don't know")				
Which group is wealthier? low	5	8	9	9	16	17	26	18	—
high	3[a]	4	4	5	0	16	23	18	—
					(% "don't know")				
Is this acceptable? low	8	6	4	4	10	0	5	20	—
high	1	2	4	4	0	6	6	14	—
					Case bases (N)				
Which group is wealthier? low	168	375	429	2,468	332	48	95	229	12
high	483[a]	256	301	323	31	96	73	57	4
Is this acceptable? low	114	248	237	1,411	178	15	38	83	2
high	375	173	219	229	25	50	36	21	0

Respondents who gave no answer have been excluded. Occupation and education are coded as in table 4.3.

[a]Read: "Of the 483 highly educated Francophones in professional and technical occupations, 78 percent reply that English Canadians are wealthier and 3 percent give a 'don't know' answer."

occupation on both of our measures of this dimension, within each language group.

It is clear that the two language communities differ systematically in their perceptions. Francophones are much more likely than Anglophones to see English Canadians as wealthier and are more likely to insist that these inequalities should be reduced. Also, Francophones are much less likely than Anglophones to say they don't know which of the two groups is the wealthier.

A further pattern that is revealed in the table is that the responses of more privileged respondents differ systematically from the responses of those who are less privileged. The higher the respondents' educational and occupational status, the more likely they are to say that English Canadians are wealthier than French Canadians, and that this inequality in wealth ought to be reduced. This relationship holds true in both linguistic communities.

The effects of education and occupation are not perfectly additive, however. The educational effect is strong among Francophones whatever their occupation, and among Anglophones mainly in the upper-level white-collar categories. Occupational differences are less clear-cut among Francophones, although it should be mentioned that the small number of highly educated farmers are noticeably likely to perceive French-English inequalities and to want to reduce them. This subset of farmers is also the least likely to give "don't know" answers.

Among Anglophones, however, occupational differences are more systematic. Highly educated upper-level white-collar workers, especially those in professional and technical occupations, are the most aware of communal inequalities and the most in favor of reducing them. Blue-collar workers are much less likely to hold these views. In contrast, within the Francophone community, blue-collar workers are not nearly as different in their outlooks from their more privileged brethren. As a consequence, the overall effect of occupational status is much stronger in the Anglophone community than in the Francophone community.

The combined effect of stratification variable and communal membership is also evident. By and large, the most-privileged Francophones are the most likely to say that English Canadians are the wealthier of the two groups, and the least-privileged Anglophones are the least likely to hold this view.

The consistently high proportion of "don't know" responses in the Anglophone community should be noted. The proportion is high regardless

TABLE 5.2

DISCRIMINATION IN EMPLOYMENT: PERCEPTIONS AND EXPERIENCE, BY EDUCATION AND OCCUPATION, BY LANGUAGE GROUP

Occupation	Francophones					Anglophones				
	PT	MP	SC	W	F	PT	MP	SC	W	F
A.										
Perception of discrimination										
Education										
				(% both have same chances)						
low	41	46	41	31	39	62	54	46	60	—
high	26	35	38	33	52	40	43	36	47	—
				(% English sometimes or often a better chance)						
low	54	41	46	54	47	10	4	8	8	—
high	55	48	49	54	36	10	6	11	8	—
				(% French sometimes or often a better chance)						
low	1	4	5	3	6	17	31	27	14	—
high	4	4	3	2	0	25	29	24	23	—
				(% qualified answer)						
low	5	9	5	7	2	8	10	17	11	—
high	13	10	8	11	13	21	16	28	17	—
				(% "don't know")						
low	0	0	3	5	5	4	0	1	6	—
high	2	2	2	0	0	4	6	1	5	—
				Case bases (N)						
low	162	375	427	2464	334	52	48	95	234	12
high	476	251	301	323	31	188	96	73	60	4

TABLE 5.2
Continued

	Francophones					Anglophones				
Occupation	PT	MP	SC	W	F	PT	MP	SC	W	F
B.										
Experience of discrimination	Education									
					(% "yes")[a]					
low	28	32	38	30	23	23	35	28	20	–
high	33	34	36	30	23	29	26	33	7	–
					(% "don't know")					
low	5	7	1	8	6	0	17	1	18	–
high	4	2	3	8	0	2	4	7	0	–
					Case bases (N)					
low	168	375	429	2,462	338	52	48	95	12	–
high	479	256	301	323	31	188	94	73	4	–

[a]Includes those who respond that either they themselves, their friends, or acquaintances have experienced discrimination.

of educational or occupational level, which lends partial support to an "avoidance" interpretation of "don't know" responses.[2]

Employment

Let us now move on to our second dimension, which deals with French-English inequalities in access to jobs. Which socioeconomic groups are most likely to perceive the labor market as being "rigged" or in some way less than impartial to ethnic origins and language? Which socioeconomic groups are most likely to report having experienced discriminatory treatment with respect to jobs and promotions? How does the impact of social stratification combine with communal membership in shaping the respondents' perceptions and experience? The data presented in table 5.2 will allow us to touch on these questions.

In the first panel of the table, we can note that here again the communal difference in perceptions of discrimination is huge. From the first set of data presented in panel A, it is clear that Anglophones are much more likely than Francophones to view French and English Canadians as competing on equal terms in the labor market. Also, from the third set of data presented in panel A, we can see a pattern of "out-group choice" whereby each communal group shows a tendency to see the other group as being relatively more privileged. This tendency is much more pronounced, of course, in the Francophone community. Finally, Anglophones are not only much more likely to give "don't know" answers, but also are more likely to give any sort of qualified answer.

The more-educated members of each language community are the least likely to believe that both groups have the same chances in the labor market. Furthermore, among Francophones, the more-educated are more likely to see English Canadians as advantaged. Of the highly educated Francophones, those in professional and technical occupations are the least likely to believe the two groups are treated equally and the most likely to view English Canadians as being advantaged.

Among Anglophones, the more educated are less likely to view the two groups as competing on equal terms, but this does not mean that the more educated are all that much more inclined to admit that English Canadians are advantaged. In fact, educational differences among Anglophones are not strongly associated with the tendency to see English Canadians as advantaged, nor with the tendency to see French Canadians as advantaged. The impact of educational differences among Anglophones, then, is to make the more educated *less* convinced of group equality in the labor market and much more likely to give a qualified answer to the question.

In both language communities, it is the more educated who are the least likely to believe that the two groups are treated equally and the most likely to give some sort of qualified answer (such as "it depends") to the question.

In the Francophone community, the unbiased belief in an unbiased labor market is strongest among the very small number of highly educated farmers. In the Anglophone community, it is strongest among the less-educated blue-collar and technical workers. Indeed, the blue-collar Anglophones are not only the most likely to believe in equal chances, but also the least likely to believe that French Canadians have an advantage, even though these workers are the ones who are most likely to work in French milieus in which the norms permitting or encouraging the use of the French language are likely to be strong.

The joint effect of education and occupation on the respondents' reported experience of discriminatory treatment at work is given in panel B of table 5.2. As we have already seen, similar percentages of each communal group report having experienced occupational discrimination, either directly or indirectly. Beyond this, within each linguistic community, those in the three white-collar categories give slightly higher reports than do those in the blue-collar and farming categories. Furthermore, within the white-collar category, the lower level, which is composed of sales and clerical staff, displays slightly higher percentages than professional and technical staff and managers and proprietors.

The effects of education are not great or systematic in either community. Where they are noticeable is among the upper-level white-collar workers: the more-educated professional and technical staff are more likely to report the experience of discrimination than their less-educated counterparts.

Business and Finance

Let us now turn to our third dimension of French-English inequalities, that dealing with the world of business and finance. The results presented in table 5.3 reveal, once again, a strong communal effect in the pattern of responses. Francophones are much more likely than Anglophones to claim that English Canadians hold the most important place in the world of business and finance and to find this situation to be abnormal. Anglophones, for their part, are more likely to reply either that both groups

TABLE 5.3

PERCEPTIONS OF COMMUNAL INEQUALITIES IN BUSINESS,
BY EDUCATION AND OCCUPATION, BY LANGUAGE GROUP

Occupation	Education	Francophones					Anglophones				
		PT	MP	SC	W	F	PT	MP	SC	W	F
A.					*(% "English")*						
Which group is dominant in business?	low	77	76	75	69	53	40	52	63	46	–
	high	85	79	86	86	77	68	62	64	62	–
				(% rather abnormal or very abnormal) (Of those replying "English")							
Is this normal?	low	69	67	66	68	74	38	32	35	17	–
	high	75	71	74	80	88	52	42	40	22	–
B.					*(% "don't know")*						
Which group is diminant in business?	low	3	6	12	8	18	6	12	16	18	–
	high	5	5	3	6	6	17	22	11	20	–
Is this normal?	low	0	1	1	2	5	0	40	0	13	–
	high	0	0	1	1	0	5	0	2	14	–
					Case bases (N)						
Which group is dominant in business?	low	168	375	427	2,468	332	52	48	91	233	12
	high	476	256	301	323	31	186	92	73	60	4
Is this normal?	low	130	285	322	1,710	176	21	25	57	106	2
	high	401	203	260	279	24	127	57	47	37	4

Occupation and education are coded as in table 4.3.   Respondents who gave no answer have been excluded.

TABLE 5.4

PERCEPTIONS OF COMMUNAL INEQUALITIES IN POLITICS,
BY EDUCATION AND OCCUPATION, BY LANGUAGE GROUP

Occupation	Education	Francophones					Anglophones			
		PT	MP	SC	W	F	MP	SC	W	F
A.										
		(% less important than it should be)								
What is position of French Canadians in Ottawa?	low	29	37	40	32	21	0	2	5	—
	high	37	41	41	50	26	14	4	10	—
		(% very or fairly similar)								
Does Quebec resemble a colonial situation?	low	24	37	38	39	41	17	50	23	—
	high	37	32	43	47	68	19	23	30	—
B.										
		(% "don't know")								
What is position of French Canadians in Ottawa?	low	13	9	13	16	25	33	18	24	—
	high	7	0	9	4	13	15	12	18	—
Does Quebec resemble a colonial situation?	low	13	6	10	15	16	12	2	23	—
	high	3	7	7	5	6	12	3	8	—
		Case bases (N)								
What is position of French Canadians in Ottawa?	low	168	375	429	2,464	332	48	95	234	12
	high	485	254	301	323	31	96	73	60	4
Does Quebec resemble a colonial situation?	low	168	375	428	2,460	338	48	95	234	12
	high	485	254	301	323	31	96	73	60	4

occupy this role equally or that they don't know. It is also clear that the more-educated members of each linguistic community are more likely to identify English Canadians as occupying the most important position in business and finance and are also more likely to view this state of affairs as abnormal.

The impact of occupational differences is clearly less important than that of educational differences. Where occupational differences *are* noticeable is in the responses of Anglophones to the second question bearing on the normative dimension. Anglophone blue-collar workers are less likely than their white-collar brethren to view the situation as abnormal.

Language-group membership and socioeconomic status exert strong and independent effects on these dependent variables. The overall picture is clear enough: educated Francophones, at one extreme, are the members of the population most likely to identify English Canadians as holding the most important position and to consider this abnormal; less-educated Anglophones, at the other extreme, are the least likely to hold these views.

Politics

Let us now turn to an examination of how social privilege variables and communal membership combine to shape perceptions of French-English inequalities in the realm of politics, the fourth of our dimensions of communal inequalities.

The data presented in table 5.4 show that Francophones are more likely than Anglophones to judge that the position of French Canadians in Ottawa is *less* important than it should be, and are more likely to say that the Quebec case is very similar or fairly similar to a colonial situation.

Here again, we can see that educational level has more of a clear-cut effect than occupational status. The more-educated respondents are more likely to say that the position French Canadians occupy in the federal government in Ottawa is less important that it should be, and they are somewhat more likely to say that the Quebec case resembles a colonial situation.

The Professions

We now turn to our fifth, and last, dimension of communal inequalities, that concerning perceptions of the relative status of Francophones and Anglophones in the areas of medicine and science.

TABLE 5.5

PERCEPTIONS OF COMMUNAL INEQUALITIES IN THE PROFESSIONS,
BY OCCUPATION AND LANGUAGE GROUP

Occupation	Francophones					Anglophones				
	PT	MP	SC	W	F	PT	MP	SC	W	F
A. Which are in general the best doctors?										
French Canadian doctors	15	19	19	22	16	2	10	7	4	–
both equally	64	66	62	60	56	41	54	41	66	–
qualified answer	4	2	2	3	1	9	8	8	3	–
English Canadian doctors	5	8	7	4	4	23	10	24	6	–
don't know	12	6	10	11	23	26	19	20	20	–
	100%	100%	100%	100%	100%	100%	100%	100%	100%	100%
	(644)	(625)	(726)	(2760)	(363)	(238)	(140)	(165)	(282)	(16)
B. In which group are the greatest scientists to be found?										
among French Canadians	7	10	7	10	13	6	0	2	3	–
both equally	48	46	4	46	41	22	34	25	34	–
qualified answer	4	4	4	4	3	6	3	3	5	–
among English Canadians	28	27	30	27	21	42	28	41	23	–
don't know	13	12	15	13	21	24	36	28	35	–
	100%	100%	100%	100%	100%	100%	100%	100%	100%	100%
	(650)	(631)	(726)	(2785)	(360)	(239)	(140)	(166)	(291)	(16)

Respondents who gave no answer have been excluded. Percentage totals may deviate from 100 because of rounding errors.

For the full text of the questions, see appendix B.

In the pattern of responses to our two measures of this dimension, there is a tendency toward what can be called reciprocal communal in-group choice, whereby members of each communal group are somewhat more likely to say that the best doctors and the best scientists are to be found in their own community. We can see, however, that this reciprocal pattern is not symmetrical: Francophones are more likely to reply that the best doctors and scientists are English Canadians than Anglophones are likely to reply that they are French Canadians. Given this complex pattern, important information may be lost if we dichotomize these dependent variables. Accordingly, in table 5.5 we present the full range of answers for each of the two measures, by occupation.[3]

Among Francophones, the impact of occupational status is minimal. There is strikingly little variation by occupation on Francophones' responses to these two questions, other than that farmers are more likely than others to give "don't know" answers and less likely to say that the best doctors and scientists either are English Canadians or are found equally in both communities.

This apparent intracommunal unanimity is not to be found among Anglophones, however. In both panels of the table, occupational differences have an appreciable impact on Anglophones' patterns of responses. The professional and technical and sales and clerical groups are the most convinced that the best doctors and scientists are English Canadians and the *least* convinced that the two groups are equal in this respect. Anglophone blue-collar workers, on the other hand, display much more egalitarian views with respect to the talents and capabilities of the two groups.

This can be seen by reading along the second and fourth rows of data in each panel of the table. In the first panel, it is clear that working-class Anglophones are much more likely than their white-collar co-communalists to express the view that French and English Canadian doctors are equally talented. In the same vein, the fourth row shows that it is working-class Anglophones who are the least inclined of all Anglophones to say that the best doctors are English Canadian.

In the second panel of the table, similar results obtain. Working-class Anglophones are the least likely to say that the best scientists are English Canadian.

The tendency of Anglophone blue-collar workers to display more egalitarian attitudes than Anglophones in white-collar occupations was first observed in my earlier research (Laczko 1978a). Earlier on, we noted that Francophones are more likely to give the egalitarian ("both equally") response to both of our measures of this dimension, namely the question dealing with the best doctors and the question dealing with the best scientists. A further observation that follows from table 5.5 is that the greater egalitarianism of working-class Anglophones makes them very similar in outlook to the entire Francophone community on these issues.

One further comment is useful here. If these two measures are compared to each other, they reveal interesting information about the uneven development of the professions in Quebec. It is noteworthy that basically egalitarian beliefs about the talents and capabilities of the two language groups are more widely diffused regarding the practice of medicine than they are regarding the practice of science. This generalization follows from the more skewed distribution of responses to the question about the best doctors: more people are likely to say "both groups equally" about doctors than they are about scientists. It also follows from the fact that the pattern of reciprocal communal in-group choice is more symmetrical in the question about the best doctors than it is in the question about the best scientists.

How can this be explained? It is not clear what importance we should attach to the fact that the population's knowledge of doctors is undoubtedly based much more on direct experience than is their knowledge of scientists. The higher proportion of "don't know" answers in both language communities for the question about the best scientists is indirect evidence of this. Notwithstanding the role of these differences in the respondents' direct experience and contact with these two sets of occupations, we should note that it is likely that historically in Quebec, the two linguistic communities have been more evenly developed in medicine than they have in (other areas of) science. Furthermore, it is interesting to note that the fact that the pattern of reciprocal communal in-group choice is more symmetrical in responses to the question about the best doctors than it is in responses to the question about the best scientists may be linked to a historical difference in the type of consolidation of the aggregate-level inequality and heterogeneity parameters in Quebec (Blau 1977).

Historically in Quebec, the range of doctors represented within each language community has probably been greater than the range of scientists represented within each community. Communal inequalities in medicine have probably been less pronounced than communal inequalities in science. As a consequence, the pattern of institutional segmentation in medicine has been less asymmetric than the pattern of segmentation or parallelism in science. We can say that by definition segmentation between communal groups is asymmetric to the extent that it differentially involves members of different social classes with each communal group. However segmented the practice of medicine has been historically in Quebec (see Brazeau 1968; Meisel and Lemieux 1972; Boudreau 1980), the historical presence of some sort of Francophone medical establishment has made for a less asymmetric pattern than has been historically the case in the sciences. A possible cumulative effect of this on the contemporary belief system in 1970 is that respondents in all categories are more likely to answer "English Canadians" to the question about the best scientists than to the question about the best doctors. The more symmetrical pattern of communal in-group choice shown on the question about the best doctors may well be linked to the more symmetrical nature of the historical segmentation of the medical world in Quebec.

THE STRATIFICATION SYSTEM AND THE STRUCTURE OF PERCEPTIONS: DISCUSSION

In the preceding section, we presented in some detail the role of educational and occupational status in accounting for variation in each of our measures of perceived communal inequalities. Let us now discuss the most significant findings in the light of our debate between the functionalist and communal competition perspectives. Following this, we shall be able to compare our results with those obtained by Roseborough and Breton (1971).

In a nutshell, the functionalist perspective predicts that the communal effect will tend to be slight and that the dominant and subordinate groups will not necessarily differ much in their assessments of the extent of communal inequalities. Also, the functionalist perspective predicts that the most privileged (white-collar, middle-class) members of the subordinate communal group would be less aware and conscious of communal inequalities because they themselves would be, in fact, "already equal" to members of the dominant communal group, and consequently more likely to perceive the two communal groups as equal.

The logic here is that if inequalities between groups are in some way the result of historical accidents and are not likely to be lasting, then they will not be seen all that differently by members of dominant and subordinate groups. Also, the more-privileged members of a subordinate group typically have far more of the resources required for advancement in the larger society than their less-privileged brethren do. A consequence of this is that in any given subordinate group, it will be the more-privileged or middle-class members of the group who will be the most integrated into the larger society, and on the most equal terms. By virtue of their educational and occupational status, middle-class members of subordinate groups are not, after all, that different from their class counterparts in the dominant communal group. For these reasons, one might expect the middle class members of subordinate communal groups to view themselves simply as members of the middle class.

The communal competition perspective, on the other hand, predicts a substantial communal effect in perceptions, because subordinate group members are more likely to feel in some way "excluded" not so much as individuals, but as members of a communal group. Similarly, it predicts that the most-privileged members of the subordinate communal group will be more aware of communal inequalities in Quebec. The mechanism at work in this hypothesis is the following: in contexts in which communal groups are in competition and in which the greatest volume of competition is at the white-collar level, it is those at the white-collar level who will be most aware of communal inequalities and most inclined to interpret inequalities of any sort as being in some way inequalities between communal groups. To the extent that the language and culture of the dominant group are dominant throughout the society's institutions, members of the subordinate group face costs and handicaps in the labor market and elsewhere that are not faced by members of the dominant group. These costs and handicaps are likely to be greatest in white-collar occupations in which language facility and a knowledge of informal cultural symbols are important for advancement (see Beattie 1975). A consequence of this is that middle-class members of the subordinate group may be especially likely to feel in some sense excluded on the basis of their language and culture. This personal experience of inequality might have the effect of making them more aware of the inequalities between the communal groups in the society as a whole.

Given the opposite predictions of these hypotheses, how should our results about the role of stratification variables be interpreted? Keeping in mind once again that confirmation is a matter of degree, we can say that on the whole these results are consonant with the predictions of the communal competition perspective. Indeed, the findings concerning the perceptions and experience of discrimination in the labor market (see table 5.2) suggest that, in Quebec in 1970, competition was indeed more intense at the white-collar than at the blue-collar level.

With respect to perceptions of discrimination, we found that the more educated members of both communal groups are indeed less likely to view both groups as having equal chances. This in itself could be seen as a function of the greater intellectual sophistication and general knowledge that come with more years of education and could be interpreted as a form of "awareness" similar to that which no doubt in part leads more-educated Anglophones to be more likely than their less-educated brethren to say that English Canadians are objectively wealthier. However, when we recall that more-educated Anglophones are not necessarily more likely than other Anglophones to come out and say that English Canadians have a better chance in the labor market, nor systematically less likely to say that French Canadians are advantaged, the higher salience of competition at the upper levels becomes clear.

Further evidence of the complexity of the situation is given by the higher proportion of qualified answers to this question among the more educated. The more a respondent is aware of the wide range of factors that need to be taken into account in assessing whether ethnic origin or language influence an individual's job chances in a segmented society such as Quebec, the more that respondent is likely to give an answer that is in some sense qualified.

Further confirmation of the communal competition perspective is obtained if we interpret these findings in light of data on objective inequalities in the occupational structure of Quebec. Hugh McRoberts and his colleagues' study (1976) of the occupational structure and Boulet's (1979) study of income distribution, both of which span the years preceding and following the administration of the survey being analyzed here, reveal that while a convergence between the Francophone and Anglophone opportunity and income structures was already evident in 1970, there were still very great inequalities at the higher levels, and indeed that it was at the higher levels that communal inequalities were (still) greatest. These inequalities included the underrepresentation of Francophones at higher levels and the lower incomes of those Francophones who *were* at higher levels. Thus, Francophones and Anglophones at higher levels in 1970 were in the best position to be aware of communal inequalities, both in their own milieus and in the society at large.

These data highlight one of the problematic assumptions of the hypothesis derived from the functionalist perspective, namely that the more-privileged members of subordinate groups are themselves less disadvantaged than their less-privileged brethren. The mechanism at work in this assumption is that more-privileged members of subordinate communal groups will compare their own individual position to that of the majority of their own communal group, on the one hand, and to that of individual members of the same social class in the other communal group, on the other. Both of these comparisons may lead the more-privileged members of subordinate communal groups to view communal inequalities as less salient than they might otherwise appear to be.

If, however, the more-privileged members of subordinate communal groups also notice that their communal group is systematically underrepresented at higher levels, their own individual equality vis-à-vis their class counterparts will probably not temper their perceptions of *communal* inequalities as being large. The mechanism that allows the more-privileged members of subordinate groups to make *individual* comparisons, in the functionalist perspective, is linked to the assumption, discussed in chapter 4, that elites of subordinate groups will tend to be less attached to their communal group and to its culture and language. We shall deal further with the important issue of the links between orientations toward cultural pluralism and perceptions of communal inequalities in the following chapter.

Although all of this indicates that there is more competition at the higher white-collar levels, it is interesting to note that those who most frequently report having directly or indirectly experienced discriminatory treatment are those in sales and clerical occupations. This holds true in both linguistic communities.

Similar findings concerning the outlook of the sales and clerical group were obtained in my previous related research (Laczko 1978b). Among Anglophones, sales and clerical workers were systematically the most likely to feel worried and concerned about Québécois nationalism, as measured by responses to a whole series of indicators of feelings of threat. This was explained by two factors. First, it was argued that the greatest volume of competition between the two linguistic communities in Quebec occurs at the white-collar level, or more precisely, above the blue-collar level (see Guindon 1964; 1978; Dofny and Garon-Audy 1969). Second, I argued that, in white-collar occupations, it is those who are at the lower levels of the white-collar hierarchy, in other words those in sales and clerical occupations, who are especially likely to feel vulnerable because their occupations are less credentialized than the occupations of the higher-level white-collar groups, which are composed of professional, technical, and managerial personnel.

Viewed against the backdrop of these previous findings, the pattern displayed in the second panel of table 5.2 is especially interesting. It suggests that the special pressures, enumerated in my previous research, facing sales and clerical workers are perhaps operative in both linguistic communities.

We should recall at this point the special pattern observed among sales and clerical workers in chapter 4. Those in sales and clerical occupations who had non–French Canadian employers were more likely than others to display a highly centrifugal outlook. That pattern is quite possibly linked to the pattern observed here. The findings of the present chapter suggest that sales and clerical workers do indeed have more grievances than others. If we assume that the discrimination experienced was at the hands of Anglophone (or more precisely, non-Francophone) employers, then this is a further reason (in addition to the lower risks involved, as argued in chapter 4) for the more centrifugal orientations of Francophone sales and clerical workers who have Anglophone bosses.

Let us conclude this discussion with a word about French-English *status* inequalities as measured by our two questions about the best doctors and the best scientists (see table 5.5). On both of these measures, a clear communal effect is evident. Francophones are more likely to give an egalitarian ("both groups equally talented") response than Anglophones.

The overall combination of class and communal factors is of the nonadditive type, since the class effect is not identical in the two language communities. The class effect is almost nonexistent among Francophones, with the exception of the special views of farmers, as we have seen. Among Anglophones, on the other hand, blue-collar workers are clearly more egalitarian than their white-collar co-communalists in their assessments of the basic talents and capabilities of French and English Canadians.

The greater egalitarianism of blue-collar Anglophones should be juxtaposed to their lower awareness of communal inequalities, especially in wealth and in business and finance. These two distinct patterns within the Anglophone community of class effects on these two dimensions of communal inequalities can best be interpreted as two sides of the same coin. Working-class Anglophones may well hold more egalitarian views about the talents and capabilities of the two groups because they are less likely to perceive any great inequalities in wealth and power between the two collectivities. Similarly, the greater egalitarianism that characterizes blue-collar Anglophones' basic outlook is not conducive to, and may indeed militate against, their evaluating French-English inequalities in wealth and business as being large.

It might also be interesting to evaluate these results in terms of the sources of support for "dominant ideologies" in industrial societies. Researchers in the United States (see Form and Rytina 1969; Huber and Form 1973) have reported that members of the dominant group of "whites" are *less* likely than the members of the subordinate group of "non-whites" to be aware of various types of inequalities. They are also *more* likely to accept explanations for these inequalities that are consonant with the "dominant ideology" of American society, for example to attribute success and failure to personal factors.

If we consider the formal equality of Francophones and Anglophones in Canada as a component of the society's "dominant ideology" (however belatedly or incompletely institutionalized), our findings suggest that members of the dominant Anglophone group in 1970 are indeed less aware of communal inequalities and more inclined to give any sort of answer ("both groups are equal," "qualified answer," "French Canadians are more privileged," "that depends," "don't know") other than one in which they would admit that English Canadians were privileged.

The explanation that I have suggested for these findings, which is derived from the communal competition perspective, is consonant with that put forth by Huber and Form for their findings. Simply put, they find general confirmation for their working hypothesis that "the dominant ideology justifying a stratification system will be most attractive to those receiving the highest rewards from it" (Huber and Form 1973:78). My explanation is similar, although it emphasizes the greater costs incurred by members of the subordinate group rather than the greater rewards accruing to members of the dominant group, is basically similar.

This similarity notwithstanding, our findings also suggest that, as we shall see presently in our discussion of the role of stratification variables, the distinction between "dominant" and "counter" ideologies is often problematic and needs to be handled carefully when applied to segmented societies composed of competing communal groups.

The findings also suggest that subscription to a dominant ideology is not necessarily strongest among those who are in every way the most privileged, and that subscription to a counterideology is not necessarily strongest among those who are in every way the most deprived.

Our findings indicate that in a segmented society such as Quebec, while members of the dominant communal group may indeed be *less* inclined than members of the subordinate group to acknowledge the existence of communal inequalities, it is not necessarily the most-privileged members within the dominant group who are the least likely to do so. Similarly, while members of the subordinate group are system-atically *more* likely to perceive communal inequalities than are members of the dominant communal group, it is not necessarily the most-deprived members of the subordinate group who are most likely to hold this view.

In other words, the position (dominant or subordinate) of an individual's communal group within the stratification system and that individual's class position (more-privileged or less-privileged) within the communal group do not always exert effects in the same direction. These findings stand in contrast to Huber and Form's general finding that race and income have an effect in the same direction on beliefs about the American stratification system. Both membership in a dominant race and membership in a higher income group contributed to shaping support for dominant ideology. Here, on the other hand, we have found that the communal effect and the individual social privilege effect combine differently. This type of combination may be due to special features of segmented societies, and the mechanisms behind it have yet to be charted theoretically. This pattern suggests that it may be useful, in segmented societies, to speak not so much of dominant ideologies and counterideologies, as of competing dominant ideologies, each of which has an institutional base. We shall return to this point in our concluding chapter.

A COMPARISON WITH
ROSEBOROUGH AND BRETON

Since this chapter has been modeled in part as a replication of the baseline study of Roseborough and Breton (1971), it is appropriate to compare the two sets of results.

Roseborough and Breton's analysis is based on the Ethnic Relations Study, carried out in 1965 for the Royal Commission on Bilingualism and Biculturalism. They use two measures taken from that study, one designed to evaluate perceptions of relative economic advantage and one designed to evaluate relative political advantage.[4] Their measure of perceptions of relative economic advantage is perhaps closest to our measure of perceived discrimination in employment, and their measure of relative political advantage is perhaps closest to our question about the role of French Canadians in Ottawa.

Although the wording of their questions is not identical to that of the questions that have been analyzed here, there is enough similarity to warrant a comparison. The central tendencies of the measures used by Roseborough and Breton are somewhat less skewed in the direction of English Canadians being perceived as advantaged than are those of the Quebec Social Movements Study measures that have been analyzed here. This is probably due to the fact that the Ethnic Relations Study covers all of Canada, while the Quebec Social Movements Study covers only Quebec.

There is substantial agreement between the two studies on communal effects and class effects. Roseborough and Breton find that those in the French ethnic category are much more likely than those whose ethnic self-identification is English or "other" to view English Canadians as being economically and politically advantaged, and much less likely to believe that all groups have equal chances.

Also, Roseborough and Breton report that the highly educated and more-privileged members of each ethnic category are the most likely to view English Canadians as being relatively advantaged. They report that the relationship between the dependent variables and stratification variables other than education are similar to those involving the education variable, but they do not report any multivariate analyses. Our bivariate relationships with education were also stronger than those with occupation, and the multivariate analyses presented in this chapter have specified that education is indeed responsible for more of the variation.

Roseborough and Breton do not draw on or refer to any explicit theoretical frameworks in their discussion of their findings, and they should not be criticized for this, since their study is put forth as a descriptive one, "an exercise in discovery, not in proof" (1971:402). Nonetheless, it may be interesting to uncover some implicit hypotheses that guided their research.

Roseborough and Breton begin by describing two possible central tendencies of their dependent variables:

> Because of the way Canadian society is organized we would expect that one or other of two viewpoints will underly Canadians' perceptions of reality. One view stresses the existence of ethnic stratification. Ethnic groups are seen as not sharing equally in the economic and political advantages of the society. The other view rejects the existence of ethnic stratification: ethnic affiliation makes no difference in the distribution of economic and political advantages; all ethnic groups share equally. (Roseborough and Breton 1971:403)

The latter view, that of perceptions of group equality and of the irrelevance or low level of relevance of ethnic factors in economic and political life, is to be expected to some extent because

> Canadian society, as a modern industrial democratic society, also has structural features which cross-cut ethnic organization. This means

that ability, competence, and performance are more important criteria for filling some positions than is ethnic affiliation. (1971:401)

This is a clear statement of what I have called the functionalist perspective,
although the authors do not refer to it as such and only mention these
points in passing.

The former view, on the other hand, that of the perception of ethnic
inequalities and of the importance of ethnic factors in economic and
political life, is also to be expected to some extent, according to
Roseborough and Breton, because of the segmented nature of Canadian
society. There are references to "ethnic blocs," "group control of institutions," and the "persistence of cultural ideas" (about the British Conquest
of New France in 1759) as a result of the high completeness of French
Canadian institutions, but these are not explicitly tied in to a recognizable
theoretical framework.

Roseborough and Breton's discussion of why those of French ethnicity are much more likely than those of English or "other" ethnicities to see
English Canadians as economically and politically advantaged refers principally to these sorts of segmentation variables. and to the "prevalence of
traditional ideas" and "low memory loss" among French Canadians about
French-English inequalities, rather than to the possibility that these perceptions might in part be generated and maintained by ongoing structural
arrangements of group competition within Quebec.

Concerning the effects of social stratification variables within each
ethnic category, Roseborough and Breton appear to have expected that
more-educated members of the English ethnic category would be more
likely than their less-educated brethren to perceive English Canadians as
privileged:

> Since they are the people with positions of advantage, we would
> expect them to see themselves at the top more frequently than would
> the English with lower status. Or, depending upon their knowledge
> of people in other ethnic groups with positions similar to their own,
> we would expect that they would see no groups as having more
> advantages than others. (1971:412)

Concerning the effects of stratification variables among the nondominant French and "other" ethnic groups, however, the authors are
surprised by their findings:

But we would expect the opposite perception of the French and the "Others." We would expect that people with lower education, with lower income, and with lower status occupations, would be the ones who would most frequently perceive the English as having greater economic advantage. Yet we find the opposite is the case. It is the French and "Others" with the most education who are more apt to perceive the English as having the economic advantage. Presumably, having positions of advantage does not lead them to see themselves as sharing with the English the economic resources of Canadian society. They are more likely than the less educated members of their ethnic groups to make invidious comparisons across ethnic lines. (1971:414)

Roseborough and Breton do not spell out the theoretical basis for their initial hypothesis. Why should one expect the less-privileged members of less-privileged cultural groups to be more aware of group inequalities? I suggest that the answer is buried in the last sentence of the paragraph just quoted. The expectation is that the more-privileged members of subordinate groups will see themselves as sharing with the dominant group in society. The implicit assumption here is that if one sees oneself as privileged *individually*, they will not see their cultural group as less privileged. This is a key assumption of the functionalist perspective, as we have seen.

There is another interesting aspect of Roseborough and Breton's implicit theory that should be mentioned. This concerns their basic study design, according to which Canada is see as a collection of "ethnic groups," some of which are more numerous and more powerful than others. The groups in question are the English Canadians, the French Canadians, and the "Others," the last-named being not so much a group as a statistical category. Each group or category is seen as being numerically dominant in a particular region of the country: the English in Ontario, British Columbia, and the Maritimes; the French in Quebec; and the "Others" in the three Prairie Provinces.

While this view may be useful as a way of describing the geographical distribution of origin groups, for sociological analyses it needs to be supplemented, whenever possible, by information about language-community membership (see Ryder 1955). Otherwise, it runs the risk of reifying the "Other" group by imputing some sort of collective group life to an aggregate residual category. More important, this view obscures the

TABLE 5.6

PERCEPTIONS OF COMMUNAL INEQUALITIES IN WEALTH, BY EDUCATION AND ETHNIC ORIGIN, BY LANGUAGE GROUP

| | Francophones | | | | | | Anglophones | | | | | |
| | French | | | Other | | | English | | | Other | | |
Ethnic origin / Education	L	M	H	L	M	H	L	M	H	L	M	H
Which group is wealthier?												
(% "English")	58	72	78	62	70	79	34	43	62	36	51	61
(% "don't know")	10	4	1	14	19	7	14	15	15	32	30	20
Case bases (N)	(3,596)	(918)	(367)	(176)	(53)	(58)	(271)	(136)	(117)	(117)	(90)	(61)
(If respondent replied "English")												
Is this acceptable?												
(% "it should be reduced")	60	68	71	41	70	78	43	49	74	42	48	78
(% "don't know")	4	2	2	20	8	9	4	5	7	30	11	5
Case bases (N)	(2,089)	(656)	(286)	(109)	(37)	(46)	(91)	(59)	(72)	(64)	(46)	(37)

language and language-community related processes by which Francophones in Quebec (the vast majority of whom are, of course, of French origin) come to hold such very different views from Anglophones. Although Roseborough and Breton barely mention the fact, their data indicate a remarkable degree of convergence between the English and the "Others" in their perceptions of the English as having the most advantages. The very different outlook of "the French" is also noted. Why is the outlook of the French so different?

Findings such as these are difficult to explain from what I have called the functionalist perspective, which views ethnicity as a receding factor in the process of industrialization. This perspective has in several ways informed Roseborough and Breton's article, although in other ways elements of a communal competition perspective (group control of institutions, and so forth) are also present elsewhere in the paper. These have been developed in Breton's later work (Breton 1978a; 1978b; 1979).

I suggest that the reason Roseborough and Breton's data show that the English and the "Others" have very similar perceptions is that the vast majority of the "Others" live in English-speaking Canada. If one conceives of Canadian society not as a set of logically equivalent ethnic groups, but as composed of two competing linguistic communities, each of which may be composed of various ethnic and cultural groups to various degrees, one would expect differences between linguistic groups, but, *ceteris paribus*, few or fewer differences between ethnic origin categories within each linguistic community.

This latter hypothesis can be tested with data that has been analyzed here from the Social Movements Study. As we did in chapter 4, let us look at the joint effects of ethnic origin and language-group membership. The data presented in table 5.6 show the combined effects of education, ethnic origin, and language group membership on our first pair of dependent variables, which deal with perceptions of communal inequalities in wealth.

The pattern is one that was observed in chapter 4: those of Other (non-French, non-English) origins are very clearly more likely than their co-communalists to give "don't know" answers, but to espouse similar views otherwise. This suggests that in a society composed of two competing linguistic communities, each with its own set of institutions, living in the context of these overarching institutions shapes people's perceptions of communal inequalities in similar ways regardless of their ethnic origins.[5] This is once again a synthesis of the functionalist and communal competition perspectives that specifies the relative utility of each. The communal competition perspective is useful for understanding the large communal difference in perceptions, and the functionalist perspective is useful for understanding the convergence in views between ethnic origin categories within each linguistic community.

CONCLUSION

In this chapter, I have attempted to provide a multidimensional picture of perceptions of French-English inequalities in Quebec as they were in 1970. We have examined how perceptions of communal inequalities in wealth, in access to jobs, in business, in politics, and in the professions are distributed among the Quebec population. In addition, we have specified how class and communal membership combine in shaping perceptions of each of these dimensions of French-English inequalities. On the whole, the central tendencies of the distributions are skewed in the direction of perceiving inequalities between the two communities along each of the dimensions. Francophones are much more likely to perceive inequalities than Anglophones, and within each community the more educated are more inclined to see inequalities than the less educated.

In part 3, we shall examine the extent to which these perceptions have changed in the ensuing decades and attempt to place the results in a broader comparative perspective. Before we do, however, let us examine the links between orientations toward pluralism and perceptions of inequalities.

6

Pluralism and Inequality: Some Dynamic Linkages

In the preceding chapters, we examined the distribution and sources of orientations toward cultural pluralism and perceptions of communal inequalities in the Quebec population. In the present chapter, we will consider the nature of the links between these two sets of dependent variables.[1] This is yet another important issue on which theoretical predictions, few and undeveloped as they are, are highly contradictory. Consequently, it may be appropriate and useful to examine the theoretical issues involved and then see what light our data might shed on them.

THEORETICAL QUESTIONS AND HYPOTHESES

As we saw in chapter 2, the functionalist perspective on intergroup relations and social change posits a clear causal connection between the extent of cultural diversity and the degree of group inequality. The reason these two attributes are so often found to be positively associated, according to this perspective, is that ethnic and cultural differences often play a role in creating group inequalities, and almost inevitably have the effect of maintaining them once they do exist. The mechanism at work here is straightforward: since members of subordinate groups typically face disadvantages to the extent that their language and culture are not the dominant language and culture of the society, the disadvantages are in some sense proportional to the magnitude or degree of cultural difference between the groups. The greater the cultural differences between subordinate and dominant groups, the less the subordinate group members will be able to participate fully in the dominant group's culture.

The extent to which the dominant group's language and culture are dominant and necessary in work organizations will be a handicap on members of the subordinate group and will have the effect of seriously curtailing their chances of mobility. Another aspect of the dilemma is that to the extent that members of the subordinate group live their lives, especially their off-the-job lives, among their fellow ethnics in segmented institutions, they may well be kept even more removed from the dominant group's language, culture, and institutions, all of which will in turn increase and perpetuate the handicaps they face in the labor market (see Migué 1970). These handicaps of individuals, when aggregated over a group, cannot help but maintain group inequalities.

In Canada, this line of thinking has been put forth forcefully by John Porter (1975). It forms the basis for Porter's skepticism about the value of ethnic and linguistic diversity in general, for his ambivalence about Canadian bilingualism, and for his very critical attitude toward Canadian multiculturalism. In a nutshell, the argument is that diversity leads to inequality. A related argument that is also often put forth is one that reverses the direction of causality. According to this position, group inequalities are often a cause of, or contributing factor to, the existence of group differences. In other words, the reason cultural differences between groups exist is that the groups are (still) unequal. As subordinate group members become more acculturated to the dominant society, they will become more equal.

According to the communal competition perspective, cultural differences are seen not so much as attributes of individuals, as resources among others likely to be used as such by communal groups competing with each other. The language and culture of a dominant communal group, to the extent that they can be imposed or made to prevail in work organizations, become transformed into valuable resources that are unevenly distributed: members of the dominant communal group almost inevitably have more of these resources than members of the subordinate group.

We might note that this perspective shares with the functionalist perspective the view that group inequalities are due to group differences. In fact, proponents of this perspective might even argue the point more strongly: the reason a subordinate group is subordinate is that it has been *excluded* by the dominant group, excluded collectively on the basis of, and because of, differences in language and culture (Balandier 1965; Memmi 1972; Blauner 1972).

According to this perspective, individuals in segmented societies are likely to have a different view of how group inequalities are to be decreased: they are to be decreased not by attempting to reduce cultural differences between the dominant and subordinate groups, in order to increase chances for individual mobility in institutions in which the dominant language and culture prevail, but by attempting to strengthen the institutions of the subordinate communal group, which means institutions that are controlled by members of the subordinate group and/or in which the subordinate group's language and culture are dominant. This strategy may also involve attempting to maximize the use of the subordinate group's language throughout the society.

How can these two perspectives be assessed with the data at hand from Quebec in 1970? One limited test that can be done is to examine the population's perceptions of how pluralism is dealt with when communal inequalities are to be reduced. What we shall investigate is in a sense the actors' own "ethno-theories" about what the causal linkages are.

Of special importance are the questions bearing on the normative dimension of cultural pluralism and communal inequalities. A key question we can ask is: for those who are most in favor of reducing communal inequalities, what strategy might they have in mind concerning the maintenance of cultural differences between Francophones and Anglophones?

The functionalist perspective would predict that those most concerned with reducing communal inequalities would be likely to want to play down cultural differences because those differences would be considered a handicap. The communal competition perspective, on the other hand, would predict that those most concerned with reducing communal inequalities would judge that to do so involves maintaining and even increasing the distinctiveness of the subordinate group's culture. This is the central mechanism involved in Hechter's (1975) "reactive ethnicity" model of ethnic solidarity. Members of subordinate groups will, according to this view, become more attached to their group's culture and language *as a result of* the group's subordinate position.

Among the many criticisms of Hechter's study of the British Isles, an important one is the simple point that "there is no evidence in Hechter's (1975) book to demonstrate such a connection between relative disadvantage of members of a group and ethnic solidarity" (Nielsen 1980:79). We

TABLE 6.1

INTERCORRELATIONS BETWEEN MEASURES OF ORIENTATIONS
TOWARD CULTURAL PLURALISM AND PERCEPTIONS OF COMMUNAL
INEQUALITIES BY LANGUAGE GROUP

	P1: (Q2-65)		P2: (Q2-76)		P3: (Q2-33)		P4: (Q2-35)	
	(French and English different?)		(Threat to French Canadians culture?)		(Should F.C. maintain ways or ...?)		(Language & culture/ standard of living?)	
Variable (high value)	F	A	F	A	F	A	F	A
Wealth								
I1 (English are wealthier)	20	20	21	21	00	03	01	-06
I2 (should be reduced)	11	14	17	16	02	17	05	29
Employment								
I3 (English better chance)	14	12	16	10	08	-08	09	01
I4 (yes, experience discrimination)	12	12	12	09	03	-01	03	10
Business								
I5 (English Canadians)	20	16	13	19	-01	15	03	-04
I6 (abnormal)	18	10	22	18	07	15	04	08
Politics								
I7 (Position of French Canadians less important than it should be)	11	-10	14	-02	05	04	05	07
I8 (Quebec resembles a colonial situation)	-06	06	01	06	02	11	00	11
Professions								
I9 (English doctors)	-05	01	-04	00	-05	-08	-01	-05
I10 (English scientists)	04	20	-01	13	-11	-05	-01	-07

F = Francophones; A = Anglophones.
Francophones (N = 3,312-5,221). Anglophones (N = 416-885).
All entries are Pearson correlation coefficients, with decimal points omitted.

Measures of orientations toward cultural pluralism are coded:
(low-centripetal, high-centrifugal), as in table 3.1.

shall return to Nielsen's critique of Hechter shortly. For the moment, let us say that criticisms such as this highlight the importance of using data about actors' perceptions as a key test of the reactive hypothesis.

TABLE 6.1

Continued

Measures of perceived communal inequalities are coded as follows:

	1	2	3
I1: (Q2-68)	French Canadians	qualified answer, equal or neither, don't know	English Canadians
I2: (Q2-72)	acceptable	qualified answer, don't know	should be reduced
I3: (Q2-77)	French Canadian has sometimes a better chance, French Canadian has often a better chance	both have the same chances, qualified answer, don't know	English Canadian has sometimes a better chance, English Canadian has often a better chance
I4: (Q2-78)	no	don't remember	yes, to myself, yes, to relatives, friends, or acquaintances;
I5: (Q2-43)	French Canadians	both equally, don't know	English Canadians
I6: (Q2-44)	very normal, fairly normal	don't know, qualified answer	rather abnormal, very abnormal
I7: (Q2-38)	more important than it should be	as important as it should be, qualified answer, don't know	less important than it should be
I8: (Q2-45)	rather different, very different	qualified answer, don't know	rather similar, very similar
I9: (Q2-37)	French Canadian doctors	both equally, qualified answer, don't know	English Canadian doctors
I10: (Q2-31)	French Canadians	both equally, qualified answer, don't know	English Canadians.

Respondents who gave no answer have been excluded.

I should mention that we already implicitly tested the reactive hypothesis in chapter 3. In accounting for the communal effect in orientations toward cultural pluralism, we operated on the working assumption that Francophones espouse more centrifugal orientations than Anglophones because they are more aware of the subordinate position of their communal group. In chapter 5, this working assumption was in turn confirmed as valid by the strong communal effect observed concerning perceptions of communal inequalities. Let us now turn to the data.

ANALYSIS AND DISCUSSION

In operational terms, the functionalist perspective would predict a negative correlation between wanting to reduce communal inequalities and espousing a centrifugal orientation toward cultural pluralism. The communal competition perspective, on the other hand, would predict a positive correlation.

Table 6.1 reports the zero-order correlation coefficients between orientations toward cultural pluralism and perceptions of communal inequalities within each language group. As can be see from table 6.1, the vast majority of the coefficients are positive.[2] Let us discuss these first. An awareness of communal inequalities and a desire to reduce them are positively associated not only with the tendency to view French and English Canadians as different, and the tendency to view French Canadian culture as being in danger, but also with the normative view that these differences should be maintained and that a people's language and culture are more important than its standard of living.

This pattern confirms the key missing perceptual links in the reactive hypothesis:

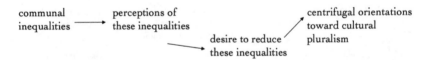

It is the positive coefficients in the two right-hand pairs of columns that provide the stronger confirmation of the reactive hypothesis, since these refer to the *normative* dimension of cultural pluralism. These coefficients are somewhat lower in magnitude than those in the two left-hand pairs columns, which refer to simple assessments of the extent of cultural pluralism.

This tendency for the coefficients dealing with assessments to be higher than those dealing with the normative dimension means that there is more debate in people's minds about the appropriate normative orientation to adapt than there is about assessments of the degree of difference. Perceiving English Canadians as privileged and advantaged is a better predictor of viewing the two groups as different than it is of saying that the differences should be maintained. This may reflect greater uncertainty about the right course to take with respect to increasing or decreasing cultural differences.

Nonetheless, the majority of the coefficients in the third and fourth pairs of columns, which deal with the normative dimension, are positive. This suggests that however much indecision there may be about what ought to be done with cultural differences in order to reduce communal inequalities, the net prevailing view is that inequalities are best reduced by *maintaining* cultural differences.

Another way to view this general reactive effect is to consider those who display the most centrifugal orientations toward cultural pluralism. These results tell us that the most centrifugal orientations are not held by those who are not aware of communal inequalities, or by those who are not "progressive" about reducing these inequalities. The reactive hypothesis, confirmed here, suggests rather that maintaining cultural differences is a part of the general strategy to reduce communal inequalities, although it is not a strategy that meets with unanimous approval.

A final point to make about the positive coefficients (that is, those dealing with inequalities in wealth, in employment chances, in business, and in politics) is that most of them are of the same sign and of similar magnitude in both linguistic communities.[3] This suggests that the processes at work behind the reactive effect are in a sense attributes of the whole of Quebec society, and not just of the Francophone community.

This means that however strong the communal differences in outlook observed in the previous chapters may be, a hidden source of structural similarity between the two communities is that the reactive effect occurs within each of them. An interesting avenue for future research would be to see if the coefficients would be positive or negative among Anglophones in the rest of Canada and among the Francophone minorities outside of Quebec.

Let us now turn our attention to the negative coefficients, most of which occur at the bottom of the table, in the rows dealing with communal inequalities in the professions. As we shall see, these are more difficult to interpret.

A first interpretation that I could put forth is that the negative coefficients are a confirmation of the hypothesis derived from the functionalist perspective. The logic here is straightforward. Perceiving the best doctors and scientists to be found among English Canadians, either because English Canadians are more talented or simply because they are richer, leads one to conclude that the way French Canadians can become more equal is to *reduce* the cultural differences between the two collectivities.

This interpretation is both logical and plausible. However, if we were inclined to accept it, we would have to explain why this pattern, which is consonant with the predictions of the functionalist perspective, is found mainly with in the dimension of communal inequalities in status, as measured by the questions about the best doctors and the best scientists, and this is difficult to do.

A more convincing explanation of this deviant pattern is based on the interpretation of the questions about the best doctors and the best scientists that I put forth earlier. This involves treating these two questions not so much as measures of group inequalities of condition as measures of inequalities in the in the talents and capabilities of the two groups.

From this point of view, the pattern of negative coefficients indicates that perceiving the two groups as equally talented and capable (in other words, not seeing English Canadians as better) makes one more inclined to want to maintain cultural differences between the two communities. Perceptions of equal talent and potential are associated with a more centrifugal orientation toward cultural pluralism.

The latter pattern, interpreted in this way, is also consonant with the communal competition perspective. The more one sees the two groups as equally capable and competent, the greater the tendency to favor the view that cultural differences between the two groups ought to be maintained as a way of strengthening Francophone institutions.

Let us note at this point that two sorts of findings shown in table 6.1 have been adduced as confirmation of the communal competition perspective. First, it has been argued that the existence of inequalities, and their perception of these inequalities, makes social actors more inclined to want to maintain cultural differences between the two communal groups. Second, it has been argued that it is the perception of certain kinds of equality that makes for a more centrifugal orientation. Let us now examine the theoretical consequences of this pattern.

THE COMMUNAL COMPETITION
PERSPECTIVE: A SYNTHESIS

The overall observed pattern discussed above brings us to an important point in our theoretical discussion. Let us recall that the work of Hechter (1975) grew out of his observing the apparent inability of what he referred to as the functional theory of ethnic change to explain the resurgence and persistence of ethnic solidarity in many contemporary Western industrial societies. The countertheory that Hechter developed as an alternative to the functional theory was what he referred to as the reactive theory of ethnic change.

Many of the mechanisms that Hechter observed at work among the Celtic minorities in Great Britain are similar to those that have been categorized here and in the previous chapters as part of the communal competition perspective. Hechter's argument is that subordinate communal groups living in segmented institutions will in many ways tend to react *as a group* and not as a set of individuals when in competition with members of a dominant communal group. The roles of territorial concentration and segmented institutions in the maintenance of group solidarity are recognized in Hechter's theory.

While these factors are recognized, even greater causal importance is given to another factor, that of group inequalities:

> The reactive theory suggests that *only* [emphasis added] when such objective cultural differences are linked to structural inequities between groups will they assume enduring significance in complex societies. (Hechter 1975:326)

This is a valuable contribution, despite the criticisms to the effect that the link was not empirically demonstrated, which is another question. Hechter's theoretical error, however, is to be so impressed by the potential importance of perceived group inequalities as to make them a necessary condition for increased group solidarity:

> The persistence of objective cultural distinctiveness in the periphery *must* [emphasis added] itself be the function of the maintenance of an unequal distribution of resources between core and peripheral groups. (Hechter 1975:37)

The problem here is one of overkill. Instead of attempting to specify the relative importance of communal inequalities and other important factors (such as setting and segmentation variables) in the maintenance of ethnic solidarity, Hechter makes group inequalities the necessary condition for its maintenance. This blunder is no doubt due to the fact that in the case that Hechter chose to study, there have long been and still are appreciable inequalities between the dominant English and subordinate Celtic groups. Nonetheless, his error is to overlook the fact that communal competition can certainly occur even when groups are relatively more equal in resources. A reactive effect is one important potential source of group solidarity, but by no means the only one. In a later essay on the topic (Hechter and Levi 1979), Hechter since recognized and corrected this oversight.

Let us now broaden the discussion and consider the contributions of another set of competition theorists. One recent example is the analysis of the linguistic conflict in Belgium by Nielsen (1980). Nielsen notes the inadequacy of the functionalist perspective in accounting for the resurgence of social movements based on ethnic solidarity in contemporary industrial societies. Two types of explanations that predict increases in ethnic solidarity are then compared. These two sets of theories of ethnic solidarity are (1) the reactive theory put forth by Hechter, and (2) competition theories.

In his exposition of competition theories, Nielsen draws mainly on the work of Barth (1969), but also examines the work of a wide range of other authors (Deutsch 1953, Lieberson 1961, Harris 1964, Van den Berghe 1967, Bonacich 1972, and Hannan 1979) and includes them under the same umbrella.

Nielsen argues that competition theories have in common an explicit or implicit reference to mechanisms of competition between groups for rewards and resources. This is a good point, but it raises the following problem. Nielsen classifies as competition theorists a wide range of authors, on the basis of their shared emphasis on mechanisms of group competition, and this general classification certainly appears to be a reasonable one. The puzzle is how Nielsen can claim that Hechter's formulation is not a competition theory. How can any reader of *Internal Colonialism* (Hechter 1975) come away with the idea that the Celtic minorities, their language, institutions, and culture have not been in competition with the dominant English language, institutions, and culture for several hundred years?

The key to the puzzle is that Nielsen apparently recognizes and classifies as competition between groups only one variant or type of competition: that occurring between groups that are equal or nearly equal in class, power, and status. Hechter's discussion of the United Kingdom is not categorized as dealing with competing groups because his study concerns unequal groups, and also because he insists on the importance of the communal inequalities. To Nielsen, competition is not really competition unless it is between groups that are relatively equal. It should be noted that this restricted definition of competition is not shared by more of the authors Nielsen quite correctly identifies as competition theorists.

Terminological problems aside, what is important to retain is that there are two broad contexts in which communal groups can be in competition. These are (1) contexts in which there are appreciable inequalities between groups, and (2) contexts in which the groups are relatively equal.

As we shall see, both Hechter and Nielsen stumble on this important analytical distinction.

Hechter's problem, as I have noted, was to attempt to build a theory of ethnic solidarity while having in mind only contexts of the first type, namely those in which the competing groups are unequal. Nielsen's problem is very similar: he considers as situations leading to communal competition only contexts of the second type, namely contexts in which the communal groups are relatively equal.

What is the prediction that Nielsen derives from his version of competition theory? The prediction is that ethnic solidarity will be greatest when and where there is a trend toward equal-status competition between groups, *when the groups have previously been much less equal.* In his study of the Flemish movement in Belgium since World War II, Nielsen quotes an observer of Belgian politics commenting on the postwar success of the *Volksunie:*

> . . . there is a paradox in this success. In former times, when the inequities suffered by the Flemish population were inestimably greater than in the period since the Second World War, the electoral support of the Flemish nationalist parties was smaller. (Hill 1974:46; quoted by Nielsen 1980:81)

Nielsen summarizes his hypothesis as follows: "Resurgences of ethnic solidarity should occur precisely where the pattern of structural discrimination breaks down and status inequalities between groups are diminished" (1980:92). Thus, it is trends toward equality which follow long-standing inequalities that make for increased solidarity. Nielsen finds general support for this hypothesis in his study.

Although the similarity is glossed over by Nielsen, his hypothesis shares with Hechter's reactive hypothesis an emphasis on the importance of group inequalities as a source of group solidarity. The two hypotheses differ in the mechanisms through which communal inequalities influence solidarity.

The reactive hypothesis posits a direct and presumably immediate increase of solidarity: objective communal inequalities lead to perceptions of these inequalities, which, in turn, lead to increased solidarity. Nielsen's time-lag formulation suggests that it is perhaps when a successful, even partial, reduction of long-standing and long-fought inequalities becomes evident, that members of historically subordinate groups develop even greater confidence and resolve to strengthen communal institutions even further.

This suggests a way of conceptualizing the latter hypothesis that is quite different from the way Nielsen himself interprets the pattern. We can hypothesize that there is a reactive effect, based on perceptions of historical inequalities, the operation of which is conditional and contingent on the substantial reduction of previously great socioeconomic disparities. This relationship between past communal inequalities and their current reduction may even be interactive in the sense that the combined impact of the reactive effect and recent relative equality might be even greater than that of either factor operating independently.

While this new hypothesis cannot be tested here, it certainly is a plausible one, and may be applicable to both Quebec and Belgium. This suggests that a similar process may be at work in the pattern of negative coefficients observed in table 6.1. In addition to the reactive effect, there is solidarity (measured here by a more centrifugal attitude) as a result of perceiving the two groups as equally competent and talented.

In sum, Nielsen's hypothesis, imbedded as it is in the dynamic argument about the impact of decreasing inequalities over time, is not diametrically opposed to the reactive hypothesis, as Nielsen claims it is. The two formulations are not diametrically opposed to one another because they both posit that communal inequalities play a key role in the generation and maintenance of communal solidarity. Where they diverge is on the conditions that lead to communal conflict.

Nielsen's hypothesis is that it is under conditions of decreasing communal inequalities and the approach of relative equality that communal solidarity (and various expressions of it, for example in electoral behavior) will be greatest. Hechter's argument, although not stated as clearly, is roughly the following: communal inequalities, once "set up" by the process of internal colonialism, become crystallized and do not necessarily decline with the process of industrialization (Hechter 1975:39). These inequalities become a permanent part of the picture and provide a constant source of grievances, which find expression in various forms of communal solidarity. While these two formulations are certainly different, they are not really diametrically opposed to one another.

As already mentioned, Hechter and Nielsen both assign a central place in their respective models to the role of communal inequalities as generators of communal solidarity. Neither author takes us very far theoretically into the uncharted territory of relations between relatively equal communal groups. Both authors (and they are not alone on this point) imply, I think erroneously, that group loyalty and solidarity would necessarily be lower were the competing communal groups equal.

It may well be that once communal groups are relatively equal, each with its own (equally strong) institutions, the potential for conflict may decrease, if only because the grievances due to inequalities are not present. But this does not mean that group solidarity and loyalty will *necessarily* decline. As McRoberts (1979; McRoberts and Posgate 1980) has noted with respect to the Quebec case, contemporary Québécois nationalism is not so much rooted in cultural difference, or in grievances about inequalities, but in institutional separateness.

SUMMARY AND CONCLUSION

Let us now try to summarize our findings. No support was found for the hypothesis derived from the functionalist perspective according to which preferences for reduced communal inequalities would lead to preferences to reduce cultural differences between the Francophone and Anglophone communities. The results support the communal competition perspective.

We then reviewed a recent debate between two authors, Hechter and Nielsen, proposing different hypotheses within the communal competition perspective. Hechter's reactive hypothesis, despite the needless primacy it was given in his earlier overall framework (1975), was found to be useful. A consistent reactive effect, whereby awareness of communal inequalities is positively associated with a more centrifugal orientation toward cultural pluralism, is definitely present.

In addition, we found some support for Nielsen's hypothesis, according to which it is basically the approaching and partial attainment of *equal-status* competition that makes for greater group solidarity. Unlike Nielsen, however, we have argued that this kind of equal-status effect can coexist with the reactive effect. Our reinterpretation of Nielsen's results on Belgium was that communal inequalities, and perceptions of them, can survive in a group's collective memory. This memory of past inequalities, combined with awareness of recent changes in the direction of more equal status, can easily coexist and may indeed exert a strong interaction effect on feelings of group solidarity. In other words, Nielsen's results can be interpreted as a confirmation of the reactive effect. This is not recognized in Nielsen's formulation.

In concrete terms, this means that the Flemish nationalist movement may well be strong now because Flemings and Walloons are more equal than they have ever been, and that the current level of support for Flemish nationalism might even be greater than that which would be predicted if the two groups had been more equal all along. This formulation is a clarification of Nielsen's discussion of Hechter, and it shows that the reactive hypothesis and the "equal-status" hypothesis are not as mutually exclusive as has been claimed.

The debate between Hechter and Nielsen that has been sketched here can also be seen as an application to communal and ethnic politics of the long-standing debate between the theories of revolution of Tocqueville and Marx. Simply put, Marx predicted that the proletariat's revolutionary potential would increase as inequalities increased and economic conditions worsened. Tocqueville, on the other hand, emphasized that groups are most inclined to revolution when conditions are visibly improving.

In the findings reported in this chapter, a similar sort of coexistence of the reactive effect and the "equal-status" effect was observed. Here the coexistence is between an awareness of inequalities making for a more centrifugal orientation, and an egalitarian attitude concerning the relative talents and capabilities of the two groups having the same effect.

In this chapter we have clarified and investigated another important question on which the functionalist and communal competition perspectives give different predictions. More research, of course, is needed. How does the magnitude of the reactive effect vary under different conditions? In particular, in which subgroups of the Quebec population is the reactive effect strongest?[4] Looking outward from this case study, we can ask in a similar vein, how does the reactive effect vary as a function of the setting variable? In particular, is the reactive effect indeed stronger in colonial situations, as Hechter has implicitly and Memmi (1972) more explicitly suggested? But these are questions for another project.

Part III

QUEBEC'S EVOLVING INTERGROUP DYNAMICS: FROM 1970 TO THE 1990s

INTRODUCTION TO PART III

As we saw in chapter 1, the 1970s was a decade marked by language legislation aimed at reversing the traditional balance of power between French and English in Quebec. Bill 101, the Charter of the French Language, was designed to allow French to become as "normal" a language in Quebec as English was in the rest of Canada. The minister responsible for the Charter, Camille Laurin, a psychiatrist by profession, argued that it was a necessary measure, not only to even the score on objective social and economic indicators, but also to foster the development of a confident "majority" psychology among Francophones. A corollary to this, of course, was that the new curtailed position of Anglophones was expected to change their psychology and outlook in the appropriate minority direction as well.

Levine describes the context in which the Charter was introduced:

> Bill 101 culminated the push, begun during the Quiet Revolution, to assert Francophone hegemony in Montreal, and the law quickly gained near-consensual support within the French-speaking community as the legal and symbolic cornerstone of the Francophone reconquest.
>
> . . . opposition to Bill 101 would become the touchstone of Anglophone resistance to the new linguistic regime. Small wonder: Bill 101 limited Anglophone rights and privileges, threatened English-language schools with a demographic crisis, and reduced the status of the Anglophone community from one of Montreal's "Charter" groups—indeed, a historically "controlling" group—to the most important of many minority "cultural communities" in a French-speaking society. (Levine 1990:119)

Anglophones eventually made some measure of peace with the new order, through a combination of strategies, including out-migration, protest and resignation, and accommodation. The latter was reflected by a rapid increase in bilingualism rates. By the early 1980s, when the new rules of the game were in place, attention turned to specific issues, such as how French-language schools were handling their new role of integrating recent immigrants, how French was spreading as a language of work, and how the rapidly expanding Francophone business class was making its presence felt in the economy. The ascendancy of the Francophone business class, which had close ties to Quebec's state-owned enterprises, was a major development.

In the 1980s, the shift toward an emphasis on market forces and privatization was felt in Quebec as it was elsewhere, and successive Quebec governments took their cues from the new private sector leadership. This dynamic led to Quebecers being among the strongest supporters of the Free Trade Agreement (FTA) between Canada and the United States in the late 1980s, and of the North American Free Trade Agreement (NAFTA) between Canada, the United States, and Mexico in the early 1990s. To many nationalists in Quebec, closer ties with the United States were viewed as one more way of distancing Quebec from the rest of Canada—a manifestation of the "Quebec more continentalist" pattern observed in chapter 4.

In the 1990s Canada has experienced two failed attempts at constitutional reform. In 1990 the constitutional amendment known as the Meech Lake Accord failed to gain the approval of all of the provinces. Subsequently, the Charlottetown Accord was defeated in the October 1992 referendum. These experiences have left Quebecers and Canadians outside Quebec with a sharpened sense of their diverging outlooks and have hardened the mood between Quebec and the rest of Canada. In this context, Aboriginal Canadians have occupied a prominent role in public debate in the 1990s.

The next three chapters cover the time span from 1970 to the 1990s, and pay special attention to a few key issues. In chapter 7, we examine how the macro-level power shift shows up in trends in micro-level perceptions of orientations toward cultural pluralism and perceptions of inequalities during the 1970s and 1980s. In chapter 8 we examine how Quebec's two linguistic segments of the larger dominant society have reacted to Native Indian movements since the 1970s, and examine changing attitudes toward immigrants, in the context of the new majority host role that the Francophone community has been called on to assume. Chapter 9 presents a few comparative observations on Quebec's restructuring of intergroup relations.

7

Pluralism and Inequality: Trends in Perceptions in the 1970s and 1980s

As we have already seen, the power shift in the direction of Franco-phones was appreciable during the 1970s and 1980s, and a wide range of objective indicators confirm this trend.[1] In this chapter, we will examine how this trend has been reflected in the perceptual structure of Quebec society. A central goal of the language legislation enacted in the 1970s was to bring about a shift not only in objective conditions, but also in mentalities and outlooks. To the extent that this has been occurring, we should look for shifts in a more egalitarian direction to show up, and indeed possibly some reversals to the patterns seen in the previous chapters. We shall examine changes in each of our original indicators for which trend data was available.

TRENDS IN ORIENTATIONS
TOWARD CULTURAL PLURALISM

Table 7.1 shows that in two of the three available indicators of orientations toward cultural pluralism, the shift in attitudes from 1970 to 1985 is in the more centrifugal direction. There is a decline in the tendency to say French and English are different, and this decline is entirely attributable to Francophones. At the same time, there is an increase in the percentage of respondents who state that French Canadians should try to maintain their

TABLE 7.1

TRENDS IN ORIENTATIONS TOWARD CULTURAL PLURALISM,
BY LANGUAGE GROUP, 1970, 1977, 1985

		1970	1977	1985
A. P1: Do you think that in their mentality and ways of living French Canadians and English Canadians are very different, fairly different, quite similar, or very similar?			(% centrifugal)	
	total Quebec	55	51	41
	Francophones	58	52	41
	Anglophones	40	42	40
Case bases (N)	Francophones	(5,215)	(1,166)	(1,753)
	Anglophones	(885)	(128)	(275)
B. P3: Do you think French Canadians should try and maintain their ways of living, or that they should become more like the other Canadians?			(% centrifugal)	
	total Quebec	50	61	
	Francophones	53	63	
	Anglophones	33	43	
Case bases (N)	Francophones	(5,207)	(1,166)	
	Anglophones	(882)	(128)	
C. P4: Which would you say it is most important for a people to maintain: its language and culture or its standard of living?			(% centrifugal)	
	total Quebec	25	36	
	Francophones	28	37	
	Anglophones	9	27	
Case bases (N)	Francophones	(5,223)	(1,753)	
	Anglophones	(884)	(275)	

N.B. The wording of the questions shown here is from the 1970 study. The 1977 and 1985 versions, which are slightly different, are given in appendix B.

---

ways of living and who say it is more important for a people to maintain its language and culture than its standard of living.

There is a decline in centrifugal orientations toward assessments of difference, but an increase in centrifugal orientations toward evaluations of its importance. In 1985, French and English Canadians are perceived as being more similar, but both language groups are more likely than before to emphasize the importance of language and culture. This would appear to be a clear sign of increased competition. In the last panel, one can note the large increase in the percentage of Anglophones who emphasize the importance of maintaining language and culture. While Francophones were 19 percent more likely than Anglophones to hold this view in 1970, the difference between the two groups drops to 10 percent in 1985. This would indicate a modest shift in the direction of a minority group reaction among Anglophones on this point.

TRENDS IN PERCEIVED COMMUNAL INEQUALITIES

Wealth

We might expect inequalities in wealth to even out more slowly than inequalities in income, which, as we have already seen, were practically eliminated by the 1980s. By 1987, half of Quebec's 100 richest people were Francophones (Moreau 1992:348), and by 1993 a majority were (Smith 1994:93). The fraction is still, however, proportionately below the 83 percent of the population who are Francophones. Interestingly enough, by 1994 nine of the ten richest individuals in Quebec were Francophones, according to a survey carried out by the business publication *Affaires Plus* (Schnurmacher 1994).

The data presented in table 7.2 show that the tendency to say English Canadians are the wealthier group remained quite stable from 1970 to 1985, with a slight increase among Francophones and a slight drop among Anglophones. The tendency to say that this gap in wealth should be reduced dropped across the board.

Employment

One of the goals of Quebec's new sociopolitical climate was to maximize pressure on corporate employers to use French and to hire Francophones. One analysis of the francization programs aimed at large private sector firms summarized the government's dilemma as one of maintaining just the right dose of "règle dure, pratique molle" (Dion and Lamy 1990). This strategy of combining strict rules with flexible enforcement practices is

TABLE 7.2

TRENDS IN PERCEIVED COMMUNAL INEQUALITIES
IN WEALTH, BY LANGUAGE GROUP, 1970, 1977, 1985

		1970	1977	1985
I1: Which of these two groups is generally the wealthier: French Canadians or English Canadians?				
			(% English Canadians)	
	total Quebec	60	65	64
	Francophones	62	67	68
	Anglophones	43	49	39
Case bases (N)	Francophones	(5,221)	(1,185)	(1,754)
	Anglophones	(879)	(128)	(274)
(If respondent named English Canadians)				
I2: Do you think that all in all the difference in wealth that exists between French Canadians and English Canadians is acceptable, or should it be reduced?				
			(% should be reduced)	
	total Quebec	61		53
	Francophones	62		54
	Anglophones	54		49
Case bases (N)	Francophones	(3,246)		(1,275)
	Anglophones	(381)		(137)

N.B. The wording of the questions shown here is from the 1970 study. The 1977 and 1985 versions, which are slightly different, are given in appendix B.

---

aimed at keeping enough pressure on employers without scaring them away. The income data reveal that bilingual Francophones have the edge as of the 1980s. One compromise often hit upon, not only in the private sector but in the federal administration as well, is to hire a Francophone who is not averse to working in English. It is not surprising, then, that both in the federal bureaucracy and in Montreal's private sector the proportion of Francophones hired has increased much faster than has the actual use of French at upper levels.

The data presented in table 7.3 reveal a clear-cut decline in the overall perception of English advantage and a corresponding increase in all other substantive responses. It is interesting to note that in 1970 the

TABLE 7.3

TRENDS IN PERCEIVED COMMUNAL INEQUALITIES
IN EMPLOYMENT, BY LANGUAGE GROUP, 1970, 1977, 1985

		1970	1977	1985
I3: In the case of job offers or promotions, do you think that a French Canadian and an English Canadian who are equally competent have the same chances of getting them, that the French Canadian has a better chance, or that the English Canadian has a better chance?				
			(% English)	
	total Quebec	45		32
	Francophones	51	56	35
	Anglophones	8		8
			(% both equally)	
	total Quebec	36		38
	Francophones	34	36	40
	Anglophones	49		24
			(% French)	
	total Quebec	6		15
	Francophones	4	5	9
	Anglophones	23		57
			(% qualified answer)	
	total Quebec	9		11
	Francophones	8		12
	Anglophones	16		9
			(% don't know)	
	total Quebec	4		4
	Francophones	3	3	4
	Anglophones	4		3
Case bases (N)	total Quebec	(6,094)	(2,028)	
	Francophones	(5,198)	(1,164)	(1,753)
	Anglophones	(885)		(275)

N.B. In 1977, this question was asked only in the French language version of the questionnaire.

single most frequent response among Francophones is "English" and among Anglophones "both equally." By 1985, the single most frequent response among Francophones is "both equally," while among Anglo-

TABLE 7.4

REPORTED EXPERIENCE OF DISCRIMINATION,
BY LANGUAGE GROUP, 1970, 1985

1970 QUESTIONNAIRE

I4: Has it ever happened to you, or to relatives, friends, or acquaintances of yours, to have less chance of getting a job or a promotion than someone of another origin, despite being equally competent?

	Franco-phones	Anglo-phones	Total Quebec
Yes, to myself	8%	8%	8%
Yes, to relatives, friends or acquaintances	21	15	20
Yes, to myself and to relatives, friends, or acquaintances	2	1	2
No	63	68	63
Don't remember	6	8	7
	100% (5,212)	100% (878)	100% (6,091)

1985 QUESTIONNAIRE

Have you ever been in a situation where you didn't have an equal chance of getting a job or promotion as people from a different language group, even though you were as qualified as they were?

	Franco-phones	Anglo-phones	Total Quebec
Yes	17%	24%	18%
No	81	75	81
Can't remember	1	1	1
	100% (1,753)	100% (275)	100% (2,029)

phones it is "French." Further symmetrical patterns are evident. As was visible in our analysis in chapter 5, in 1970 it is Anglophones who are the more likely to give a "hedging" response, (i.e., to say both equally, give a qualified answer, or say don't know) or, in other words, to exhibit a "majority group" reaction of sorts. By 1985, it is Francophones who are more likely to give hedging responses, which indicates a modest shift toward majority status. Looking at the totals for Quebec society as a whole, it is significant that by 1985 the overall single most frequent response was "both equally," which was far from being the case in 1970.

Experience of Discrimination

Responses to two questions about the experience of unfair treatment are shown in table 7.4. Notice that the wording of the 1970 question concerns origins, while the 1985 question refers to language group. In 1970, only 8 percent of the respondents in each language group claimed a personal experience of unfair treatment, with Francophones reporting slightly more such experiences among their friends, relatives, and acquaintances than Anglophones. By 1985, the percentage of respondents reporting having personally experienced unfair treatment doubled to 17 percent among Francophones, and tripled to 24 percent among Anglophones. These increases no doubt reflect the extensive politicization of language over the period in question. Note also that the percentage of respondents reporting they can't remember drops to 1 percent in 1985. The climate obviously helps people remember.

If in any "normal society" model it is minorities who adjust to the rules set by majorities, then this structural pattern would indicate that it is now Anglophones who have (a little) more of a "minority" response. This is one more small reflection of the changing balance of power. From the point of view of the overall legitimacy and stability of the system, it is significant that a vast majority of both groups report no experience of unfair treatment.[2]

Business and Finance

The data presented in table 7.5 show the trends in perceptions about which group has the dominant position in the world of business and finance in Quebec. Over all, there is a clear decline in the percentage of respondents who say the English do, and an increase in the percentage who say the French do. While both of these shifts are present in both language groups, they are much stronger among Anglophones than among Francophones. By 1985 the percentage of Anglophones saying the French have the dominant position in the world of business and finance is almost as high as the percentage saying the English do, while Francophones are still much more likely to say the English do.

It is interesting to compare these results with the responses to a similar question asked by Kornberg and Clarke in three cities across Canada in 1980

TABLE 7.5

TRENDS IN PERCEIVED COMMUNAL INEQUALITIES
IN BUSINESS AND POLITICS, BY LANGUAGE GROUP, 1970, 1980, 1985

		1970	1985
I5: Do French Canadians or English Canadians hold the most important place in the world of business and finance in Quebec?			
		(% English)	
	total Quebec	71	61
	Francophones	74	65
	Anglophones	56	38
		(% French)	
	total Quebec	5	14
	Francophones	5	11
	Anglophones	4	31
		(% don't know)	
	total Quebec	9	10
	Francophones	8	9
	Anglophones	17	14
Case bases (N)	Francophones	(5,212)	(1,754)
	Anglophones	(874)	(275)
(If respondent named English Canadians)			
I6: On the whole, how do you evaluate this state of affairs: is it normal, fairly normal, rather abnormal, or very abnormal?			
		(% rather or very abnormal)	
	total Quebec	67	64
	Francophones	70	66
	Anglophones	35	36
Case bases (N)	Francophones	(3,827)	(1,591)
	Anglophones	(490)	(237)

(presented at the bottom of table 7.5). The vast majority of the residents of Trois-Rivières, Quebec, are Francophones, just as the vast majority of the residents of Peterborough, Ontario, and Lethbridge, Alberta, are Anglophones. Keeping in mind that the proportion of "don't know" responses is much higher outside Quebec than in Trois-Rivières, and higher among Anglophones than among Francophones within Quebec in both 1970 and 1975, it is clear that Anglophone Quebecers' views fall in between those of Francophone Quebecers and the views of Anglophones in Ontario and

TABLE 7.5
continued

		1970	1985
I8: Some people claim that the situation of Quebec is similar to that of other parts of the world that were or still are colonies. Other people claim these situations are different. Would you say they are very similar, fairly similar, rather different, or very different?			
		(% very or fairly similar)	
	total Quebec	37	26
	Francophones	39	27
	Anglophones	27	21
Case bases (N)	Francophones	(5,218)	(1,749)
	Anglophones	(885)	(272)

KORNBERG AND CLARKE'S 1980 SURVEY OF THREE CANADIAN CITIES

"Which group has the most important place in the world of business and finance?"

	Trois-Rivières	Peterborough	Lethbridge
French Canadians	6	37	41
English Canadians	60	27	26
both same chance	24	7	10
Don't know, no answer	10	28	22
Number of cases	(350)	(308)	(303)

Source: adapted from Kornberg and Clarke (1992:53)

Alberta. The view of the latter group that French Canadians are dominant in business and finance deserve further investigation. It may reflect the prominence of a few business leaders, the overall perceived power of Francophones and of Quebec over the federal state, or a combination of such factors. We shall return to this point in a later chapter.

In the responses to the question about whether the Quebec case resembles a colonial situation, there is an overall decline in affirmative answers from 37 percent to 26 percent, and also a decline in the communal effect (the extent to which the two language groups hold different views), from 12 percent to 6 percent. This decline parallels the shift in dominant nationalist discourse over the period. The colonial analogy was indeed

TABLE 7.6

TRENDS IN PERCEIVED COMMUNAL INEQUALITIES IN THE
PROFESSIONS, BY LANGUAGE GROUP, 1970, 1985

	Francophones		Anglophones	
	1970	1985	1970	1985
A. I9:Which do you think are in general the best doctors: French Canadian doctors, or English Canadian doctors?				
French Canadian doctors	20%	23%	5%	7%
both equally	61	35	51	41
qualified answer (that depends, etc.)	3	4	7	6
English Canadian doctors	5	15	15	22
don't know	11	23	22	22
	100%	100%	100%	100%
	(5,172)	(1,750)	(860)	(274)
B. I10: In which of the following two groups do you think one finds the greatest scientists: among French Canadians, or among English Canadians?				
among French Canadians	10%	3%	13%	14%
among both equally	46	24	28	11
qualified answer (that depends, etc.)	4	3	5	1
among English Canadians	27	35	33	39
don't know	14	25	31	33
	100%	100%	100%	100%
	(5,206)	(1,751)	(875)	(275)

Respondents who gave no answer have been excluded.
Percentage totals may deviate from 100% because of rounding.
I9 refers to question 2-37. I10 refers to question 2-31.

---

common in the early independence movement of the 1960s, but has receded since the Parti Québécois has become a governing party and as the sovereignty movement has become mainstream and sophisticated.

Professions

The data presented in table 7.6 shows an increase in communal polarization in perceptions of the talents and capabilities of the two groups.

Between 1970 and 1985, there is a marked decline in the percentage of respondents who say that the best doctors and scientists are equally likely to be found in either group, and there is a corresponding increase in the percentage who say that either French Canadians or English Canadians are the best doctors and scientists.

Interestingly enough, the tendency to see one or the other of the groups as more talented increased in both language subsets. In 1985, a higher percentage of both Francophone and Anglophone respondents viewed French Canadians as the better doctors, English Canadians as the better doctors, French Canadians as the better scientists, and English Canadians as the better scientists than they did in 1970. The "don't know" responses doubled among Francophones over this period, reflecting heightened uncertainty on these issues. By 1985, this uncertainty was shared almost equally by Francophones and Anglophones. These patterns are another consequence of the heightened communal competition over this period.

STATUS INEQUALITIES: A FURTHER LOOK

The responses to questions about the professions that we have just analyzed measure perceptions of group status indirectly. Given the symbolic and emotional importance of relative group status issues throughout the 1970s in Quebec, it may also be useful to examine responses to a very straightforward and direct question bearing on the issue. The data presented in table 7.7 show how members of each language group respond to a point-blank question about how they think the other group sees their own group.

The full weight of history is clearly at work in the asymmetric pattern whereby the single most frequent response among Francophones is that English Canadians see French Canadians as inferior, while the single most frequent response among Anglophones is that French Canadians see English Canadians as equal to themselves. Here again, there is evidence of polarization between 1970 and 1977, with a decline in the percentage of respondents in both language groups who say "equal to themselves," and a stable or increased tendency to say either "superior" or "inferior." While the central tendencies are differently located in the two language groups, the overall pattern reveals much variation and much overlap, reflecting the fact that the past has left inequalities that are best seen as relative, not absolute.

It might be useful to mention the related findings of Genessee and Holobow (1989), who carried out a matched-guise experiment with a small

TABLE 7.7

TRENDS IN PERCEIVED COMMUNAL INEQUALITIES
IN STATUS, BY LANGUAGE GROUP, 1970, 1977

French questionnaire			English questionnaire		
What do you think is the attitude of English Canadians toward French Canadians: do they see French Canadians in general as being superior, equal, or inferior to themselves?			What do you think is the attitude of French Canadians toward English Canadians: do they see English Canadians in general as being superior, equal, or inferior to themselves?		
	1970	1977		1970	1977
superior	3	3		10	22
equal	38	32		47	32
inferior					
to themselves	44	56		11	15
qualified answer	7	2		14	12
don't know	7	7		18	19
	100%	100%		100%	100%
	(4,290)	(1,184)		(872)	(127)
Personally, have you ever felt or not that English Canadians are superior to French Canadians in a number of areas?			Personally, have you ever felt or not that French Canadians are superior to English Canadians in a number of areas?		
		1977			1977
yes		36			22
no		60			60
don't know		3			17
		100%			100%
		(1,165)			(126)

sample of students in the mid-1980s in Montreal. They found that more "Francophone respondents generally rated the Canadian English and European French speakers as having higher status occupations than did the Anglophone respondents" and that ". . . the status results for French Canadian respondents could not be accounted for by actual socioeconomic advantages associated with English" (Genessee and Holobow 1989:33,17). As already suggested, if the observed tendency of Francophone respondents to judge Francophones as inferior cannot be accounted for by present conditions, then the explanation must lie in the enduring weight of past conditions in shaping present perceptions.

SURFACE CHANGE AND "DEEPER" CHANGE

Researchers have probably long been aware of the distinction between changes in univariate distributions of a given variable over time and changes in relationships between variables over time. Nonetheless, as Laslett (1980) points out, this issue has received little attention, theoretical or methodological, among scholars. To Duncan, change in relationships between variables (as opposed to change in univariate distributions) involves "social change in a deeper sense of the term" (1975:57). The distinction may well be one useful way of conceptualizing the distinction between surface change and deeper change. This can be illustrated by examining an example of each type.

Quite a few instances of both types of social change have been observed in this chapter. Consider the finding reported in the second panel of table 7.1, in which the overall percentage of the Quebec population giving a centrifugal response to the question about whether French Canadians should maintain their ways of living increased from 50 to 61 percent between 1970 and 1977. The rate of increase was identical in both language groups, and the 20 percent communal gap between Francophones and Anglophones remained exactly the same over this time span. This is an example of surface change.

Now let us consider a different type of pattern. According to the data presented in Table 7.4, the overall volume of reported incidents of unfair treatment more than doubled between 1970 and 1985. The increase was higher among Anglophones than among Francophones: in 1970, it was Francophones who were slightly more likely to report unfair treatment; in 1985, it was Anglophones who were more likely to do so. This reversal of the communal effect is a sign of deeper social change.

CONCLUSION

How can these trends in orientations toward cultural pluralism and in perceptions of communal inequalities best be summarized? The approach adopted here has emphasized looking at shifts in the overall distribution of perceptions, as well as shifts in the way members of the two language groups differ from each other. On the whole, the perceptual structure reveals much continuity, as well as much change. The pattern appears to reflect an evening-out of the macro-level power relationship between French and English rather than a full-blown reversal. Francophones have acquired some "majority mentality" characteristics, without, however, leaving their long-held minority outlook completely behind them.[3] Similarly, Anglophones now display some minority-outlook reactions, but have not relinquished all signs of past majority status.[4] On balance, the two groups appear to have converged to meet on a middle ground on which both majority and minority reflexes are simultaneously present in both communities.

Indeed, in the context of group competition, the minority outlook may well be maintained not because it is an atavistic remnant of earlier times, but because it can be a useful resource. Francophones may believe that ceasing to see and report English domination could jeopardize the continued advancement of the evening-out process or even hasten the return of English domination. Similarly, Anglophones may well display more of a minority outlook because this has become a useful way for them to channel claims against their competitors. As we shall see shortly, in its restructuring Quebec is similar to other parts of the world where similar power shifts have occurred and where past inequalities still color present perceptions.

8

Aboriginals, Immigrants, and the Language Cleavage

In chapter 1, we saw that Quebec and Canada have a complex ethnic and linguistic pluralism that can be understood by distinguishing between three axes of differentiation: the relationship between Aboriginal or Native peoples and the larger society; Canada's historic French-English dualism; and the relationship between certain immigrant ethnic groups and the larger society. To understand change, we need to trace the evolution of each of these distinct axes, and examine the changing relationship between them.

The research reported in the preceding chapters was focused explicitly on the second of these axes within Quebec, that dealing with linguistic dualism. This guided our choice of dependent variables, and also our choice of linguistic community membership as a key independent variable. Given the central focus of this study on the restructuring of the overarching linguistic cleavage within Quebec, it might be interesting and instructive to relate these results to research on the structure of mass perceptions of the two other principal axes of ethnic differentiation. This is all the more appropriate since the past two decades have been a period in which native peoples, as well as immigrant communities, have slowly come "out of irrelevance" and onto center stage in Quebec.

Before we begin, we should recall a point made in the beginning of our study—that Quebec's internal pluralism is the key to Canada's outlier position as a state with a higher-than-expected level of pluralism given its high level of development. We should also recall that Quebec's historic

French-English dualism has affected the two other axes of differentiation: both Quebec's aboriginal peoples and its immigrant ethnic communities display characteristics not shared by their counterparts elsewhere in Canada. We can add that, in the past two decades, just as Quebec's Anglophone community has been called upon to redefine itself as a Quebec minority rather than as a fraction of Canada's English-speaking majority that happens to live in Quebec, so Quebec's aboriginal and immigrant ethnic communities have been called upon to redefine themselves as Quebec minorities distinct from their counterparts in the rest of Canada.

In the first section of this chapter we will examine the structure of attitudes toward Native peoples and discuss how it has evolved from the 1970s to the 1990s. In the second section, we will examine the structure of attitudes toward immigrants and immigrant integration over the same period.

ATTITUDES TOWARD NATIVE PEOPLES

We shall begin by referring to a study of the dominant (non-Native) Canadian population's perceptions of Indian affairs and Indian issues in the 1970s (Ponting and Gibbins 1980). In that study, based on data from a 1976 national survey, Ponting and Gibbins constructed what they referred to as an "Indian Sympathy Index." One of the most clear-cut sources of variation in scores on that index was language group membership. When the views of Francophones from Quebec were compared to those of Anglophones from across Canada, the shapes of the distributions were similar. Beyond this, however, the authors report that

> Francophones on the average received higher (more sympathetic) scores. Thus our general attitudinal measure confirms a general pattern; Francophones demonstrate a more positive outlook towards Indians and Indian issues than do Anglophones. (Ponting and Gibbins 1980:86)

Ponting and Gibbins add that Francophones exhibited greater sympathy toward Indians and Indian issues than do Anglophones even though, according to their data, Francophone respondents tended to be less well-informed about Indian issues than Anglophone respondents. They conclude that

> On balance, although not consistently, Francophone respondents were also more approving of Indian protest. With respect to the major

differences between Indians and non-Indians, Francophones were much more prone to mention cultural differences, while at the same time deemphasizing differences in personality and economic opportunity. In describing the main problems faced by contemporary Indians, Francophones were more likely to mention white prejudice and the problems associated with assimilation. (Ponting and Gibbins 1980:90)

In Ponting's follow-up study based on data from a 1986 survey, this pattern was maintained. On scales designed to measure sympathy for Indians as well as support for special status and for self-government, Quebec showed the highest average score of all the provinces (Ponting 1987:21).

Pineo's investigation of the relative status of ethnic categories in French and English Canada yielded similar results. Respondents were asked to rank a list of ethnic group labels according to "social standing." While "Canadian Indians" was a label that was ranked near the bottom of the list by both the English and the French respondents, it is interesting to note that the French respondents gave it a higher score than the English sample did (32.5 as opposed to 28.3) (Pineo 1977).

What this pattern reveals is that there may be a structural source of sympathy at work here. It may well be that since Francophones are more conscious than Anglophones are of French-English differences and the diverse problems that Anglophone domination have caused for Francophones (see chapters 3 to 7) they are also, as a consequence more aware of the somewhat similar problems faced by Indians in their relationship with the larger society. This has, in fact, been a recurrent if not always dominant, strand in Quebec writings about Francophone-Aboriginal relationships (see Vincent 1992).

Francophones may well be more sympathetic than Anglophones to Indian protest because Indian grievances and claims involve a territorial component and, more importantly, a demand for *collective* rights within the larger society. These two characteristics of the Native peoples' movements in Canada are, of course, quite similar to the characteristics of the historical struggles of French Canada for autonomy via-à-vis English Canada. As mentioned earlier, this similarity between the two sets of grievances may well be a source of the greater sympathy of Francophones for Indian protest and Indian rights.

In terms of our early theoretical discussion about types of settings in which intergroup relations take place, both French Canada and the Indians of Canada were incorporated into the Canadian state structure as a result of conquests and annexations that were less than voluntary. Both of these axes of differentiation, notwithstanding their many dissimilarities in other respects, fall into the same category in the frameworks of Lieberson (1961), Blauner (1972), and Schermerhorn (1978), by virtue of the fact that they trace their origins to less than voluntary inclusion into the state structure at the hands of culturally alien agents of that state structure. Both French Canadians and Native peoples became indigenous subordinate groups in the larger Canadian context.

In the 1970s and 1980s, the Quebec state formulated its own policies with respect to "its" Native peoples, and the special sympathy for the rights of Native peoples displayed by Francophones in Quebec was in a sense matched by more favorable objective conditions there. On many indicators covering this period, Native people in Quebec are relatively less disadvantaged than their counterparts elsewhere in Canada. For example, the family incomes, educational levels, and housing conditions of Native peoples in Quebec, while clearly below the levels of non-Native Quebecers, nonetheless indicate that they have less of a relative disadvantage than do Native peoples in other Canadian provinces. In similar fashion, suicide rates among Native peoples are lower in Quebec than elsewhere in Canada (Salée 1992:373). The higher rates of ancestral language retention among Native peoples in Quebec have already been mentioned.

The dynamics behind all of this are complex. The Francophone nation-building Quebec state wanted to extend its influence and authority over all groups residing in its territory. The Indians and the Inuit of Northern Quebec, however, had a tradition of dealing directly with the federal government. Moreover, many of Quebec's Native communities had, over time, come to use English as their main language for communication with the state. A new accommodation has often taken the form of increasing the use of French *and* aboriginal languages, in exchange, so to speak, for a reduced use of English. As we shall see, there are parallels between the "new social contract" that the Quebec state is attempting to forge with its Native communities and that which it is attempting to forge with various immigrant ethnic communities.

Across Canada in the late 1970s and 1980s, aboriginal political mobilization increased significantly. The National Indian Brotherhood clearly revealed the adoption of nationhood as a basis for advancing claims against the state and the larger society by becoming the Assembly of First Nations. This development was in some ways inspired by and modeled on the successful Francophone political mobilization on the basis of nationhood that has occurred in Quebec. Within Quebec, Native groups pressed their case for greater autonomy against the government, and in 1985, the Quebec National Assembly officially recognized the existence of aboriginal nations within Quebec (Vincent 1992:770).

Since 1990, relations between Aboriginals in Quebec and the government and larger society have become more tense and polarized. In the summer of 1990, the federal constitutional amendment known as the Meech Lake Accord, which would have provided for recognition of Quebec as a distinct society within Canada, failed to gain the assent of all of the provinces. The Manitoba legislature did not give its assent because one of its members, a Native Indian, refused to approve the Accord on the grounds that it put Quebec's needs ahead of those of Canada's First Nations. While this gesture is understandable as a protest against Indian exclusion, in Quebec it was widely interpreted as an anti-Quebec and anti-French stand, of the sort that have repeatedly marked the history of Western Canada. To some Quebecers, Native people as a group were seen as the ones who, in collusion with a hostile English Canada, had killed the constitutional agreement. Later in the summer of 1990, the Oka crisis, a land dispute between a municipality and Mohawk leaders, erupted near Montreal. One police officer was killed in an altercation, and a major bridge was blockaded for some weeks in a tense standoff involving some Mohawks, the Sureté du Québec (the provincial police force), and the Canadian army. All of this brought international media attention to Native grievances in Quebec. Since then, the Cree have mounted an ultimately successful international campaign against the proposed expansion of the James Bay hydroelectric project in Northern Quebec.

All of these changes in the sociopolitical climate have had a marked effect on the patterns observed in opinion surveys. The pattern that had been consistent for two decades whereby Quebec and Francophone respondents displayed higher levels of sympathy for aboriginal rights has given way to a more ambiguous overall picture, in which Quebecers often take a harder line than other Canadians on Indian issues. Of particular interest, given our focus on perceived group inequalities, is some very new data on the way the non-aboriginal population of Quebec views the standard of living enjoyed by Indians:

> Despite hard facts to the contrary, more than half of Quebec Francophones believe that Quebec Indians living on reserves have a higher standard of living than non-aboriginal Quebecers, according to a recent poll. . . . While 52 percent of Francophones thought the quality of life in native communities was "a lot better" or "a little

better" than in the rest of Quebec, only 26 percent of anglophone Quebecers thought the same way, according to the poll conducted earlier this month by the SOM polling firm for La Presse and Radio Quebec. (Lalonde 1994)

This newspaper report suggests that one reason for this skewed perception may well be Francophones' sense of being "victimized" by the antisovereignty and antinationalist statements of a number of Indian leaders. Whatever the mechanisms involved, this kind of pattern clearly indicates the impact the macropolitical context can have on group outlooks, leading sometimes to perceptions quite dissonant with reality. It is unclear if this result will show up in trend data or if it is simply an example of the volatility of perceptions under certain conditions.

Before moving on, I might mention one further point that gives pause for reflection. The percentage of Francophones holding the view that Indians have a higher standard of living than other Quebecers, reported in the newspaper article cited above (52 percent), is not far below the percentage of Francophone respondents in table 7.2 who perceive English Canadians as richer than French Canadians. The proportion of the latter remained fairly stable at over 60 percent between 1970 and 1985. Similarly, the 26 percent gap between Francophones and Anglophones in their responses to the question about the standard of living of Quebec Indians is of the same order of magnitude as that observed in responses to the French-English wealth question in table 7.2. More research needs to be done the possible linkages between these different sets of beliefs.

ATTITUDES TOWARD IMMIGRANTS
AND IMMIGRANT INTEGRATION

We now turn to attitudes toward immigrants and look at how they have been evolving under Quebec's ongoing power shift. We shall begin by examining the results of a few well-known studies on the issue from the 1970s.

In their investigation of Canadian attitudes toward immigration and the then recently-enacted federal multiculturalism policy, Berry, Kalin, and Taylor (1977) report that French-speaking Canadians displayed a less favorable attitude toward non-French and non-English ethnic origin groups than English-speaking Canadians did. Similar differences are reported concerning attitudes toward immigration and toward the federal multiculturalism policy.

In a similar vein, Curtis and Lambert (1976) report that French Canadians were systematically more likely to voice a greater "preference for cultural uniformity" than were English Canadians.[1] In other words, these results suggest that Francophone Canadians displayed less acceptance of ethnic and religious diversity than do Anglophone Canadians. Along the same lines, in Pineo's study (1977) referred to earlier, it is indeed the case that the French respondents gave most group labels lower rankings than the English respondents did.

If the results of these various studies are put together with our own findings reported earlier, the following rudimentary picture about the structure of attitudes in the 1970s emerges. Francophones were more convinced than Anglophones were of the differences between French and English culture and were more likely to insist on the value of the differences being maintained. Francophones were also more likely than Anglophones to display a sympathetic attitude toward Indian protest activities. Francophones were less likely than Anglophones, however, to display a sympathetic attitude toward ethnic and cultural diversity that has been produced by immigration. Why is it that during the 1970s Francophones were apparently *more* sympathetic than Anglophones were to Indian affairs, and *less* sympathetic than Anglophones to immigration and the ethnic diversity that it has produced?

The higher sympathy of Francophones for Indian affairs has already been linked to a sense of shared collective minority status within the Canadian state. What about Francophones' lower level of approval of immigrants and immigrant diversity? Their lower level of acceptance of French-speaking Canadians of immigration and of the federal multiculturalism policy is no doubt linked to their overriding concern for protecting the institutions of the Francophone collectivity. It is quite likely that immigration has not been viewed as favorably in French Canada as in English Canada because French Canada has historically benefited from immigration much less than has English Canada. Since the majority of immigrants to Canada, and even to Quebec, have in the past tended to become more integrated into the Anglophone community than into the Francophone community, the lower proportion of relatively recent immigrants and their descendants in the Francophone community has in itself been a direct and important reason for the less favorable view of immigration that the Francophone community displays.

Beyond this, however, there is the perception that immigration has been harmful to the Francophone community precisely because it has historically been disproportionately absorbed by the Anglophone community. To the extent that immigration has been used to strengthen and buttress Anglophone institutions both within Quebec and across Canada—and there is no doubt that this has been the case throughout Canadian history—it is natural that Francophones should display a healthy skepticism toward it.

A further reason for the lukewarm attitude of Francophones toward immigration, and toward ethnic diversity in general, is that the integration of immigrants as *individuals* into the Anglophone community constitutes, in a sense, an acceptance by immigrants of the Anglophone offer of *individual* incorporation that has long been collectively resisted by Francophones. The lack of enthusiasm among Francophones for the federal multiculturalism policy can be understood in similar terms. Multiculturalism is viewed as granting immigrant ethnic groups some sort of *collective* rights, which have heretofore been granted, however grudgingly, only to Indians and to Francophones (and to Anglophones as well, of course). This reduces the distinctive legal status of the Francophone community, in the eyes of many observers (see Rocher 1973). According to this view, Canada's historic dualism is cheapened. Multiculturalism is seen as all the more dangerous because many of the groups being granted symbolic collective rights are viewed as by and large already assimilated into the larger Anglophone community across Canada. So in the 1970s, just as the federal Official Languages Act was viewed by many Francophones as doing too little too late for Quebec, so the federal multiculturalism policy was viewed as an inappropriate policy for Quebec since it would naturally favor the already more multiethnic Anglophone community.

If this was the summary picture in the 1970s, how has the situation evolved since then? As a consequence of the provincial-state led reforms of the 1970s, immigrant integration is an area in which some of the most significant structural and institutional changes have occurred. Part of the impetus for the legislation of the 1970s was the realization on the part of Francophone elites that Anglophone institutions in Montreal had been able to maintain and even expand their power base by absorbing several waves of immigrants. The aim of the new legislation was to allow Francophone institutions to take over the immigrant integration process, a role in keeping with, and essential to, the goal of building a French-language society in which mere ethnic differences would eventually be transcended. This aspect of Quebec's normalization process—that of having the institutions of the demographic majority finally fulfill their natural majority role—would also have the effect of cutting Anglophone institutions back to more reasonable and modest dimensions and leave them with a much narrower demographic base. The new measures were aimed at correcting the harmful overdevelopment that Anglophone institutions had been allowed to undergo in the past, due to unfair power arrangements, and simultaneously at building up Francophone institutions to the point of permitting them to assume their rightful dominant role.

One of the striking features of Quebec's new immigrant absorption policy is that it is more explicitly state-directed than that of, for example, English Canada and the United States. This is so because in Quebec "the market" cannot be counted on to do the job, and in a sense cannot be counted on to work in the same direction as the state. Quebec's immigrant integration policies are one more example of the use of the Quebec state by Francophone elites to counteract the forces of the larger continental marketplace. Societies whose dominant culture and language are powerful enough to have immigrants inevitably adopt them to some extent, sooner or later, (for example, the United States or English Canada) will have no serious objection to a policy of multiculturalism. Indeed, what harm can there be in letting immigrants think they are keeping their own culture, if one is sure that in the long run everyone will integrate. In Quebec, a feeling of confidence based on a high probability of long-term convergence is absent. Rather, the fear is that, in the short run as well as in the long run, immigrants will turn to English rather than French, with the consequence of exacerbating the *minorisation* of Francophones. Hence the need for strong state measures to counteract the forces of the market and the hegemonic position of English in the larger North American environment.

The broad policy shift that mandated French-language institutions as immigrant integrators on a broad scale has already produced a number of interesting consequences. Here once again, there is evidence that Francophones are indeed slowly adjusting to the new majority role that they and their institutions are expected to play regarding immigrants, but their defensive minority reflexes are also still evident.

One example of the complexity of the dynamics at work can be gleaned from the data presented in table 8.1. These data show the distribution of a summary measure of comfort with immigrants.[2] The two panels present the joint effect of ethnic origin and language, and ethnic origin and Quebec residence.

The results indicate that Quebecers and Francophones have lower scores than other Canadians and Anglophones, indicating they feel the need to exercise a greater caution with immigrants, as has been reported in past studies. These differences remain even if social privilege variables are controlled. What these data allow us to show is that if ethnicity and either language or Quebec residence are examined simultaneously, as is being done

TABLE 8.1

MEAN COMFORT LEVEL WITH IMMIGRANTS, BY LANGUAGE GROUP
AND ETHNIC ORIGIN AND BY REGION AND ETHNIC ORIGIN, CANADA, 1991

A.		Language of Questionnaire	
Ethnic Origin		English	French
Aboriginal		5.74	5.24
		(39)	(31)
French		5.92	5.08
		(156)	(586)
British		5.96	5.31
		(1,334)	(62)
Other		5.86	5.30
		(902)	(84)

B.		Region of residence	
Ethnic Origin		Outside Quebec	Inside Quebec
Aboriginal		5.91	5.08
		(37)	(33)
French		5.92	5.07
		(163)	(579)
British		5.96	5.63
		(1,275)	(121)
Other		5.88	5.43
		(845)	(141)

Mean value of 13 variables each of which is a 7 point scale coded (1 = not at all comfortable) and
(7 = completely comfortable). Details are given in appendix B.

here, then it is clear that ethnic origin is less important than either Quebec
residence or language. In other words, it is living in Quebec, or answering in
French, that lowers the score, and this mechanism operates in all ethnic origin
categories, as can be seen by reading across the rows of the table.

What this means is that when people of any and all ethnic origins are
socialized into the Francophone community through the French language
and culture, they adopt the somewhat more cautious orientation toward
immigrants that is characteristic of the Francophone community. The same
type of effect is exerted by residence in Quebec. Phrased differently,
residence outside Quebec and answering in English are both associated
with higher comfort levels with immigrants.

One of the special features of this data set (in contrast to the earlier ones used for the analyses in previous chapters) is that the ethnic origin question includes a category of respondents who designated themselves Aboriginals, that is either Indian, Métis, or Inuit. When the respondents' ethnic origins are recoded into four categories corresponding roughly to the different types of incorporation discussed in chapter 2 and earlier in this chapter, then a further detail emerges from the table. Although ethnic origin is much less important overall than either language or Quebec residence, we can see that within Quebec or within the Francophone community it is still Aboriginals and those of French origin (the two categories of indigenous subordinates, in Lieberson's framework) who have somewhat lower scores than those of British or "other" origins. This shows a lesser effect of ethnic origin within the much larger and more important effect of language and territory. Although the number of cases drops prohibitively if we attempt to examine the joint effect of language and ethnic origin just within the Quebec sample, the overall result is the same. These results show that concern about immigration is an attribute of Quebec society as a whole, and also more specifically of Francophones as the majority language group, and is not restricted to those of French origin.

These results, that language and territory are more important factors than ethnic origin in shaping outlooks, are consonant with the state-mandated shift in recent decades toward a majority role for Quebec's Francophone institutions, in which the French language serves as a unifying medium. Quebec's ongoing state-sponsored shift from ethnic to linguistic and civic group boundaries has many parallels with the similar shift from ethnic to linguistic and civic group boundaries that began over a half-century earlier in the English-speaking parts of Canada (see Breton 1988). In both contexts, changes in group boundaries are linked to the expanding majority group's transition from an ethnic group to a broader multiethnic linguistic and civic category. Just as the defining characteristics of English Canadian nationalism have slowly evolved from an emphasis on shared British "stock" and ethnic origins to an emphasis on shared territory and the use of the English language, so it is that Quebec nationalism is undergoing a similar shift, but with a much later start.

Given the head start that English-speaking Canada has gained in this process, and given the minority position of the French language in Canada, it is not surprising that Francophones and Quebecers still display less comfort with immigrants than Anglophones and respondents in the rest of Canada. Is this communal difference rooted in semi-permanent structural differences and thus likely to be enduring? Or does it rather represent a temporary lag that is a consequence of the way an uneven development process has shaped the Francophone and Anglophone communities?

No definite answer can be given to this question. In broad terms, it makes sense to view this communal difference in discomfort as being rooted in history, and to some extent as a lag that is a predictable part of Quebec's uneven development process. It is due to the following factors, among others: (1) Francophone Quebec's late start in the immigrant integration business, (2) a (still) lower proportion in the Francophone community of recent immigrants and their descendants, (3) the Francophone community's still subordinate (and/or still perceived to be subordinate) economic position, and finally (4) the feeling of being a threatened demographic minority. As these factors change over time, the communal difference in comfort levels can be expected to decline as well. In this connection, it is noteworthy that one study has found that differences between Francophones and Anglophones in Montreal in their attitudes toward immigration and multiculturalism are largely attributable to concerns about the future of the French language in Quebec, once socioeconomic differences are taken into account (Bolduc and Fortin 1990). This suggests that some sort of lagged convergence might be taking place on this issue, both between Francophones and Anglophones in Quebec and between Quebec and other regions of Canada. More will be said on this point in a later chapter.

CONCLUSION

The findings presented in this chapter clearly suggest that more research needs to be done on how the three types of diversity enumerated at the beginning of the chapter combine and coexist within Quebec and Canadian society. Some important questions for further research are: Are the other social bases (in addition to language group membership) of sympathy for Indian affairs and comfort with ethnic diversity related to the other social bases of orientations toward French-English dualism and perceptions of communal inequalities that were analyzed in previous chapters? If so, how? How are the different sets of dependent variables related to each other? How is the perception of French-English inequalities related to the perception of Native peoples as relatively advantaged or disadvantaged? Does a highly centrifugal orientation toward French-English dualism and a perception of communal inequalities involve more or less sympathy for Indian protest? More or less acceptance of immigration and ethnic diversity?[3]

Quebec's New Dynamics: Some Comparative Observations

So far in our analysis of Quebec's internal restructuring, I have made a few comparative references in passing. Now is the time to develop a few of these. In this chapter I shall sketch a few comparative reference points and observations that could guide more systematic research. We shall begin close to home, in Canada and North America, then move on to other contexts in Europe and further afield.

UNEQUAL PARTNERS IN QUEBEC, CANADA, AND THE UNITED STATES

In chapter 4, I mentioned some parallel bases of Canadian and Quebec nationalism. Just as Ontarians and more-educated English Canadians are the strongest supporters of Canadian nationalism, so it is that more-educated Francophones in Quebec are the strongest supporters of Quebec nationalism. We went on to see that a similar "weaker partner/stronger partner" dynamic is at work in explaining the different views of Francophones and Anglophones within Quebec. Membership in the historically subordinate group has led Francophones to be systematically more aware of their group distinctiveness and of French-English inequalities. We also saw that as an educated aboriginal leadership mobilized Native peoples, advancing its own claims of nationhood against Quebec nationalism, Francophone sympathy for the First Nations cause declined.

We have seen that although our analysis has focused on competition between groups within one territory, many of the dynamics are similar to those between competitors in different territories. This suggests that it may be possible to integrate the literature on intercommunal relations within states or regions with theoretical work on relationships between regions or states. I might mention, in this respect, that the pattern of intercommunal relations observed in Quebec also appears in relationships between states in the international arena.

For example, the theoretical discussion of combinations of class and communal effects in chapter 4 provides a link between our results, which deal with the outlook of high-status members of a subordinate communal group in one segmented society, and discussions of the orientations of elites in many other parts of the world. In Weberian terms, membership in a national community in the international state system can be seen as analogous to, and not all that different from, membership in a communal group *within* a given state in the international system. For example, Lipset has discussed the orientations of elites in less-developed and peripheral countries in the following manner:

> Many in the elite of the poorer part of the world see themselves as the leaders of oppressed peoples; the radicalism of the intellectuals, university students, military officers, and the like in the less developed nations *can be related to the social and economic inferiority of their countries, rather than to their position in the class structure* [emphasis added]. Such considerations take us far afield from the conventional Western sociological concerns with class relationships, but they clearly are relevant to any effort at specifying the source of class behavior and ideologies. As sociology becomes more comparative in outlook and research, we may expect efforts to link class analysis of individual nations to the facts of international stratification. (Lipset 1979:55)

Here, Lipset is referring to situations in which a knowledge of where a state or country stands within the international system is as important to understanding individual motivations as is a consideration of social class membership within that state or country.[1] From this point of view, membership in a communal group within a state or region and membership in a country or state within the international system can be considered to be two types of Weberian status group. Each of these types of status group can be more or less correlated with social privilege variables, and each has the property of aggregating the impact of social privilege variables in a specific way.

What we can add to all of this is that the dyadic competitive relationship between Francophones and Anglophones in Quebec appears to share many of the characteristics of relationships between small states and their larger, more powerful neighbors. Jacek (1993) has identified such unequal relationships as being characterized by the weaker or smaller partner (1) displaying a greater sense of cultural identity and concern about the relationship, (2) having greater recourse to more collective forms of social organization, and (3) making greater use of the state. Jacek has applied this framework to the Canada/United States relationship and to the Austria/Germany relationship and has found many similarities in the functioning of these two dyadic pairs of unequal part- ners. At face value, this framework is also useful for understanding the Francophone/Anglophone relationship within Quebec, as well as the Quebec/Canada relationship.

DOMINANT MINORITIES IN
QUEBEC AND ENGLISH CANADA

In chapter 7, we saw that while some very noticeable shifts in the structure of perceptions of French-English inequalities have occurred in recent de- cades, Francophones are still much more likely than Anglophones to view English Canadians as wealthier than French Canadians and as dominant in business. Specifically, in table 7.5 we saw that residents of Lethbridge, Alberta, and Peterborough, Ontario, quite unlike residents of Trois-Rivières, Quebec, named French Canadians as having the dominant role in the world of business and finance. What is it about these small cities in Alberta and Ontario, where French is almost never heard and where Francophones are very rare, that leads the respondents who live in them to see French Canadi- ans as dominant? We might also ask, what is it about Trois-Rivières, where Anglophones are rare and where, as elsewhere in Quebec, there is now a large Francophone business class, that leads the respondents who live there to be so unanimous in their view of English dominance?

These questions cannot be answered definitively here, but I suggest that this pattern shows the importance of history, on the one hand, and macropolitical dynamics, on the other, in shaping current perceptions of group inequality. The residents of Trois-Rivières, the vast majority of whom live their lives entirely in the French language and have very little contact with Anglophones, may well still have very vivid memories of Quebec's old order. In the early decades of Quebec's industrialization, English Canadians wielded influence and power out of all proportion to their numbers. In a community with great intergenerational demographic continuity, this historical fact may simply remain, so to speak, a part of the present. Survey questions about present communal inequalities may be asked in the present tense, but each respondent's sample of observations is historically deep.[2]

What about the residents of Lethbridge, Alberta, and Peterborough, Ontario? They do not live in communities that have been historically industrialized by a migrant business class from Quebec or from France, that came in and set up its own set of institutions apart from those of the local majority. Their parents and grandparents were almost certainly never told they had to learn French to get a good job. The local business classes of Lethbridge and Peterborough have not had to accommodate historically to the presence in their towns of French or Quebec-based multinational corporations bringing their own personnel and customs with them. So their perceptions are not the result of still-remembered past economic inequities, but they reply that it is French Canadians who are dominant in business and finance. Where do their perceptions come from?

The answer may lie elsewhere in Canadian history, or in the way the Canadian federal system channels power and influence. For several decades, the Quebec question has been at the heart of Canada's national political agenda. Residents of Ontario and Alberta are reminded daily in the media of the prominent place that Quebecers and Francophones have in the federal government, and most of them have grown up in a period where the prime minister has been from Quebec, as has been the case for 27 of the past 28 years. And, while their parents and grandparents probably never had to learn French, in recent decades they have been told that if their children learn it their chances of getting a federal job will improve. This has led to a diffuse feeling that Quebec and Francophones have too much influence over the lives of people in the rest of Canada. The endless constitutional debates of the past few years have no doubt contributed to these feelings, just as they have left Quebecers with the feeling that the rest of Canada is intransigent, uncompromising, and unable to accommodate Quebec within the Canadian federation.

QUEBEC, ENGLISH CANADA, AND THE WORLD

Some evidence of these diverging views regarding the national political climate is shown in table 9.1. As we have seen, the centerpiece of Quebec's language legislation of the 1970s was a shift in the direction of territorial unilingualism, as a way of making the English language less legitimate and hence less dominant than in the past in Quebec.

Here we see a familiar bifurcation, in this instance regarding minority language rights, between Quebec and the rest of Canada. Canadians outside Quebec are much less likely than Quebecers to see English rights in Quebec as being well respected. Quebecers, in turn, are much less likely than other Canadians to see French rights outside Quebec as being well respected. Since the top panel of the table refers to all of Canada, the contrast between Quebec and the rest of Canada is actually sharper than that shown. For example, in 1991, the percentage of respondents in the Canada-wide sample stating that English rights inside Quebec are well protected, 37 percent, includes the Quebec respondents of whom 79 percent hold the same view. Outside of Quebec, the percentage of respondents holding the same view ranges from 14 percent in British Columbia to 27 percent in the Atlantic provinces (not shown). In parallel fashion, the percentage of respondents in the 1991 Canada-wide sample who hold that French rights are well protected outside Quebec, 68 percent, includes the Quebec respondents, of whom only 25 percent hold the same view. Outside of Quebec, the percentage of respondents holding this view is over 80 percent in all regions (Bozinoff and MacIntosh 1991). This pattern has deep historical roots. The history of Quebec has been shaped by an awareness of the declining position of French minorities in Western Canada over the past century. The position of French minorities in the western provinces declined for a number of reasons, but chief among them were the decisions of provincial governments to curtail use of the French language and pursue a policy of Anglo-conformity.

Responses in Quebec and in the rest of Canada are probably shaped by current sociopolitical dynamics as well as by historical memories. More research needs to be done on the relative importance of these two sets of causal factors, as well as on how these types of perceptions are linked to perceptions of economic and social inequalities.

Let us now attempt to locate this feature of Canada's ongoing internal dynamics in a larger international context. The first panel in table 9.2 shows responses collected in sixteen countries to a statement about the distinctiveness of French culture in North America.

TABLE 9.1

PERCEIVED PROTECTION OF MINORITY LANGUAGE RIGHTS,
QUEBEC AND ALL OF CANADA, 1987–1991

Protection of English rights inside Quebec			Protection of French Rights outside Quebec		
From what you have read, seen, or heard, would you say the language rights of English-speaking Canadians inside Quebec are very well protected, fairly well protected or not at all well protected?			From what you have read, seen, or heard, would you say the language rights of French-speaking Canadians outside Quebec are very well protected, fairly well protected or not at all well protected?		
very/fairly well protected	not at all well protected	don't know	very/fairly well protected	not at all well protected	don't know
Year					
CANADA (INCLUDING QUEBEC)			CANADA (INCLUDING QUEBEC)		
1991	37%	54%	9%	68%	24%	9%
1989	41	51	8	65	27	8
1987	46	43	11	68	24	9
QUEBEC			QUEBEC		
1991	79	16	4	25	64	11
1989	81	15	5	25	68	7
1987	80	15	5	36	57	7

Total N=1004. Percentages may not add exactly to 100 due to rounding.
Source: Bozinoff and MacIntosh 1991.

As might be expected, respondents in Quebec are the most likely to agree with the statement that "the French-speaking population in Canada has a unique culture which makes it a distinct society in North America." Notice, however, that respondents in the English-speaking regions of Canada (outside Quebec) are less likely to agree with the statement than are, for example, respondents in the United States and Mexico or Europe. People in the English-speaking regions of Canada are in fact the most likely by far to disagree with the statement, as the second row of the table shows. What does this reveal? Respondents in the English-speaking regions of Canada, unlike those in other countries, read political meaning into the question in the context of ongoing constitutional debates. Since the phrase "distinct society" was used in the failed Meech Lake Accord, it is possible that the use of the phrase in this survey statement triggered a negative reaction. At the same time, as we can see from the second panel in table 9.2, people in English Canada would be the most saddened if Quebec were to become independent. This comparison further illustrates how the

TABLE 9.2

DOMESTIC AND INTERNATIONAL PERSPECTIVES ON
THE NATIONAL CLIMATE IN CANADA, 1992

	Canada	Quebec	English regions	USA/ Mexico	Europe	Asia
A. "The French-speaking population in Canada has a unique culture which makes it a distinct society in North America."						
Agree	67	87	60	76	69	57
Disagree	31	11	38	16	11	17
B. "How would you react if Canada split into two countries and Quebec became independent?"						
Happy	15	33	9	6	14	9
Unmoved	20	14	21	59	48	52
Sad	63	49	69	31	36	29

Source: Reid Report (1993:25,28)

macropolitical context in which communal competition takes place can shape responses to survey questions.

OTHER SETTINGS

Switzerland

Research on both Switzerland and Belgium is relevant to understanding how the patterns observed in Canada fit into a wider perspective. Schmid (1981) found that, unlike Anglophone Canadians, German-speaking Swiss do not have a majoritarian (dominant group) outlook, even if they are a demographic majority in roughly similar proportions to Anglophones in Canada. The French-speaking Swiss, who constitute a lower percentage of the population than do Francophones in Canada, display a mild kind of minority outlook.

McRae (1983) reports that the French-speaking Swiss are more conscious of their linguistic identity than the German-speaking Swiss are, and that this stems from their minority position in the Swiss Confederation. Similarly, "French-Swiss and Italian-Swiss intellectuals also react instinctively against any sign of 'Helveticism,' a term loosely applied to any measure that looks towards a common cultural outlook for the whole country" (McRae 1983:108). On these two points, the French-Swiss are certainly like Francophones in Canada.

The main difference between the Swiss and Canadian contexts, of course, is that in Switzerland, the two main language groups are roughly equal on most socioeconomic indicators and are relatively equal in status. This relative equality has been long-standing, and as a result the overall pattern in the structure of attitudes and perceptions of relative equality is a positive one.

Two conclusions that might be relevant for understanding the course of Quebec's restructuring can be drawn from the Swiss experience. First, the pattern of positive attitudes in Switzerland has been rooted in a long-standing objective equality between groups; hence, it might be that perceptions and outlooks will not change immediately in Quebec, but only over time. Secondly, even though there has been long-standing socioeconomic equality between groups, the French-Swiss and Italian-Swiss still display minority outlooks simply because they are demographic minorities. Thus, given the Canadian and continental demographic context, even if Quebec's historic inequalities are completely eliminated on all possible indicators, a minority outlook of some sort on the part of Francophones may still be expected to prevail.

Belgium

We have already mentioned the Belgian case in chapter 6. In Belgium, in contrast to the pattern in Switzerland, negative attitudes and perceptions of inequality between members of the historically subordinate Dutch-speaking community and the historically dominant French-speaking community are widespread. These perceptions are rooted in structured inequalities set up by historical development patterns. McRae (1986) notes that the negative attitudes and perceptions of inequality have persisted in recent decades even though the historic inequalities between the two language communities have been very much reduced. While the structural basis for the perceptions no longer exists, the collective memory of less egalitarian times still exerts a powerful effect on mass perceptions. This pattern echoes in some respects what we have found in Quebec. Blais's (1991) comparison of feeling thermometer scores shows Canada's language cleavage to be more severe than that of Switzerland, but less severe than that of Belgium.

Since the Second World War, economic and political changes in Belgium have polarized relations between the Dutch and French language groups even as socioeconomic indicators have evened out. The demographic majority Dutch-speaking Flemings have become dominant without fully relinquishing their minority reflexes. Similarly, the historically dominant French-speaking Walloons have developed threatened-minority reflexes. So in the Belgian case, as well, it appears more accurate to speak of an evening-out or rebalancing of power relations rather than of a strict reversal or reconquest. Both French-speakers and Dutch-speakers now display a combination of majority and minority group outlooks.

Quebec's new language policies, inspired as they are by the principle of territoriality, find a natural comparative point of reference in Belgium, where linguistic territoriality has been implemented since the 1960s. Since historically subordinate Flanders is now a unilingual Dutch-language territory, one particularly interesting question concerns the fate of the historically privileged French-speaking minority of Flanders.

> The Francophone population of Flanders, long a prime target of the Flemish Movement, is now seldom mentioned. . . . From an official or legislative standpoint, the Francophones of Flanders no longer exist. In a sociological sense, however, a minority of this size, historical importance, and economic resources does not vanish overnight. Yet it is worth noting that the language laws of 1962-63 did not produce the dramatic consequences that might have been imagined beforehand. There was no discernible wave of outmigration of French speakers from Flanders. . . . (McRae 1986:277)

McRae argues that the Francophones of Flanders for the most part adjusted to the new language rules within one generation:

> The tentative conclusion for Flanders is that many Francophone elite families have been able, after a transitional period, to adjust to the change of language patterns and to retain a significant share of their traditional position in Flemish society. (1986:285)

A central difference between Flanders and Quebec is that in Quebec the erstwhile dominant minority in Quebec has not so much been ruled out of existence, as its extensive array of public institutions have had their autonomy circumscribed. Beyond this, though, there is much evidence that an elite adjustment similar to that of Francophones in Flanders has been occurring in Quebec, although given the Canadian and North American context, "exit" has been a much more frequently chosen adjustment strategy in Quebec than in Flanders. Indeed, the existence of this safety valve, as well as the steady replacement of out-migrants with new immigrants from elsewhere (see table 1.2), has contributed to making the transition process relatively peaceful.

Finland

During this century, the historically dominant Swedish minority in Finland has been gradually transformed into a nondominant minority. The Swedish minority, which was once overrepresented in the ruling groups of society, is now best described as slightly more white collar in its occupational composition than the Finnish majority. Liebkind's description of the staying power of perceptions rooted in past stratification patterns is very much in line with our earlier discussion about memory:

> The primary reasons for the tenacious retention in Finland of the popular stereotype of the Swedish-speaking minority as an upper-class population must be sought more in the historical symbol value of this image than primarily in statistical facts. The memory of the necessity in the past for Finns to adopt the Swedish language in upward social mobility does not fade away as quickly as the objective cultural, political, social and economic mobility of the Finnish-speaking population actually has taken place. Once a stereotype based on the perceived differences between two groups is firmly established, even a minor existing difference will suffice for its maintenance or revival. (Liebkind 1982:377)

Another parallel suggested by the case of Finland is the existence of the Swedish Peoples Party, a party dedicated to defending the interests of the Swedish minority, many of whose members fear the continual decline of their language group in numbers and influence. The parallel in Quebec would be the existence of the new Equality Party, mentioned in chapter 7. At present it appears unlikely, however, that the Equality Party will be an enduring part of the Quebec political scene. The Quebec Liberal Party is likely to continue to gather the votes of most non-Francophones in provincial elections in the foreseeable future. Francophone voters, of course, have been divided between the Parti Québécois and the Liberal Party.

South Africa

Another context similar to that of Quebec is the long-standing rivalry between the two white European dominant segments in South Africa. Starting a decade or more earlier than Francophones in Quebec, the Afrikaner group, which had been in a subordinate position to the English-speaking group, undertook a state-sponsored evening-out program similar to the one undertaken by Francophones in Quebec that was effective in building up an Afrikaner business class. Adam and Giliomee's argument (1979) is summarized by Banton:

> . . . the economy has been refashioned in the service of Afrikaner group interests. In 1948 the average income of Afrikaners in the cities was around half that of the English group. Though 59 percent of the white population had Afrikaans as their mother tongue, in 1954 the Afrikaner share of the national income was one quarter. In mining, the Afrikaner share was 0.5 percent and in retail trade but 6 percent of the annual turnover. The new government in 1948 set out to help those who had voted for it and in the first five years the index of real white wages rose by over 10 percent while that of blacks fell by 5 percent. The government used the public or semi-state corporations to promote Afrikaner economic progress to spectacular effect. Afrikaners already dominated the public services, including the police, holding posts from top to bottom. . . . Most of the English group . . . have since come to resent the way in which the public sector of the economy has been built up and state power used to favour nationalist private industry. By the end of the 1950s the poor whites had disappeared. By 1976 those Afrikaners who were in employment were earning on average the same as members of the English group; given the power they enjoyed in so many settings, it could be said that they had attained equality. . . . (Banton 1983:235)

Malaysia

Over the past twenty-five years, Malaysia has undergone a restructuring of intercommunal relations between the Malay majority and the non-Malay, mainly Chinese and Indian, minorities. The politically dominant Malays instituted a New Economic Policy in order to systematically eliminate the historical inequalities between the economically better off non-Malays and the Muslim Malay majority.

Coupled with unchallengeable political hegemony, the NEP has produced a veritable socio-economic revolution in Malaysia that has elevated the Malays to near economic parity with the non-Malays. Further, the faces of cities and towns, university campuses, banks and financial institutions, and corporate boardrooms have radically changed in twenty years from a situation where not many Malays or Islamic symbols were visible to one where there are mostly Malays and Islamic symbols. (Mauzy 1993:114)

Despite the many obvious differences between the two societies, Malaysia's New Economic Policy and Quebec's language reforms of the 1970s display several remarkable similarities. The first is their timing. The NEP was instituted in 1969, after serious intercommunal rioting, the same year as Canada's federal Official Languages Act and Quebec's Bill 63 language law were passed. The second similarity is the rationale behind the two sets of measures. In both cases, the measures were adopted because the economically privileged groups (the Chinese in Malaysia and the Anglophones in Quebec) were seen as not having kept their side of the implicit bargain to open up the private sector to full participation by the less–economically privileged groups (the Malays in Malaysia and the Francophones in Quebec). In both societies, voluntary measures were judged to have been ineffective, thus making more coercive measures both legitimate and necessary. One important difference was that the willingness to sacrifice economic growth, if necessary, in order to promote intergroup equality was explicit in the Malaysian program, but was left unclear in the Quebec reforms. We shall return to this point in the concluding chapter.

India

In Assam, in northeastern India, the indigenous Assamese majority shares the territory with in-migrant Bengalis who have settled in urban areas over the past century. The Bengali majority in neighboring states vastly outnumber the Assamese, who total only 6 million people and who fear that their territory is being "taken over" by Bengalis. In recent decades, legislation has established Assamese as the official language of the state of Assam, and as the medium of instruction in schools. Weiner describes the way this particular case combines the question of identity and the question of job competition, two features found to exist side by side in the Quebec case as well:

Since it touched upon the issue of employment and cultural identity, language policy became the focal point of controversy between the two communities. For the Bengalis, who favored the use of both languages, a dual language policy would give equal status to the Assamese and Bengalis, and would therefore mean equality of opportunity in employment and political and social status. The Assamese, however, viewed a dual language policy as a perpetuation of Bengali domination in both the cultural and employment spheres.

It is not easy to separate the issue of cultural identity from the struggle over access to jobs. While one could plausibly explain the conflict between Bengali Hindus and Assamese strictly in terms of competition for public employment on the part of their respective middle classes, the explanation would ignore the element of cultural conflict and the deep emotional content of the struggle. Certainly the Assamese would have developed a sense of their own cultural identity even in the absence of a large "alien" migration, for regional identities have been emerging everywhere in India. What characterized the Assamese quest for a cultural identity was their need to distinguish themselves from the Bengalis in their midst. . . . (Weiner 1978:112)

BIPOLAR SETTINGS AND ETHNIC POLITICS

It is unclear if political developments will move Quebec's intergroup relations closer toward or further away from the ethnically bipolar pattern identified by Milne (1981). In this pattern, found in a number of multiethnic societies in different parts of the world, one group, often the demographic majority, is dominant in politics and the other group (or broad coalition of smaller groups), often historically overrepresented in cities and in the economy, is less represented in the state machinery. In recent years, in Quebec politics, Francophones have been divided into federalist and independentist camps, and almost all non-Francophones have been on the federalist side. In some respects, Quebec already bears a resemblance to Guyana, Malaysia, and Fiji, three multiethnic states that display an interesting bipolar pattern in their political organization. In all three states, the ethnic group that is politically dominant attempts to find ways of translating its political power into economic power.

In these contexts, the group that is *not* politically dominant (the Chinese and the Indians in Malaysia, the Indians in Guyana and in Fiji) often displays higher rates of avoidance of politics, alienation from politics, and outmigration. Quebec has long displayed some signs of such a bipolar pattern, but in different directions in federal and provincial politics. Until the 1960s, the English-speaking business class of Montreal had considerable behind-the-scenes influence on Quebec politicians, while at the mass level Anglophone interest and participation in provincial politics and elections lagged behind that of the Francophone majority (Bernard 1976). In near-symmetric fashion, Francophone interest and participation in federal politics was lower than that of Anglophones, and Francophone Quebecers have long been less attached to the federal government than other Canadians. Francophone Quebecers have long been more attached to their provincial government than Canadians in other provinces are to theirs (Pinard 1975). Also, Anglophone Quebecers, along with Francophones outside Quebec, as numerical minorities in their respective provinces, have long displayed higher levels of attachment to the federal government than have the numerical majority groups.

This pattern provides one framework that allows us to interpret the pattern of "don't know" responses found in the various surveys analyzed in this research. Anglophones repeatedly displayed higher "don't know" rates, and a possible explanation offered in chapter 5 was that this was related to the fact that these surveys deal with language and politics, areas in which Anglophones are increasingly *non*dominant in Quebec. Seen in this broader bipolar framework, the higher rate of Anglophone "don't know" responses, as well as the higher rate of Anglophone nonresponse to this survey and to many other surveys in Quebec, can be interpreted as indicators of Anglophone discomfort or ambivalence. This is in keeping with the more general historical pattern, found by Bernard (1976) of higher Anglophone abstentionism in provincial elections (see Rudin 1985:260-262).

Bernard also found that Francophones, for their part, have historically had higher abstentionism rates in federal elections. Is there any counterpart to this in these surveys? One small sign of such a pattern is evident. In their responses to the questions about comfort with immigrants analyzed in the previous chapter, Francophones systematically display higher "don't know" rates, and they do so not only to the questions analyzed, but to many others in the survey as well. Could it be that this touches on an area in which it is Francophones, this time, who feel less secure and more alienated? In a broader sense, Anglophone "don't know" responses and nonresponses to Quebec surveys are possibly expressions of ambivalence, or at least a way of laying low. In similar fashion, Francophone "don't know" responses to questions about immigrants may well be expressions of ambivalence about diversity that is troubling. More research needs to be done on these issues, and the observations made here should be viewed as tentative.

SUMMARY

In this chapter, we have seen that Quebec's restructuring can be examined through quite a few comparative lenses.[3] The sketches given here need to be followed up by systematic research.

CONCLUSION

Some Lessons From the Quebec Case

Let us now take stock of what has been done in this book. What lessons can be learned from this look at the Quebec case? After a short review of the findings, a few specific themes will be developed.

THE FINDINGS

We began with the important issue of communal conflict in segmented societies. How can one account for the incidence of communal conflict? Its intensity? Its distribution in time and space?

We noted in the introduction that Canada has an exceptionally high level of pluralism given its high level of development. Contemporary Quebec is thus a very appropriate setting in which to examine the links between the development process and intergroup relations.

In part I, the historical and theoretical background for our study was presented. The background to contemporary Quebec as a setting was sketched in chapter 1. The two theoretical perspectives outlined in chapter 2, the functionalist perspective and the communal competition perspective, lead to rather different predictions about the impact of industrialization and modernization on intergroup relations in polyethnic societies. As we saw, the functionalist perspective, in its many variant forms, predicts that the degree of cultural diversity and the extent of group inequalities within a society will decrease over time. According to the various currents and strands of thinking that make up the communal competition perspective, however, there is no assumption that cultural diversity and group inequalities will necessarily be reduced by any automatic processes of social change.

The empirical analyses carried out in part II consisted of a series of tests of hypotheses aimed at linking these two competing macrosociological theoretical perspectives with the data on Quebec society. This detailed study held time constant, and provided a portrait of how the historical macro-level balance in favor of English was reflected in the way perceptions were distributed within Quebec society in 1970.

In chapters 3 and 4, hypotheses derived from the two broad theoretical perspectives were put to the test with respect to the structure of orientation toward cultural pluralism. It was found that the distributions of our measures of orientations toward cultural pluralism tend to be skewed in a centrifugal (toward more pluralism) direction. Also, Francophones systematically display more centrifugal orientations than Anglophones, and the more-privileged (white-collar, more-educated) members of the Francophone community espouse a more centrifugal outlook than their less-privileged brethren. In fact, language-group membership and socioeconomic status exert strong and independent effects on the dependent variables. The more-privileged Francophones are the most centrifugal in their orientations, and the less-privileged Anglophones are the least centrifugal.

It was also found that an important component of a less-centrifugal attitude is a lack of information about Quebec society and history, which is more widespread among the less educated and among those with a low cumulative lifetime exposure to Quebec society. Because of these factors, "don't know" answers are more frequent among Anglophones than among Francophones, and more frequent among those of other (non-French, non-English) origins in each linguistic community. While those of "other" ethnic origins are more likely to give "don't know" answers to each of our dependent variable measures, there is little evidence of a clear-cut "other ethnic" effect in the structure of centrifugal orientations.

Among those with the most-centrifugal orientations, namely the more-privileged and more-educated Francophones, it was found that education and occupation have independent effects. Within the upper-level white-collar group, those in professional and technical occupations systematically hold more-centrifugal views than managers and proprietors. As predicted by theorists of nationalism in general, and authors on contemporary Québécois nationalism in particular, employment in the public sector, and especially in the Quebec provincial civil service, is a further source of highly centrifugal views.

In chapter 5, the structure of perceptions and evaluations of French-English inequalities in Quebec was examined. It was found that the five dimensions of communal inequalities investigated were not perceived to be equally severe. Inequalities between the two communities were perceived to be greatest in the basic dimension of wealth, and in the world of business and finance. Francophones were systematically more likely than Anglophones to perceive inequalities between the two communal groups, and to judge that English Canadians are favored and advantaged by the workings of the system. More-privileged (white-collar, more-educated) Francophones were the most likely to be aware of inequalities, and to insist that they ought to be reduced. Less-privileged Anglophones, on the other hand, were the *least* likely to be aware of communal inequalities, and the least likely to insist on their being reduced.

In chapter 6, the findings concerning the linkages between orientations toward cultural pluralism and perceptions of communal inequalities clearly support the predictions of the communal competition perspective. Those most aware of communal inequalities and most insistent on their being reduced tend to hold the view that cultural differences between the two communities ought to be maintained rather than reduced. The retention of cultural differences can be seen as part of the overall strategy of those most concerned with reducing group inequalities, as predicted by the communal competition perspective. This holds true in both linguistic communities.

In part III, some of the ways Quebec's intergroup dynamics have changed since the 1970s were examined. In chapter 7, shifts in the structure of orientations toward cultural pluralism and perceived communal inequalities were traced. The heightened politicization of language during this period increased concerns for cultural security among both Francophones and Anglophones. The overall evening out of the power relationship and the objective reduction in French-English inequalities that has taken place since the 1970s is reflected to some extent in changes in the population's perceptions, but there is much stability as well. Francophones have come to assume some signs of a majority group outlook without relinquishing their minority reflexes. Similarly, Anglophones have developed some minority group patterns in their perceptions, without losing their majority outlook.

The data presented in chapter 8 showed that for much of the 1970s and 1980s, Francophone sympathy for Native peoples in Canada was higher than that of Anglophones, but that this pattern changed in the 1990s, when Indian mobilization on the basis of nationhood clashed with

Quebec nationalism. Francophones display lower levels of comfort with immigrants than Anglophones, partly as a result of the later start of Francophone institutions as integrating milieus, which is itself due to the past uneven development process. This more cautious outlook is shared, however, by all those interviewed in French, regardless of their ethnic origins.

Chapter 9 sketched a few ways in which changes in Quebec's intergroup relations over the past few decades display parallels with a number of other contexts around the world. Let us now turn to a few lessons that can be learned from this study.

HUGHES'S FRENCH CANADA IN TRANSITION: A LOOK BACKWARD

How does the development process shape the course of intergroup relations? We began this study by considering a wide family of functionalist approaches, with their implicit emphasis on individual competition, and contrasted their predictions with those of a similarly broad family of approaches emphasizing group competition. We then considered Hughes's study, formulated as it was in terms of the impact of industrialization and modernization on ethnic relations. In short order, however, our study was analyzing the role of the state, and specifically the Quebec state.

As we saw in chapter 2, Hughes posited that, in broad terms at least, the process of adjustment and accommodation between indigenous locals, their elites, and economically powerful newcomers was likely to be the same the world over. He also added that this basically similar process was likely to be complicated by the presence of ethnic differences between locals and newcomers. But how will ethnic differences modify an otherwise similar process? Will the locals simply take longer to adapt culturally to the incoming dominant group's language and way of doing things than they otherwise would? Or will the local elites mobilize politically to modify the terms of the relationship?

Hughes took the political status quo of the 1930s as a given, as an apparently natural and unchanging part of the backdrop. He was, of course, not alone in this regard. As I have mentioned, his study was carried out during a lengthy period of relatively stable class alliances between the English Canadian bourgeoisie and the French Canadian political and clerical elites. This old order was to break down only after the Second World War. The course of events in Quebec suggests that a crucial factor in determining the outcome of the adjustment process between locals and newcomers is the local group's elites' capacity for collective action on the part of their members. The more the indigenous subordinate group has access to organizational resources, and specifically to state power, the more likely a collective counteroffensive can be launched, drawing on the subordinate group's language and culture as symbols and weapons in a counter struggle. In the Quebec case, a power shift within the Francophone community, and specifically the ascendancy of the new bureaucratic middle class, triggered the reorienting of Francophone collective political goals in a more interventionist direction.

This raises the important question of the interplay of economic and political factors in the development process. In periods of political stasis, when an unequal balance of power between elite groups is relatively stable for long periods of time, it is easy to take this context as a constant rather than a potentially changing variable. Hughes begins the second paragraph of the preface to the 1963 edition of his book, which was written in the early years of Quebec's Quiet Revolution, by observing that "There is no reason to believe that the higher management of the leading industries is not as English now as then. I wager that more French have come up in the service end of the industries . . . and that the lower supervisors are predominantly French" (Hughes 1963:xiii). This would appear to suggest that the higher management was (still) predominantly English because not enough time had yet passed for the French presence to "naturally" and gradually make itself felt there.

Yet, interestingly enough, Hughes goes on to refer to the Quebec of the early 1960s as an anachronism, and his reason for doing so is suggestive of his appreciation of the importance of how political factors can modify the impact of economic development on intergroup relations. Hughes compares the Quebec case to that of the Flemings and Walloons in Belgium, the Catholic Rhinelanders and North German Protestants in Germany, and the Afrikaners and the English in South Africa:

> But if one puts Quebec with these cases, it appears archaic. For the
> Flemings have taken over Belgian politics; and the Catholic center
> party born in the Rhine country, is, in effect, in power in Germany,
> while in South Africa the former minority, the Afrikaners, are firmly
> in the political saddle. (Hughes 1963:xiv)

What was archaic, then, about Quebec in the early 1960s was that French Canadians had not yet exerted their political power to the same extent as their counterparts in these other settings had. What is implicit here is the possibility that if such political power ever were to be fully exerted, the ethnic and linguistic division of labor might change a little faster.

Has Quebec's rapid leveling out of historic inequalities actually occurred as a result of the language legislation and other public policy measures enacted in the 1960s and 1970s, or would the same changes have come about "naturally" through the gradual play of market forces, specifically the arrival on the market of so many highly educated Francophones from the 1960s onwards? The evidence suggests that the public policy measures definitely contributed to reducing linguistic inequalities (Levine 1990), but that during the same period neither Quebec's overall economic position in Canada, nor many other structural features of Quebec's internal stratification system have changed for the better.

COMMUNAL INEQUALITIES
AND CLASS INEQUALITIES

In his foreword to the 1963 edition of Hughes's work, Keyfitz noted that in the early 1960s Quebec faced two major challenges. These were to find solutions to its chronically high unemployment rate and to the predominance of Anglophones as leaders of industry, a situation that had existed for decades (Keyfitz 1963:vi). By the 1980s, most top managers were French, a majority of Quebec's wealthiest people were Francophones, and the gap in incomes between Francophones and Anglophones had become negligible. Yet Quebec's higher-than-average unemployment rate remains. It has been argued that Quebec's reforms have really only solved one half of the historical "double inferiority" (or source of inequality) of Quebec Francophones, that between French and English within Quebec, but not that between Quebec and Ontario or the rest of Canada. Indeed, not only has Quebec's unemployment rate remained high, its overall poverty rate in 1986 was higher than that of all other provinces except Newfoundland and Saskatchewan (Noel 1993:377).

Furthermore, ". . . in the 15 years between 1977 and 1992, Quebec families have systematically become poorer than their Ontario equivalents. This trend is common to both French and English-speaking Quebeckers" (Hébert 1994). In similar fashion, Quebec's share of Canada's total economic production has been declining, if only because of the more rapid increase in Ontario and Western Canada. From a broader perspective, then, Quebec's internal restructuring may well have shifted the internal linguistic inequality into inequalities between Quebec and the rest of

Canada. Recent critical analyses have argued that Quebec's reforms may, in the process of consolidating the hegemony of the French segment of the Quebec bourgeoisie over the English segment, have actually weakened the Quebec economy as a whole. The consolidation has been achieved in part by the English segment's partial exit, at considerable cost to the provincial treasury in foregone taxes (Arbour 1993). Similarly, it has been argued that while Quebec's state interventions have indeed succeeded in reducing internal linguistic inequalities, they may well have impeded the economy from growing as it otherwise would have, with the net result that the gap between Quebec and Ontario remains as large as ever (Smith 1994).[1]

On the whole, then, Quebec's largely successful internal communal restructuring has occurred alongside a relative decline in Quebec's demographic and economic position within Canada. It is still unclear whether this is a coincidence, both processes being due to other factors, whether the relative decline allowed or facilitated the internal equalization, or whether the internal equalization policies hastened the decline. Whatever the explanation, the phenomenon raises some interesting questions about the links between economic development, regional inequalities, and ethnic inequalities within a given territory. During the first half of this century, when Montreal was the most important city in Canada and was under the ascendancy of an English-Canadian business class, French-English inequalities were at their highest. As Montreal and the whole of Quebec have become proportionately less important parts of Canada, French-English inequalities have declined within Quebec, leaving regional inequalities between the whole of Quebec and the more affluent provinces of Ontario, Alberta, and British Columbia.

Quebec's state measures have largely succeeded in removing the ethnic and linguistic coloring of its historical class inequalities, while apparently leaving the volume of these class inequalities largely intact. Quebec has become a "more normal" society in that a majority of its rich as well as a majority of its poor are now French-speaking. Also, to the extent that the large head-office sector in Montreal is more evenly distributed in its linguistic composition than in the past, it is also true that much of the past asymmetry between the occupational structures of the two language groups at all levels has been removed.

In this connection, we might note that in the 1970 survey, Francophones were only slightly more inclined than Anglophones (49 percent compared to 45 percent) to say that "the degree of inequality that exists between the rich and the poor" was "very large." This is a much narrower gap than the persistent communal gap in perceived French-English inequalities, as we have already seen. While Francophones are much more likely than Anglophones to perceive French-English inequalities, they are not always more likely to perceive class inequalities, according to a cursory examination of responses to several questions about class inequalities in the 1970 study. More research needs to be done on the links between the extent of perceived class inequality and the extent of perceived communal inequalities.

We might add that the slight 4 percent communal gap in perceptions of class inequalities in Quebec can be contrasted with the very large and systematic gaps between France and Great Britain found by Gallie (1983). Gallie reports that respondents in France are much more likely to see social inequalities as being very large than are respondents in Great Britain, even if according to objective indicators the degree of class inequality is quite comparable in the two countries. Seen against the backdrop of Gallie's research, the low communal gap in perceived class inequalities in Quebec is no doubt due to the fact that Francophones and Anglophones in Quebec do live in the same territory and share a political system and economy. This contrast between Gallie's results and these Quebec results concerning perceived class inequalities is an example of differences in outlooks between residents of independent national states being much greater than differences between communal groups within a given state. The relatively low communal gap between Francophones and Anglophones concerning class inequalities illustrates the cumulative impact of a common state structure in shaping a common outlook among residents of a given territory, even if the level of structural pluralism between the two language communities is very high, as we have seen. It remains to be seen if the kinds of national differences observed in Europe by Gallie will be reduced over time with continuing European integration.

THE SHIFTING BASES OF COMMUNAL COMPETITION

We have already noted that, on the whole, the empirical results of this research tend to lend greater support to the hypotheses derived from the communal competition perspective than to those derived from the functionalist perspective. Let us now try to go beyond a simple juxtaposition or comparison of the competing predictions and sets of results and consider a few points that suggest how they might be fruitfully combined.

Let us begin by returning for a moment to the findings reported in Chapters 4 and 5 about the relative impact of ethnic origin and language group membership on our two sets of dependent variables. We found that concerning both orientations toward cultural pluralism and perceptions of communal inequalities in wealth, there is relatively little systematic variation due to ethnic origin *within* each linguistic community. Francophones and Anglophones of "other" (non-French, non-English) ethnic origins display views that are, by and large, similar to those of their co-communalists of French and British origins. The ethnic origin effects, although complex at times, are clearly less important than the overriding communal effect of language-group membership.

We noted that this pattern can best be accounted for by drawing on both theoretical perspectives. The noticeable and enduring effect of language-group membership is consonant with the predictions of the communal competition perspective, and the convergence of views among those of different ethnic origins *within each* communal group is consonant with the predictions of the functionalist perspective.

In chapter 4, I also suggested why it might be that language differences have become more important than other types of group differences. In both Quebec and Belgium, the boundaries of the groups engaged in communal competition are now defined principally in terms of language. This trend in both of these segmented societies represents a shift away from definitions of group boundaries in terms of race, religion, and ethnic origin, to name only the most commonly used labels in both societies over the past century.

As mentioned in chapter 4, one reason for this shift is that language is a relatively (and only relatively) more achieved and less ascribed characteristic than race, religion, or ethnic origin. This shift, while consonant with the predictions of the functionalist perspective on social change, should not, however, be viewed as an ineluctable consequence of the processes of industrialization and modernization. Rather, it should be viewed in the light of some identifiable mechanisms that have been at work in the international system since the Second World War.

These mechanisms are linked to the widespread adjustment of a majority of the world's state elites to the rules of the game of the international system (see Meyer, Boli-Bennett, and Chase-Dunn 1975; Meyer 1980; Boli-Bennett 1980), as well as to the values of "modernity" (Guindon 1978). Meyer argues that the world political system has granted a special legitimacy to the nation-state as a particular type of formal organization:

> The nation-state system is given world-wide support and legitimacy, and is importantly exogenous to individual societies. This system confers great and increasing powers on states to control and organize

societies around the values (modern notions of rationality and progress) established in the world political culture. (Meyer 1980:109)

In this evolving worldwide system of structurally similar nation-
states, state elites are given legitimated control over their territory, their
population, and the means of violence. Also, other organizational forms
that might compete with state structures are increasingly delegitimated. In
exchange for the monopoly of the legitimate control of their territory and
population, state elites are faced with certain internationally recognized
obligations. Chief among these is the obligation to pursue modern "progress" on behalf of their populations. State elites are expected to espouse
the values of modernity. Although the concept of modernity has been given
quite a variety and range of operational definitions around the world, it is
widely interpreted as involving, among other things, a certain secularization of social and political life, and also a certain "delegitimation of ethnic
primordiality" (Meyer 1980:113).

Following this line of reasoning, one could deduce that state elites
are increasingly expected to organize their internal membership criteria,
or citizenship rights and obligations, so as to make them applicable,
according to universalistic criteria, to all citizens or residents of the state's
territory.

The Quebec state, historically much weaker than it is now, for a very
long period shared its power and authority with the Catholic Church.[2] The
Quebec state has also long assumed the special role of being a protector
of French Canadian interests. In the past three decades, many of the
church's social service and educational functions have been taken over by
the Quebec state, and the authority of the church has been drastically
delegitimated.

This "disestablishment" of the Catholic Church in Quebec has been
felt in all areas of social life and has been an important component of the
modernization of the society. One consequence is that intercommunal
relations are no longer referred to in terms of religious group boundaries.
In Quebec and elsewhere in Canada, as in Belgium and in Switzerland, a
consequence of the secularization of these societies is that the religious
factor has receded in importance as a criterion used to define communal
membership.

Another trend that is discernible, but is much less developed and
clear-cut, is a shift away from ethnic origin per se as a criterion of
communal group definition and membership. A persistent structural
source of tension in the system stems from the state elites' obligation to

reconcile the historical role of the Quebec state as a special guarantor and protector of the French language and culture, with its newer role of providing a whole range of services, including the symbolic service of providing an "identity," to all members of Quebec society, regardless of their language and ethnic origin. This newer role of being the state of all Quebecers is part of the broad shift from ethnic to civic nationalism in Quebec in recent years (see Breton 1988).

This shift toward a civic territorial definition of the Quebec nation resembles similar shifts that have occurred elsewhere in the developed world over the same time period, notably in the Basque country and in Catalonia (Linz 1985). In its emphasis on language as a key component of this shift, the Quebec case resembles Catalonia rather more than the Basque country (see Conversi 1990). As in both of these Spanish contexts, the last decade in Quebec has been marked by a heightened concern, in intellectual and political circles, for developing some sort of inclusive Quebec identity based on nonascriptive criteria.

Modern state elites are increasingly expected to adjust the structures of their societies in order to minimize, as far as possible, selection on the basis of ascribed characteristics. This helps explain the shift toward "more legitimate" bases of exclusion and selection, given the worldwide diffusion and acceptance of the rules of the game for state actors in the international system. These rules basically involve tacit guarantees of noninterference by other states in the internal legislation of a given state, provided certain basic human rights are respected in theory and to a lesser extent in practice (Boli-Bennett 1980).

The increasing emphasis on language in Quebec in recent decades, as reflected in the progressively more complex and all-encompassing legislation of the 1970s, can be seen as part of the general attempt on the part of the provincial elites to modernize Quebec society. The legislation promoting the use of the French language allows the Francophone community to improve its competitive position vis-à-vis the Anglophone community because members of the former are likely, *ceteris paribus*, to have a better command of the French language than members of the latter. This is a way of improving the competitive position of the subordinate communal group without insisting that preferential treatment be given to Francophones or to those of French origin.

Selection on the basis of language proficiency is more legitimate than selection on the basis of other, more ascribed, criteria, such as ethnic origin or religion. This is because language, unlike the other two criteria, is at least in part a functional instrument of communication central to the operation of modern societies. Selection on the basis of language proficiency can easily be legitimated by reference to the technical and functional requirements of a modern society. Thus, in industrialized, segmented societies, selection on the basis of language proficiency can be seen as similar to the process of selection on the basis of educational credentials that has become the norm throughout the industrialized world. However strongly language proficiency and educational credentials may be correlated with ascribed characteristics, both are legitimate means of differentiating between competing candidates.

Viewed in this light, the language legislation of the 1970s in Quebec should be seen as an extension of the educational reforms of the Quiet Revolution of the 1960s. Both sets of measures were carried out as part of a broad program aimed at modernizing Quebec society. In sociological terms, both sets of measures can be seen as having modernized the structures within which competition, selection, and exclusion take place.

This parallel is suggested by Murphy's (1979: chapter 11) analysis of the changes in education in Quebec and Canada during the 1960s. In his view, the expansion of the educational system, the creation of comprehensive or polyvalent high schools, and the increase in the importance of optional programs as opposed to compulsory programs have had the effect of allowing schools to transmit social inequalities in a more legitimate, if perhaps less efficient, fashion than they did before. The *sponsored* mode of ascent that was characteristic of the long classical college era in Quebec has been replaced by a *contest* mode of ascent that operates in an institutional system based on the formal equality of those who are served by it. Both systems transmit social inequalities from generation to generation, but the second system does it less blatantly. Murphy argues that these structural changes have been widely adopted throughout the industrialized world partly because they provide "superior means of legitimating social inequalities" (Murphy 1979:209).

The point that we can use from this line of thinking is that structures can be "modernized" in order to allow social processes of competition, selection, and exclusion to operate more legitimately than would otherwise be the case. The emphasis on universalistic criteria such as language use can be viewed as a way of promoting the collective interests of the Francophone community without necessarily excluding non-Francophones as a group. The criterion of language proficiency provides a way of redressing communal inequalities that is more likely to be perceived as legitimate than other mechanisms, such as quotas, for example.

It is for this reason that language legislation to redress communal inequalities has been adopted in quite a number of settings around the world. In analyzing the Indian context, Weiner writes:

> In India the exercise of political power to "correct" a perceived status and economic imbalance must take place within a narrowly prescribed political framework. The Assamese cannot bar the province to migration, since the constitution guarantees freedom of movement. ... Under some conditions there can be restrictions on employment and on admissions into schools and colleges. In any event, such restrictions would not affect most of the Bengali Hindus in Assam, as they were born in Assam. Language policy, on the other hand, does affect the descendants of migrants as well as the migrants themselves, and it is a "legitimate" area of state intervention, justified on grounds other than the protection of a specific ethnic group. (Weiner 1978:116)

In Canada, as in India, the federal political framework imposes constraints on what provincial governments can do, and freedom of movement is similarly guaranteed. Clashes with the federal government have, not surprisingly, been over the conflicting language policies, and over control of international immigration.

In each of these areas, the Quebec government has reactively developed its own policy, distinct from that of the federal government. In opposition to the federal government policies of bilingualism, the Quebec government developed a policy of one official language, French, with due protection given to English and aboriginal languages. In opposition to the federal multiculturalism policy, the Quebec government has put forth a policy of interculturalism, which puts greater emphasis on sharing in the larger context of French as a common public language.

The essential difference between the federal and provincial policies in both of these areas is that the provincial policies put a greater emphasis on the primacy of French, to compensate, in a sense, for the actual, empirical, historical, and still-present dominance of English in many areas of Montreal. With respect to immigrant integration, the Quebec government's goal is to bring about a *convergence culturelle* between "cultural communities" and Quebec's French majority through the shared public language, French. These new policies are, of course, put forth to counteract the possibility, left open in the federal policy, that immigrants are (still) free to integrate to either French or English since both French and English are official languages of Canada.

Whatever their differences, the language and immigrant integration policies of both levels of government share the basic assumption that language is a basis for aggregating ethnic diversity. In the federal policy, either of the two official languages, or both, are to be used by people of any number of cultures and ethnic origins. In the Quebec policy, the one official language, French, is to be used in public by all even if the cultural communities do retain various characteristics. The shared language is to become the medium of a new, shared public culture, the evolving content of which is something larger than the culture of the French Canadian majority.

Finally, I also touched upon an important question regarding the operation of an industrialized liberal democracy whose ethnic pluralism stems from different types of incorporation of different ethnic groups into the larger whole. How do the initial conditions of differential group incorporation (involuntary versus voluntary, indigenous versus immigrant) combine with the universalizing and unifying forces of an industrial occupational structure and a liberal state? In chapter 8, we saw an example of the joint impact of these two sets of factors with respect to the issue of comfort with immigrants. It was found that Francophones are (still) less comfortable with immigrants and that their attitude is shared by all those who answered the question in French, not just those of French origin. This phenomenon can be taken as confirmation that the complex processes by which people of different ethnic origins spanning different types of incorporation are subsumed under larger, more modern linguistic community umbrellas are indeed at work in Quebec society. That these ethnicity-aggregating processes are at work even in responses to potentially sensitive questions on intergroup relations such as those analyzed in parts II and III of this study, only adds to the weight of the evidence. The policies of both the federal and provincial governments, whatever their differences, share the general goal of having ethnic origin be subsumed under a larger official language umbrella, as we have already seen.

The other results analyzed in table 8.1 illustrate the effects of the late starting-position of the Francophone community as an immigrant integrator and ethnicity aggregator. We saw that within the Francophone community, ethnic origin has more of an effect on people's outlook than it does within the Anglophone community. Similarly we found that within Quebec, ethnic origin has more of an effect on people's outlook than it does outside of Quebec. This relatively more important role of ethnic origin within the Francophone community attests to the (still) weaker operation of ethnicity-aggregation processes within it.

Ethnicity "still matters" more within the Francophone community than within the Anglophone community, and within Quebec more than outside of Quebec, simply because these are two terrains on which the majority has not had as clear a field as elsewhere on which to become a hegemonic ethnic-origins-aggregating integrator, as we saw in chapter 1. These findings can be taken as micro-level counterparts of the macro-level objective indicators referred to in part 1, namely that because of Quebec's de facto "dual majority" history, not only has neither majority become hegemonic, despite the best attempts of each to do so, at different points in history, but also both aboriginal and immigrant communities display signs of being less and/or less rapidly integrated into the larger dominant society.

POSSIBLE FUTURE TRENDS

What impact would a shift in Quebec's political status in the direction of greater independence have on Quebec's internal ethnic dynamics? Would such a political shift lead to the creation of two new successor states, each more homogeneous than its predecessor? Put differently, would a sovereign Quebec be more predominantly French-speaking, and the new (rest of) Canada (without Quebec) more homogeneously English-speaking? Such predictions are consonant with the ideology of the modern nation-state as a linguistically homogeneous entity (McNeill 1986). According to one formulation consonant with this perspective, the complexities of Canada as a bilingual federal state are holding back the "natural" development of two smaller, more unilingual states. In this view, both Quebec and the rest of Canada would develop more "normally" if there were two new independent states instead of the current federation.

Such questions are impossible to answer with any accuracy, involving, as they do, a large number of unknowns. In a hypothetical Canada without Quebec, there is little doubt that the French language would be less important than it is now, since it would be the language of less than five percent of the population. Whether policies toward Native peoples and with respect to immigrant integration would be any different is difficult to say. What about the position of non-Francophone minorities in an independent Quebec? The expectation among some nationalists may well be that a shift in Quebec's political status toward greater or full independence should signal a trend toward decreased autonomy for Quebec's minorities, the better to fully integrate them into the institutions of the Francophone majority. Pressures on the state in this direction would certainly be helped along by an outmigration of non-Francophones, which could be expected to some unknown extent.

Such pressures on the state are likely to be balanced, however, by opposite pressures on the state, flowing from geopolitical considerations. An independent Quebec, with world attention turned on it, would be expected to make explicit guarantees concerning the maintenance of Anglophone and aboriginal minority rights. As a consequence, Quebec's structurally exceptional position as an outlier in the overall inverse relationship between level of development and degree of pluralism is quite likely to be maintained, regardless of possible changes in the province's political status. Quebec is likely to continue to display a higher level of pluralism as well as more complex internal plural dynamics than any other province in Canada. Its Francophone majority is now unquestionably in power as never before, but, as we have seen, still displays a mix of majority and minority characteristics. Its Anglophone minority has become quite different from the rest of the English-speaking world in that it no longer shares the mixed blessing of its language being so hegemonic that the vast majority of even its educated native speakers never have any real need to learn any other language. The differences between Quebec Anglophones and those elsewhere are also likely to continue to intensify, given that the ongoing communal competitive process in part concerns how the Anglophone community is to be defined. However defined, it is unlikely to be assimilated or to go away completely, or to be split up and decomposed into its constituent ethnic parts, thereby reducing the remaining core English group to the status of just another ethnic minority. Even if its numbers are reduced over time, it is likely to retain a full network of autonomous and relatively powerful institutions.

As for aboriginals in Quebec, as we have seen, they already have more autonomy and higher levels of cultural retention than their counterparts elsewhere in Canada. Similarly, immigrant minorities in Quebec have long displayed higher levels of cultural retention than their counterparts in other parts of Canada (see Bourhis 1994). This trend has not decreased in the post-1970 modern period, and, although evidence is scarce, the argument can be made that in many ways it has increased. Looking to the future, one might in fact argue that, if anything, the cultural retention and, in some cases the institutional completeness of aboriginal and immigrant communities may well increase. Why?

First of all, because there are signs of a conscious strategy on the part of the Quebec state to build up or at least tolerate minority ethnic institutions, provided they make use of the French language (Rosenberg and Jedwab 1992). This is a conscious compromise strategy aimed at reducing the minority communities' identification with the overarching English community, thereby weakening the latter's overly imperialistic reach of decades past. As mentioned in chapter 8, this pattern is similar to what has been occurring with respect to aboriginal organizations. So a likely future trend is for members of immigrant communities in Quebec to have high rates of French-English bilingualism, in addition to maintaining a continued higher-than-elsewhere retention rate of ancestral languages.

Secondly, it is clear that over time conditions in schools and elsewhere will reinforce the already evident development of a common culture based on the French language. At the same time, though, the late start, as well as the full weight of past cautious reflexes long imbedded in traditional French Canadian culture, may well dampen the extent to which full assimilation will occur and may limit its overall volume. This is likely to be true even if the English community is completely kept out of the immigrant integration process in the future, as state planners and nationalists alike hope it will be.

In fact, there is also the possibility that the relative autonomy of Quebec's Anglophone, aboriginal, and immigrant communities may well even increase further, such autonomy being in some sense negotiated in exchange for political loyalty. These considerations are not negligible, given the disruption potential of appeals to the United Nations and to the international media on the part of Anglophone and aboriginal pressure groups, of the sort that have occurred intermittently in recent years. This would be the continuation of an old Canadian pattern—the Canadian state's development alongside a larger and more powerful United States has led to a pattern of rather higher pluralism in Canada than in the United States.

Just as the higher level of pluralism in Canada is traceable to the development of the Canadian state in the shadow of its larger neighbor (Laczko 1994), so the continued high level of pluralism within Quebec may be maintained or even accentuated because of a newly independent Quebec's competitive position against a more powerful "rest of Canada." And just as Canada's existence as a national entity independent of the United States has involved a complex pattern of compromises resulting in a higher level of internal pluralism, so it may well be that an independent Quebec, to peacefully consolidate its new status, would follow a similar pattern of compromises with its internal minorities. The ironic result is that a sovereign Quebec might continue to be for all practical purposes bilingual, while the rest of Canada, especially the nine provincial governments, might drift back into the unilingual English pattern that characterized so much of its history. This possibility parallels the situation in the new successor states of former Czechoslovakia, where Slovakia, the smaller and weaker former partner, continues to be much more internally heterogeneous than the larger and stronger former partner, the Czech Republic.

In a broad sense, Quebec's state and nation-building of the past few decades is very much in the Canadian tradition of defensive expansionism identified by Aitken (1967). Just as the Canadian state was used to consolidate the settlement and development of Western Canada, in order to ward off the American presence there, so the Quebec state's measures concerning its various minorities can be seen in the same light. The Quebec state's defensive expansionism consists of extending its influence over internal minorities with the express goal of removing them from the historic influence of English-language and federal institutions. This represents a major shift in strategy quite in contrast to the long-standing defensive retrenchment of traditional French Canadian institutions (see Taddeo and Taras 1987), and is in keeping with the shift toward a secular Quebec state-based nationalism that has largely replaced the earlier Canada-wide "French Canadian" minority nationalism that was based on ethnicity and religion (see Balthazar 1993).

All in all, Quebec's restructuring displays a pattern of lagged or delayed convergence both with respect to the role of the dominant language in society, and also with respect to the issue of immigrant integration. In Quebec, the language of the demographic majority, French, has belatedly assumed the functions that English has long assumed in the other Canadian provinces. The society has converged in form and symbolism to the larger normal society model of "one dominant language, many of 'one's own' minorities" (see Handler 1987), but rather less completely than its larger English-speaking neighbors. This less-complete convergence toward a hegemonic role for one dominant language is partly due to the late start, and is an instance of what Lieberson has called "asymmetric causality" (1985). Because the state measures to make French the dominant language have been taken in a context in which English has long been present and dominant, the effective hegemony that will be brought about by such measures is likely to be more limited than would be the case had they been adopted earlier or in the absence of the powerful rival.

Still, although the dominance of the French language does face constraints by virtue of history, the continental context, and the worldwide spread of English as the language of technology, its hegemony compares favorably to that found in other small societies. It is worth noting that the percentage of Quebecers reporting a knowledge of English is much lower than the percentage of people reporting a knowledge of English in the smaller societies of Northern Europe. In a recent European survey, 77 percent of respondents in the Netherlands and 74 percent in Sweden report being able to speak English.[3] Although the measures may not be completely comparable, in 1986, 30 percent of Quebec Francophones (44 percent in Montreal) reported knowing both French and English (Conseil de la langue française 1992:6). The Quebec percentages are very close to those of France, where 31 percent report being able to speak English. More research needs to be done on the meaning of such questions asked in different national contexts.

On the whole, Quebec's substantial, if not total, reversal of the historical power relationship is recent and, as such, is still seen as fragile by large segments of the Francophone majority. Now that Francophones are in full political control and Quebec is increasingly in charge of integrating its own new immigrants, a group more racially and religiously diverse than ever before, the challenge for the coming decades will be to continue to find ways of fully sharing the new evolving majority culture with those who have historically not been exposed to it.

DEVELOPMENT, PLURALISM, AND CONFLICT

Nearly three decades ago, Inglehart and Woodward (1967) examined the link between development, linguistic pluralism, and political stability. It might be interesting to close by locating our research against the backdrop of their results. They found that the association between pluralism and political stability was mediated by a state's level of political development. Their analysis of cross-national data from the 1960s revealed a curvilinear pattern. At low levels of political development, in traditional polities, there was no association between pluralism and political stability. At intermediate levels of political development, in transitional polities, pluralism was associated with political instability. At high levels of political development, in developed polities, pluralism was not associated with political instability; in fact, their highly plural developed societies were all classified as politically stable.

From the data at hand at the time, Inglehart and Woodward identified a small set of 6 states as being simultaneously developed polities, linguistically plural societies, and with a high degree of political stability. These were Belgium, Canada, Czechoslovakia, Israel, Switzerland, and the U.S.S.R. Some three decades later, this short list would be shorter still. The Soviet Union and Czechoslovakia have both divided into a number of successor states, which, in the latter case, have maintained some measure of political stability, and in the former case have not. The other four (Belgium, Canada, Israel, Switzerland) have all experienced internal communal conflict to greater or lesser degrees over this period. Seen in this perspective, Quebec's extensive yet relatively peaceful internal restructuring over the past three decades is yet another manifestation of Canada's exceptional outlier position.

APPENDIX A
ABOUT THE SURVEYS

1970 QUEBEC SOCIAL MOVEMENTS STUDY

The 1970 Quebec Social Movements Study was designed by Professor M. Pinard of McGill University to analyze the support of the Quebec population for the independence movement and the Parti Québécois. It was administered during the winter of 1970-71 to a cross-sectional sample of Quebec residents aged 18 and over.

A total of 1982 respondents were interviewed at home by trained personnel in either French or English, with French and English questionnaires, according to each respondent's preference.

The sample for the study was drawn following the standard sampling model of Quebec devised by the Centre de Sondage de l'Université de Montréal. It was developed for a multistage stratified proportional sample of about 2,400 from a total population of about 1,367,000 households as of 1966. This excluded residents of inaccessible communities, Indian reserves, and "unorganized territories," that is, about 2 percent of Quebec's total population.

1977 QUEBEC POLITICAL ATTITUDES STUDY

The 1977 Quebec Political Attitudes Study was commissioned by the Canadian Unity Information Office. A total of 1,297 in-person interviews were conducted in May and June of 1977. The fieldwork was done by L'Institut de cueillette de l'information in Montreal.

1985 QUEBEC OMNIBUS REPLICATION STUDY

The 1985 Quebec Omnibus Replication study was designed by the author as a replication of several items from the 1970 Quebec Social Movements Study. It was administered in April 1985 to a cross-sectional sample of Quebec residents aged 18 and over.

A total of 2,030 interviews were completed by telephone in French or English. The sample was selected by random-digit dialing, which allowed possible inclusion of all residential telephone numbers in Quebec, including those not listed in a directory, but excluded those in some remote northern areas where operator assistance is required. The fieldwork was carried out by the Centre de Sondage de l'Université de Montréal.

All three of these Quebec studies underrepresent non-Francophones to a certain extent, due to their lower response rate.

1991 MULTICULTURALISM AND CITIZENSHIP ATTITUDES SURVEY

The 1991 Multiculturalism and Citizenship Attitudes Survey was commissioned by the federal government's Department of Multiculturalism and Citizenship. The fieldwork was carried out by the Angus Reid Group:

> The total sample involved a base sample of 2,500 Canadian adults along with 'booster' samples in each of Toronto, Montreal and Vancouver in order to include at least 500 respondents in each of the three major urban centers in Canada. The total augmented sample was 3325.
>
> The survey was administered by telephone through the Angus Reid Group's national network of eight telephone interviewing centers across Canada. All telephone interviewing was conducted between June 29th and July 17th, 1991. Interviews were conducted in either English or French, according to the language preference of the respondent. (Reid 1991:7)

APPENDIX B
QUESTIONS FROM THE SURVEYS

In the three Quebec surveys, all questions were first drafted in French for the French-language questionnaire and then translated into English for the English-language version. The English-language version is presented here. For the pan-Canadian survey, the English-language version presented here is the original.

1970 QUEBEC SOCIAL MOVEMENTS STUDY

1-51   Are you a French Canadian, an English Canadian, an Italian Canadian, or a Canadian of some other origin? (IF OTHER ORIGIN OR NOT CANADIAN): Of what origin are you?

French Canadian _____ English Canadian _____ Italian Canadian _____ Canadian of other origin (specify) _____ Not Canadian (specify) _____

1-67   Have you ever lived or worked outside the province of Quebec?

Yes _____ No _____

2-31   In which of the following two groups do you think one finds the greatest scientists: among French Canadians, or among English Canadians?

Among French Canadians _____ Among English Canadians _____ Among both equally _____ Qualified answer (that depends, etc.) _____ Don't know _____

2-33   Do you think French Canadians should try and maintain their ways of living, or that they should become more like the other Canadians?

Maintain their ways of living _____ Become more like the other Canadians _____ Both _____ Qualified answer (that depends, etc.) _____ Don't know _____

2-35   Which would you say it is most important for a people to maintain: its language and culture or its standard of living?

Its language and culture _____ Both are equally important _____ Its
standard of living _____ Qualified answer (that depends, etc.) _____
Don't know _____

2-37 Which do you think are in general the best doctors: French Canadian doctors, or English Canadians doctors?

French Canadian doctors _____ English Canadian doctors _____
Both equally _____ Qualified answer (that depends, etc.) _____
Don't know _____

2-38 What do you think of the position of French Canadians in the
Federal government in Ottawa: is it more important, as important, or less
important than it should be?

More important _____ As important _____ Less important _____
Qualified answer (that depends, etc.) _____ Don't know _____

2-43 Do French Canadians or English Canadians hold the most important place in the world of business and finance in Quebec?

French Canadians _____ English Canadians _____ Both equally
_____ Don't know (PROCEED TO QUESTION 2-45) _____

2-44 On the whole, how do you evaluate this state of affairs: is it very
normal, fairly normal, rather abnormal, or very abnormal?

Very normal _____ Fairly normal _____ Rather abnormal _____
Very abnormal _____ Qualified answer (that depends, etc.) _____
Don't know _____

2-45 Some people claim that the situation of Quebec is similar to that of
other parts of the world that were or still are colonies. Other people claim
these situations are different. Would you say they are very similar, fairly
similar, rather different, or very different?

Very similar _____ Fairly similar _____ Rather different _____ Very
different _____ Qualified answer (that depends, etc.) _____ Don't
know _____

2-65 Do you think that in their mentality and ways of living French Canadians and English Canadians are very different, fairly different, quite similar, or very similar?

Very different _____ Fairly similar _____ Quite similar _____ Qualified answer (that depends, etc.) _____ Don't know _____

2-68 Which of these two groups is generally the wealthier: French Canadians or English Canadians?

French Canadians _____ English Canadians _____ They are equal _____ Neither is wealthier _____ Qualified answer (that depends, etc.) _____ Don't know _____

2-72 Do you think that all in all the difference in wealth that exists between French Canadians and English Canadians is acceptable, or should it be reduced?

Acceptable _____ Should be reduced _____ Qualified answer (that depends, etc.) _____ Don't know _____

2-76 To what extent do you think that the culture and way of life of French Canadians are in danger of disappearing: are they in great danger, in a little danger, or in no danger of disappearing?

In great danger _____ In a little danger _____ In no danger _____ Qualified answer (that depends, etc.) _____ Don't know _____

2-77 In the case of job offers or promotions, do you think that a French Canadian and an English Canadian who are equally competent have the same chances of getting them, that the French Canadian has a better chance, or that the English Canadian has a better chance?

Both have the same chances _____

(IF ONE HAS A BETTER CHANCE)

Does the (French Canadian *OR* English Canadian ACCORDING TO THE ANSWER TO THE PREVIOUS QUESTION) often have a better chance, or only sometimes?

French Canadian has sometimes a better chance _____ French Canadian has often a better chance _____ English Canadian has sometimes a better chance _____ English Canadian has often a better chance _____ Qualified answer (that depends, etc.) _____ Don't know _____

2-78   Has it ever happened to you, or to relatives, friends or acquaintances of yours, to have less chance of getting a job or a promotion than someone of another origin, despite being equally competent?

Yes, to myself _____ Yes, relatives, friends, or acquaintances _____ Yes, myself AND relatives, etc. _____ No _____ Don't remember _____

4-29 & 4-30   Are the members of the top level management of this organization French Canadians, English Canadians, Canadians of some other origin, or non Canadians? (CHECK SEVERAL RESPONSES IF NECESSARY)

French Canadians _____ English Canadians _____ Canadians of some other origin _____ Non Canadians _____ Don't know _____

4-52   How many years of study did you complete yourself?

Number of years _____

1977 QUEBEC POLITICAL ATTITUDES SURVEY

Q17   In your opinion, would French Canadians be better off maintaining their ways of living or becoming more like the other Canadians?

Maintain their ways _____ Become like others _____ Both at the same time _____ Qualified answer _____ Don't Know _____

Q24   Do you think that in their mentality and ways of living French Canadians and English Canadians are very different, fairly different, quite similar, or very similar?

Very different _____ Fairly different _____ Quite similar _____ Very similar _____ Qualified answer _____ Don't know _____

Q25   Which of these two groups is generally the wealthier, is it . . .

The French Canadians _____ The English Canadians _____
Equal _____ Qualified answer _____ Don't know _____

The other 1977 questions were worded exactly as they appear in the tables in chapter 7.

1985 QUEBEC OMNIBUS REPLICATION STUDY

Q46   Now let's go on to a few questions about the Francophone-Anglophone relationship. In your opinion, which would you say is the most important for a people to maintain: its language and culture *or* its standard of living?

Language and culture _____ Standard of living _____ Both _____
Qualified answer (that depends) _____ Don't Know _____

Q47   Would you say that from the standpoint of their mentality and lifestyle, Francophones and Anglophones are very different, fairly different, fairly similar, or very similar?

Very different _____ Fairly different _____ Fairly similar _____
Very similar _____ Qualified answer (that depends, etc.) _____
Don't Know _____

Q48   Do you think that it's mainly the Francophones or mainly the Anglophones who dominate the business and financial world in Quebec?

Mainly Francophones _____ Mainly Anglophones _____
Both equally _____ Qualified answer (that depends, etc.) _____
Don't Know _____ (If Don't Know: GO TO Q50)

Q49   Generally, do you feel that this situation is very normal, fairly normal, rather normal, rather abnormal, or very abnormal?

Very normal _____ Fairly normal _____ Rather abnormal _____
Very abnormal _____ Qualified answer (that depends, etc.) _____
Don't Know _____

Q51 In which of the following two groups do you think one finds the greatest scientists: mostly among Francophones or mostly among Anglophones?

Mostly among Francophones _____ Mostly among Anglophones _____ Both equally _____ Qualified answer (that depends, etc.) _____ Don't Know _____

Q52 In general, who do you think for the most part make the best doctors: Francophone doctors or Anglophone doctors?

Francophone doctors _____ Anglophone doctors _____ Both equally _____ Qualified answer (that depends, etc.) _____ Don't know _____

Q53 Some people believe that the Quebec situation is similar to the situation in other places in the world which were, or still are, colonies. Other people feel the opposite is true. In your opinion, are these situations fairly similar or fairly different?

Fairly similar _____ Fairly different _____ Qualified answer (that depends, etc.) _____ Don't know _____

Q54 Of the two groups, is it mostly the Francophones or mostly the Anglophones who are the wealthiest?

Mostly the Francophones _____ (GO TO Q55) Mostly the Anglophones _____ (GO TO Q55) Both are equally wealthy _____ (GO TO Q56) Qualified answer (that depends, etc.) _____ (GO TO Q56) Don't know _____ (GO TO Q56)

Q55 Do you feel that the differences in wealth between the two groups are on the whole acceptable, or should they be decreased?

Acceptable on the whole _____ Should be decreased _____ Qualified answer (that depends, etc.) _____ Don't know _____

Q56 In terms of job offers and promotions, do you believe that a Francophone and an Anglophone who are equally qualified have the same chance of getting a job or promotion, that the Francophone has a better chance, or that the Anglophone has a better chance?

Both have the same chance _____ Francophone has better chance _____ Anglophone has better chance _____ Qualified answer (that depends, etc.) _____ Don't know _____

Q57 Have you ever been in a situation where you didn't have an equal chance of getting a job or promotion as people from a different language group, even though you were as qualified as they were?

Yes _____ No _____ Can't remember _____

1991 CANADIAN MULTICULTURALISM AND CITIZENSHIP STUDY

Q10 I would like you to think of recent immigrants to Canada. These are people who were born and raised outside of Canada. How comfortable would you feel being around individuals from the following groups of immigrants. How about . . . (read British first outside of Quebec, French first in Quebec, then rotate)

For each of 13 ethnonational group labels, respondents are asked to rate "how comfortable" they would feel with recent immigrant members of the group on a 7-point scale, with 1 = not at all comfortable and 7 = completely comfortable. The labels are: British, French, Ukrainians, Sikhs, Indo-Pakistanis, Germans, Chinese, West Indian Blacks, Jews, Arabs, Italians, Portuguese, Moslems.

NOTES

Introduction

1. The raw data, mainly from the 1960s, are compiled from Taylor and Hudson (1972). Unfortunately, the data on ethnic and linguistic cleavages were not updated in the third edition of this handbook which appeared in 1983.

   The equation of the regression line is
   INDEX OF PLURALISM = 47.34–0.01 × GNP/CAPITA
   (N = 129; R squared = 0.096)

   The extent to which a case is an outlier is measured by the size of its residual, which is simply the vertical distance between the data point and the regression line.
2. For a discussion of the theoretical importance of examining the perceptual structure, see Dahl (1971).
3. These dimensions are used in a descriptive way in Smooha (1978).

Chapter 1

1. The historical literature on Quebec is voluminous. Useful overviews are provided by Ryerson 1945; Cook 1969; Ouellet 1980; Trofimenkoff 1983; Monière 1977; Linteau, Durocher and Robert 1983.
2. This study by Raynauld, Marion, and Béland, as well as the different ways discrimination can be measured, are discussed in McRoberts (1988:177, n.6,465). The broad parameters of the wide-ranging inequalities during this period are well documented (see Hughes 1963; Porter 1965; Royal Commission on Bilingualism and Biculturalism 1969; Breton and Roseborough 1971; Carlos 1973; Milner and Milner 1973; Laporte 1974; Beattie 1975; H. McRoberts et al. 1976; Raynauld, Marion, and Béland 1965; Sales 1979).
3. All of these data are taken from Conseil de la langue française (1992).

Introduction to Part II

1. Levine (1990:chapter 5) provides an excellent overview of this period.

Chapter 3

1. It should be noted that the roughly synonymous concepts of institutional parallelism, segmentation, segmented pluralism, and structural pluralism are all variable attributes of a *society*. Breton's related concept of institutional completeness (R. Breton 1964) is a variable attribute of an ethnic or linguistic *group* within a society.
2. The indicator used is the language of the questionnaire, French or English. This can be viewed as a measure of a respondent's preferred public or official language.

Chapter 4

1. These results are also relevant to those interested in applying the popular concept of a "new class" to segmented societies. I will not attempt to do so here, partly because it would lead us too far off the track and partly because I think the problems of definition involved with this concept appear so formidable as to cast doubts on its utility. For discussions of the "new class" concept, see Gouldner 1979; Bruce-Biggs 1979; Brint 1980; Konrad and Szelényi 1979. For an application of the concept to the Quebec context, see Grand-Maison (1979) and the review by Laurin-Frenette (1980).
2. This formulation is put forth keeping in mind the probabilistic view of theory advanced by Lieberson (1992).
3. Whichever interpretation one prefers, it is interesting to note that Cuneo's data do *not* support a rather different but equally time-honored view of the French Canada/English Canada/United States triangle. According to this view, as Max Weber put it almost a century ago in one of his rare passing references to Canada, "The loyalty of the French Canadians toward the English polity is today determined above all by the deep antipathy against the economic and social structure, and the way of life, of the neighboring United States; hence membership in the Dominion of Canada appears as a guarantee of their own traditions" (Weber 1978:397).
4. For a discussion of how and why anti-American sentiment in Canada may be strongest among upper-level white-collar workers, see Friedenberg (1978).

Chapter 5

1. Much of this chapter appeared in Laczko (1987).
2. It is possible and even likely that the tendency of Anglophone respondents to give "don't know" answers is in some sense a reflection of their greater discomfort in answering many of these questions. Answering "don't know" to these questions should be interpreted as one possible way of *not* answering that English Canadians are wealthier, or more privileged. At the same time, it makes sense to interpret the high proportion of "don't know" responses among Anglophones in the context of

the general reaction of the Anglophone community to this study when it was carried out in late 1970 and early 1971. As mentioned in appendix A, one of the reasons Anglophones are underrepresented in the sample survey is that they had a lower response rate than Francophones. It is unclear whether this reticence to participate can be attributed to the general sociopolitical climate at the time (only shortly after the October Crisis), to the fact that the study was clearly labeled as bearing on social and political trends in Quebec, to the fact that the principal investigator (M. Pinard) is a Francophone, to the fact that the covering letter identified the study with a French-language institution (the Centre de Sondage de l'Université de Montreal), to the fact that many of the interviewers were identifiably of French mother tongue, or to other reasons.

3. The joint effects of education and occupation are not given because the presentation of these effects for each dependent variable category would be too cumbersome. These results were examined, though, and they do not reveal systematic independent effects of education in either language community, other than that of slightly reducing the proportion of "don't know" responses.

4. The question from the Ethnic Relations Study that Roseborough and Breton used as a measure of relative economic advantage is as follows: "In general, who has the most chances of getting the best jobs in Canada: the English Canadians, the French Canadians, or Canadians of another group?"

    The question used as a measure of relative political advantage is as follows: "When the federal government makes decisions which affect all of Canada, does the opinion of one of the following groups count for more than the opinion of others: the opinion of English Canadians, the opinion of French Canadians, or the opinion of Canadians of some other group?" (Roseborough and Breton 1971:403-405).

5. The exact multivariate relationship is not identical for each of our ten dependent variable measures, but the general pattern of communal differences being greater than intracommunal ethnic differences is consistent, as is the higher proportion of "don't know" responses on the part of those of other (non-English, non-French) origin.

    One interesting interaction effect occurs concerning the reported *experience* of discrimination. This is the one question that is worded in such a way that no direct mention is made of French-English relations as such. While the overall ethnic and communal differences here are *low*, there is an ethnic effect among the minority who have the most education, and in this subset only. The most-educated (those who have some university experience) Others are clearly the most likely to report the direct or indirect experience of discrimination. This holds true whether this subset is compared to their less-educated ethnic and communal brethren or to their highly educated counterparts of French and English origin.

    This again points to the higher incidence and intensity of competition at the white-collar level in Quebec.

Chapter 6

1. A slightly different version of this chapter appeared in Laczko (1986).
2. Further analyses were carried out to check the possibility that these results might be spurious because of the strong effect of education on both sets of dependent variable. These yielded only the most minor types of changes in the pattern shown here. When the effect of education is controlled, the results remain substantially the same.
3. There might be an interaction effect present, since there is a tendency for the coefficients in the two right-hand pairs of columns to be higher among Anglophones. Indeed, 13 of the 20 pairs of coefficients between perceptions of communal inequalities and normative orientations toward cultural pluralism that appear in the right-hand side of the table display a stronger correlation among Anglophones. This slightly weaker reactive effect among Francophones indicates that there may be greater uncertainty and indecision among Francophones as to the appropriate strategy to adopt concerning the maintenance of cultural differences. This reflects the great diversity of interests and opinions within the Francophone community in 1970, and could be one further consequence of the greater costs that Francophones incur as members of the historically subordinate communal group.
4. Most of the variables used here correlate positively, if often weakly, with indicators of Quebec nationalism and support for the separation of Quebec from Canada. For an attempt to specify the conditions under which perceived communal inequalities in chances for employment can lead to support for separation among Francophones, see Bélanger and Pinard (1991).

Chapter 7

1. In addition to the sources already cited, other useful sources include Sales and Bélanger 1985; Boulet and Lavallée 1983; Murphy 1981; Lacroix and Vaillancourt 1981; Arnopoulos and Clift 1980; Coleman 1984; Langlois et al. 1990; Conseil de la langue française 1992; Moreau 1992; Vaillancourt 1992; Vaillancourt 1993; Smith 1994.
2. If the 1985 responses are broken down by a trichotomized mother tongue variable, Francophones remain at 17 percent, with both Anglophones and Allophones at 24 percent. In general, on other questions, the "allophone" statistical category displays responses falling in between those of French and English mother tongues. This reflects the fact that the allophone category contains members oriented toward both overarching linguistic communities, a pattern already seen earlier. We shall be returning to this point in the following chapter.
3. In this connection, it is interesting to note that in a 1981 national survey, Francophones' achievement motivation scores were clearly higher than those of Anglophones (Baer and Curtis 1988). Baer and Curtis suggest that this constitutes a possible reversal from earlier periods, although comparable data are not readily available.

4. For a discussion of the how this new minority feeling among Anglophones led many of them to support a new single-issue English-rights Equality Party in the late 1980s and early 1990s, see Rudin (1993).

Chapter 8

1. This preference for cultural uniformity is measured by a two item index composed of the following items drawn from the 1968 Canadian Federal Election Study: "Canada would be a better place if all the people had the same national origin," and "Canada would be a better place if all people had the same religion" (Curtis and Lambert 1976:192). Further explorations of the issue are reported in Lambert and Curtis 1982; 1983.

2. These data are analyzed further from the perspective of citizenship theory, but without any regional breakdowns, in Laczko 1995.

3. Does being on the receiving end of discrimination or injustice lead to more favorable or less favorable attitudes toward other minorities? It would appear to depend on the context. We have seen that the relationship can be positive, as was suggested in our interpretation of Francophones' higher level of sympathy for Native peoples during the 1970s and 1980s, or negative, as was suggested in our interpretation of the recent reversal of this pattern. Consider the results of a recent American survey commissioned by the National Conference of Christians and Jews:

   > The survey found that 80 percent of blacks, 60 percent of Latinos and 57 percent of Asian Americans surveyed felt that their groups did not have equal opportunity with whites. But among white respondents, 63 percent said blacks have equal employment opportunity, 57 percent said the same of Latinos and 63 percent said it of Asians. . . . (Duke 1994)

   The survey also found that members of minority groups are more likely than whites to hold negative stereotypes about other minority groups:

   > For instance, 33 percent of Latinos, 22 percent of Asians and 12 percent of whites surveyed agreed with the statement, "Even if given a chance, (black Americans) aren't capable of getting ahead."

   On Jews, 54 percent of blacks, 43 percent of Latinos, 35 percent of Asians and 27 per cent of non-Jewish whites agreed with the statement "When it comes to choosing between people and money, Jews will choose money." (Duke 1994)

   Notice that the rank orderings of perceived discrimination correlate very highly with the rank orderings of negative attitudes.

Chapter 9

1. This point is central to Wallerstein's critique of the modernization perspective (see Wallerstein 1979).

2. This process is analogous to the "low memory loss" evoked in the research of Roseborough and Breton (1971), which is discussed in chapter 5.
3. Other useful comparative perspectives are found in Baker 1977; Montcalm 1984; and Zolberg 1975.

Conclusion

1. This point brings us to what appears to be a difference between Quebec's reforms and those carried out in Malaysia. There, the willingness to reduce economic growth, if necessary, in order to reduce internal inequalities, was made explicit (Mauzy 1993). A similar proviso has only been implicit in Quebec, in the context of the Quebec government's commitment to maintaining the province's overwhelmingly French character.
2. This powerful historical "quasi state" role of the Catholic Church in Quebec stems from the Quebec Act of 1774, as mentioned in chapter 1. While the Anglican Church became the established church of Canada as a British colony, that status was in a sense shared with the Catholic Church which had authority over the majority French Canadian population, which was almost entirely Catholic. This pattern had spinoff effects in other provinces in the course of Canada's development. Concessions of semi-official status were granted to the Catholic Church in several provinces. In several provinces today, Protestant and Catholic schools are supported by the state as public schools.
3. These figures are from Reader's Digest International Eurodata (1991:24), table 6.1. I am indebted to Jean Laponce for mentioning the existence of these data and making them available.

REFERENCES

Adam, Heribert, and Hermann Giliomee. 1979. *Ethnic Power Mobilized. Can South Africa Change?* New Haven: Yale University Press.

Aitken, Hugh G. J. 1967. "Defensive Expansionism: The State and Economic Growth in Canada." in *Approaches to Canadian Economic History,* ed. W. T. Easterbrook and M. H. Watkins. Toronto: McClelland and Stewart.

Aguirre Beltran, Gonzalo. 1957. *El proceso de aculturación.* Mexico City: Universidad Nacional Autonoma de Mexico.

Anctil, Pierre. 1984. "Double majorité et multiplicité ethnoculturelle à Montréal." *Recherches Sociographiques* 25(3):441-456.

Arbour, Pierre. 1993. *Québec Inc. et la tentation du dirigisme.* Montreal: L'étincelle.

Arnopoulos, Sheila M., and Dominique Clift. 1980. *The English Fact in Quebec.* Montreal: McGill-Queen's University Press.

Baer, Douglas E., and James E. Curtis. 1988. "Differences in the Achievement Values of French Canadians and English Canadians." Pp. 476-484 in *Social Inequality in Canada: Patterns, Problems, Policies,* ed. James Curtis, Edward Grabb, Neil Guppy, and Sid Gilbert. Scarborough, Ont: Prentice-Hall.

Baker, Donald G. 1977. "Ethnicity, Development and Power: Canada in Comparative Perspective." in *Identities: The Impact of Ethnicity on Canadian Society,* ed. Wsevolod Isajiw. Toronto: Peter Martin Associates.

Balandier, Georges. 1965. "The Colonial Situation." in *Africa: Social Problems of Change and Conflict,* ed. P. L. Van den Berghe. San Francisco: Chandler.

Balthazar, Louis. 1993. "The Faces of Quebec Nationalism." in *Quebec: State and Society,* 2d ed., ed. Alain-G. Gagnon. Scarborough Ont: Nelson Canada.

Banton, Michael. 1983. *Ethnic and Racial Competition.* New York: Cambridge University Press.

Barth, Fredrik, ed. 1969. *Ethnic Groups and Boundaries.* Boston: Little, Brown.

Beattie, Christopher. 1975. *Minority Men in a Majority Setting: Middle-level Francophones in the Canadian Public Service.* Toronto: McClelland and Stewart.

Bélanger, Sarah, and Maurice Pinard. 1991. "Ethnic Movements and the Competition Model: Some Missing Links." *American Sociological Review* 56(4):446-457

Bernard, André. 1976. "L'abstentionnisme des électeurs de langue anglaise du Québec." in *Le processus électoral au Québec,* ed. Daniel Latouche, Guy Lord, and Jean-Guy Vaillancourt. Montreal: Hurtubise HMH.

Berry, John W., Rudolf Kalin, and Donald M. Taylor. 1977. *Multiculturalism and Ethnic Attitudes in Canada.* Ottawa: Supply and Services.

Bibby, Reginald. 1987. *Fragmented Gods: The Poverty and Potential of Religion in Canada.* Toronto: Irwin Publishing.

Blais, André. 1991. "Le clivage linguistique au Canada." *Recherches Sociographiques* 32(1):43-54.

Blau, Peter. 1977. *Inequality and Heterogeneity: A Primitive Theory of Social Structure.* New York: Free Press.

Blauner, Robert. 1972. *Racial Oppression in America.* New York: Harper and Row.

Blumer, Herbert. 1965. "Industrialization and Race Relations." in *Industrialization and Race Relations,* ed. Guy Hunter. London: Oxford University Press.

Boeke, J. H. 1953. *Economics and Economic Policy of Dual Societies, as Exemplified by Indonesia.* New York: Institute of Pacific Relations.

Bolduc, Denis and Pierre Fortin. 1990. "Les francophones sont-ils plus 'xénophobes' que les anglophones au Québec? Une analyse quantitative exploratoire." *Canadian Ethnic Studies* 22(2):54-77.

Boli-Bennett, John. 1980. "Global Integration and the Universal Increase of State Dominance, 1910-1970." Pp. 77-107 in *Studies of the Modern World System,* ed. Albert Bergesen. New York: Academic Press.

Bonacich, Edna. 1972. "A Theory of Ethnic Antagonism: The Split Labor Market." *American Sociological Review* 37(5):547-559.

———. 1979. "The Past, Present, and Future of Split Labor Market Theory." Pp. 17-64 in *Research in Race and Race Relations,* ed. C. Marrott and C. Leggon. Vol. 1. Greenwich, Conn.: JAI Press.

Boudreau, Françoise. 1980. "The Quebec Psychiatric System in Transition." *Canadian Review of Sociology and Anthropology* 17 (2):122-137.

Boulet, Jac-André. 1979. *L'évolution des disparités linguistiques de revenus de travail dans la zone métropolitaine de Montréal de 1961 à 1977.* Document no. 127, Conseil économique du Canada.

Boulet, Jac-André, et Laval Lavallée. 1983. *L'évolution des disparités linguistiques des revenus de travail au Canada de 1970 à 1980.* Document no. 245, Conseil économique du Canada.

Bourdieu, P., and J. C. Passeron. 1970. *La reproduction.* Paris: Éditions de minuit.

Bourhis, Richard Y. 1994. "Ethnic and Language Attitudes in Quebec." Pp. 322-360 in *Ethnicity and Culture in Canada: The Research Landscape,* ed. J. W. Berry and J. A. Laponce. Toronto: University of Toronto Press.

Bozinoff, Lorne, and Peter MacIntosh. 1991. "Two Solitudes Apparent in Language Domain." *Gallup Report.* 5 December.

Brass, Paul. 1991. *Ethnicity and Nationalism: Theory and Comparison.* London: Sage.

Brazeau, Jacques. 1968. "The Practice of Medicine in Montreal." in *Canadian Society: Sociological Perspectives,* 3d ed., ed. Bernard R. Blishen, Frank E. Jones, Kaspar D. Naegele, and John Porter. Toronto: Macmillan.

Breton, Albert. 1964. "The Economics of Nationalism." *Journal of Political Economy* 72 (August):376-386.

Breton, Raymond. 1964. "Institutional Completeness of Ethnic Communities and the Personal Relations of Immigrants." *American Journal of Sociology* 70 (September):193-205.

———. 1978a. "Stratification and Conflict between Ethnolinguistic Communities with Different Social Structures." *Canadian Review of Sociology and Anthropology* 15(2):148-157.

———. 1978b. "The Structure of Relationships Between Ethnic Collectivities." Pp. 55-73 in *The Canadian Ethnic Mosaic: A Quest for Identity,* ed. Leo Driedger. Toronto: McClelland and Stewart.

———. 1979. "Ethnic Stratification Viewed from Three Theoretical Perspectives." Pp. 270-294 in *Social Stratification: Canada,* 2d ed. ed. James E. Curtis and William G. Scott. Scarborough, Ont: Prentice Hall.

———. 1988. "From Ethnic to Civic Nationalism: English Canada and Quebec." *Ethnic and Racial Studies* 11(1):85-102.

Breton, Raymond, Jeffrey G. Reitz, and Victor Valentine. 1980. *Cultural Boundaries and the Cohesion of Canada.* Montreal: The Institute for Research on Public Policy.

Breton, Raymond, and Howard Roseborough. 1971. "Ethnic Differences in Status." Pp. 450-468 in *Canadian Society: Sociological Perspectives.* 3d ed., abridged, ed. Bernard R. Blishen, Frank E. Jones, Kaspar D. Naegele, and John Porter. Toronto: Macmillan.

Brint, Steven. 1980. "'New Class' or New Scapegoat?" *Contemporary Sociology* 9 (September):651-653.

Bruce-Biggs, B., 1979. *The New Class?* New Brunswick, N.J.: Transaction Books.

Carlos, Serge. 1973. *L'utilisation du français dans le monde du travail du Québec.* Quebec: L'éditeur officiel du Québec.

Clark, S. D. 1968. *The Developing Canadian Community.* 2d ed. Toronto: University of Toronto Press.

Clement, Wallace. 1977. "Macrosociological Approaches Toward a 'Canadian Sociology'." *Alternate Routes: A Critical Review.* Vol. 1.

Coleman, William D. 1984. "The Class Bases of Language Policy in Quebec, 1949-1983." Pp. 388-409 in *Quebec: State and Society,* ed. Alain-G. Gagnon. Toronto: Methuen.

Collins, Randall. 1975. *Conflict Sociology: Toward an Explanatory Science.* New York: Academic Press.

Connor, Walker. 1977. "Nation-Building or Nation-Destroying?" in *Race, Ethnicity, and Social Change,* ed. John Stone. North Scituate, Mass.: Duxbury Press.

Conseil de la langue française. 1992. *Indicateurs de la situation linguistique au Québec.* Quebec: Gouvernement du Québec.

Conversi, Daniele. 1990. "Language or Race? The Choice of Core Values in the Development of Catalan and Basque Nationalisms." *Ethnic and Racial Studies* 13(1):50-70.

Cook, Ramsay. 1969. *French Canadian Nationalism.* Toronto: Macmillan.

Coser, Lewis. 1956. *The Functions of Social Conflict.* New York: Free Press.

Cuneo, Carl. 1976. "The Social Basis of Political Continentalism in Canada." *Canadian Review of Sociology and Anthropology* 13(1):55-70.

Curtis, James E., and Ronald D. Lambert. 1976. "Educational Status and Reactions to Heterogeneity." *Canadian Review of Sociology and Anthropology* 13(2):189-203.

Dahl, Robert A. 1971. *Polyarchy: Participation and Opposition.* New Haven: Yale University Press.

D'Anglejean, Alison. 1984. "Language Planning in Quebec: An Historical Overview and Future Trends." Pp. 29-52 in *Conflict and Language Planning in Quebec,* ed. Richard Y. Bourhis. Clevedon, England: Multilingual Matters.

Deutsch, Karl W. 1953. *Nationalism and Social Communication: An Inquiry into the Foundations of Nationality.* Cambridge: M.I.T. Press.

Dion, Stéphane. 1992. "Explaining Quebec Nationalism." Pp. 77-121 in *The Collapse of Canada?,* ed. R. Kent Weaver. Washington, D.C.: Brookings Institution.

Dion, Stéphane, and Gaëtane Lamy. 1990. "La francisation de la langue de travail au Québec: Contraintes et réalisations." *Language Policy and Language Planning* 14(2):119-141.

Dofny, Jacques, and Muriel Garon-Audy. 1969. "Mobilités professionnelles au Québec." *Sociologie et Sociétés* 1(2):277-301.

Duke, Lynn. 1994. "Survey Shows a Deeply Divided U.S." *Montreal Gazette,* 3 March. (Reprinted from *Washington Post*).

Duncan, Otis Dudley. 1975. *Introduction to Structural Equation Models.* New York: Academic Press.

Enloe, Cynthia. 1973. *Ethnic Conflict and Political Development.* Boston: Little, Brown.

Federalist, The (1788). *The Federalist.* New York: Modern Library, n.d. Section reprinted in *Class, Status and Power,* 2d ed., ed. Reinhard Bendix and Seymour Martin Lipset. New York: Free Press, 1966.

Fenwick, Rudy. 1981. "Social Change and Ethnic Nationalism: An Historical Analysis of the Separatist Movement in Quebec." *Comparative Studies in Society and History* 23(2):196-216.

Fischer, Claude S., et al. 1977. *Networks and Places: Social Relations in the Urban Setting.* New York: Free Press.

Fishman, Joshua A. 1968. "Some Contrasts between Linguistically Homogeneous and Linguistically Heterogeneous Polities." *Sociological Inquiry* 36 (spring):146-158.

Form, William H., and Joan Rytina. 1969. "Ideological Beliefs on the Distribution of Power in the United States." *American Sociological Review* 34(1):19-31.

Fournier, Marcel. 1977. "La question nationale: les enjeux." *Possibles* 1(2):7-18.

Friedenberg Edgar Z. 1978. "Changing Canadian Attitudes Toward American Immigrants." Pp. 135-146 in *The Canadian Ethnic Mosaic,* ed. Leo Driedger. Toronto: McClelland and Stewart.

Furnivall, J. S. 1948. *Colonial Policy and Practice: A Comparative Study of Burma and Netherlands India.* Cambridge: Cambridge University Press.

Gagnon, Lysiane. 1969. "Les Conclusions du Rapport B.B." in *Economie Québécoise,* ed. Robert Comeau et al. Montreal: Les Presses de l'Université du Québec.

Gallie, Duncan. 1983. *Social Inequality and Class Radicalism in France and Britain.* Cambridge: Cambridge University Press.

Gellner, Ernest. 1964. *Thought and Change.* London: Weidenfeld & Nicolson.

Genesee, Fred, and Naomi E. Holobow. 1989. "Change and Stability in Intergroup Perceptions." *Journal of Language and Social Psychology* 8 (1):17-38.

Gouldner, Alvin W. 1979. *The Future of Intellectuals and the Rise of the New Class.* New York: The Seabury Press.

Grabb, Edward G. 1979. "Relative Centrality and Political Isolation: Canadian Dimensions." *Canadian Review of Sociology and Anthropology* 16 (3)

Grand'Maison, Jacques. 1979. *La nouvelle classe et l'avenir du Québec.* Montreal: Stanké.

Guindon, Hubert. 1964. "The Social Evolution of Quebec Reconsidered." Pp. 137-161 in *French Canadian Society,* ed. Marcel Rioux and Yves Martin. Toronto: McClelland and Stewart.

————. 1968. "Social Unrest, Social Class and Quebec's Bureaucratic Revolution." in *Canada, A Sociological Profile,* W. E. Mann. Toronto: Copp Clark.

————. 1978. "The Modernization of Quebec and the Legitimacy of the Canadian State." *Canadian Review of Sociology and Anthropology* 15(2):227-245.

————. 1988. *Quebec Society: Tradition, Modernity, and Nationhood.* Toronto: University of Toronto Press.

Handler, Richard. 1987. *Nationalism and the Politics of Culture in Quebec.* Madison: University of Wisconsin Press.

Hannan, Michael T. 1979. "The Dynamics of Ethnic Boundaries in Modern States." Pp. 253-275 in *National Development and the World System: Educational, Economic and Political Change, 1950-1970.* ed. Michael T. Hannan and John Meyer. Chicago: University of Chicago Press.

Harris, Marvin. 1964. *Patterns of Race in the Americas.* New York: Walker.

Hartz, Louis. 1964. *The Founding of New Societies.* New York: Harcourt Brace.

Haug, Marie. 1967. "Social and Cultural Pluralism as a Concept in Social System Analysis." *American Journal of Sociology* 73 (November):294-304.

Hébert, Chantal. 1994. "Salary Data Counter Myth of Official Bilingualism as Pro-Francophone Plot." *Ottawa Citizen,* 28 March.

Hechter, Michael. 1975. *Internal Colonialism: the Celtic Fringe in British National Development.* Berkeley: University of California Press.

Hechter, Michael. 1976. "Ethnicity and Industrialization: on the Proliferation of the Cultural Division of Labor." *Ethnicity* 3:214-224.

Hechter, Michael. 1978. "Group Formation and the Cultural Division of Labor." *American Journal of Sociology* 84 (September): 293-318.

Hechter, Michael, and Margaret Levi. 1979. "The Comparative Analysis of Ethnoregional Movements." *Ethnic and Racial Studies* 2(3):260-274.

Hill, Keith. 1974. "Belgium: Political Change in a Segmented Society." Pp 29-107 in *Electoral Behaviour: A Comparative Handbook,* ed. Richard Rose. New York: Free Press.

Horowitz, Donald L. 1971. "Multiracial Politics in the New States: Toward a Theory of Conflict." Pp. 164-180 in *Issues in Comparative Politics,* ed. Robert J. Jackson and Michael B. Stein. New York: St. Martin's Press.

————. 1980. *Coup Theories and Officers' Motives: Sri Lanka in Comparative Perspective.* Princeton: Princeton University Press.

————. 1985. *Ethnic Groups in Conflict.* Berkeley and Los Angeles: University of California Press

Horton, John. 1966. "Order and Conflict Theories of Social Problems as Competing Ideologies." *American Journal of Sociology* 71(May):701-713.

Hroch, Miroslav. 1985. *Social Preconditions to National Revival in Europe.* Cambridge: Cambridge University Press.

Huber, Joan, and William H. Form. 1973. *Income and Ideology: An Analysis of the American Political Formula.* New York: Free Press.

Hughes, Everett C. [1943] 1963. *French Canada in Transition.* First Phoenix edition. Chicago: University of Chicago Press.

Inglehart, Ronald F., and Margaret Woodward. 1967. "Language Conflicts and Political Community." *Comparative Studies in Society and History* 10(1):27-45.

Jacek, Henry J. 1993. "Unequal Partners: The Historical, Political, Economic and Cultural Dimensions of the Austria-FRG/Canadian-U.S. Dyads." in *Unequal Partners: A Comparative Analysis of Relations Between Austria and the Federal Republic of Germany and Between Canada and the United States,* ed. Harald von Riekhoff and Hanspeter Neubold. Boulder: Westview Press.

Juteau-Lee, Danielle. 1981. "Visions partielles, visions partiales: visions (des) minoritaires en sociologie." *Sociologie et Sociétés* 13(2):33-47.

Kerr, Clark, John R. Dunlop, Frederick Harbison, and Charles Myers. 1960. *Industrialism and Industrial Man.* Cambridge: Harvard University Press.

Keyfitz, Nathan. 1963. Foreword to *French Canada in Transition,* by Everett C. Hughes. Chicago: University of Chicago Press.

Konrad, G., and I. Szelényi. 1979. *The Intellectuals on the Road to Class Power.* New York: Harcourt Brace Jovanovich.

Kornberg, Allan, and Harold D. Clarke. 1992. *Citizens and Community: Political Support in a Representative Democracy.* New York: Cambridge University Press.

Kraus, Richard, William E. Maxwell, and Reeve D. Vanneman. 1979. "The Interests of Bureaucrats: Implications of the Asian Experience for Recent Theories of Development." *American Journal of Sociology* 85 (July):135-155.

Kuper, Leo. 1970. "Stratification in Plural Societies." in *Essays in Comparative Social Stratification*, ed. L. Plotnicov and A. Tuden. Pittsburgh: University of Pittsburgh Press.

Lacroix, R., and F. Vaillancourt. 1981. *Les revenus et la langue au Québec (1970-1978)*. Quebec: Conseil de la langue française.

Laczko, Leslie S. 1978a. "English Canadians and Québécois Nationalism: An Empirical Analysis." *Canadian Review of Sociology and Anthropology* 15(2):206-217.

———. 1978b. "Feelings of Threat Among English-speaking Quebecers." in *Modernization and the Canadian State*. ed. D. Glenday, H. Guindon, and A. Turowetz. Toronto: Macmillan.

———. 1986. "On the Dynamics of Linguistic Cleavage in Quebec: A Test of Alternative Hypotheses." *International Journal of Sociology and Social Policy* 6(1):39-60.

———. 1987. "Perceived Communal Inequalities in Quebec: A Multidimensional Analysis." *Canadian Journal of Sociology/Cahiers canadiens de sociologie* 12(1-2):87-110.

———. 1994. "Canada's Pluralism in Comparative Perspective." *Ethnic and Racial Studies* 17(1):20-41.

———. 1995. "Feelings of Fraternity Towards Old and New Canadians: The Interplay of Ethnic and Civic Factors." *Nationalism and Ethnic Politics* 1(3): 43-61.

Lalonde, Michelle. 1994. "Perception of Indians is Skewed, Poll Finds." *Montreal Gazette*, 12 March.

Lambert, Ronald, and James Curtis. 1982. "The French- and English-Canadian Language Communities and Multicultural Attitudes." *Canadian Ethnic Studies* 14(2):43-58.

———. 1983. "Opposition to Multiculturalism among Québécois and English Canadians." *Canadian Review of Sociology and Anthropology* 20(2):193-207.

Langlois, Simon, Jean-Paul Baillargeon, Gary Caldwell, Guy Fréchet, Madeleine Gauthier, and Jean-Pierre Simard. 1990. *La société québécoise en tendances 1960-1990*. Quebec: Institut québécois de recherche sur la culture.

Laporte, Pierre. 1974. *L'usage des langues dans la vie économique au Québec: Situation actuelle et possibilités de changement*. Quebec: L'éditeur officiel du Québec.

———. 1984. "Status Language Planning in Quebec: An Evaluation." Pp. 53-80 in *Conflict and Language Planning in Quebec*, ed. Richard Y. Bourhis. Clevedon, England: Multilingual Matters.

Laslett, Barbara. 1980. "Beyond Methodology: The Place of Theory in Quantitative Historical Research." *American Sociological Review* 45(2):214-228.

Laurin-Frenette, Nicole. 1980. Review of *La nouvelle classe et l'avenir du Québec*, by Jacques Grand'Maison. *Recherches Sociographiques*. 21(1-2).

Leslie, Peter. 1989. "Ethnonationalism in a Federal State: The Case of Canada." Pp. 45-90 in *Ethnoterritorial Politics, Policy, and the Western World*, ed. Joseph R. Rudolph, Jr. and Robert J. Thompson. Boulder: Lynne Rienner Publishers.

Levine, Marc. 1990. *The Reconquest of Montreal: Language Policy and Social Change in a Bilingual City*. Philadelphia: Temple University Press.

Lieberson, Stanley. 1961. "A Societal Theory of Race and Ethnic Relations." *American Sociological Review* 26(6):902-910.

———. 1985. *Making It Count: The Improvement of Social Research and Theory*. Berkeley and Los Angeles: University of California Press.

———. 1992. "Einstein, Renoir, and Greeley: Some Thoughts About Evidence in Sociology." *American Sociological Review* 57(1):1-15.

Liebkind, Karmela. 1982. "The Swedish-Speaking Finns: A Case Study of Ethnolinguistic Identity." in *Social Identity and Intergroup Relations*, ed. Henri Tajfel. Cambridge: Cambridge University Press.

Lijphart, Arend. 1977. *Democracy in Plural Societies: A Comparative Exploration*. New Haven: Yale University Press.

Linteau, Paul-André, René Durocher, and Jean-Claude Robert. 1983. *Quebec: A History 1867-1929*. Toronto: James Lorimer.

Linz, Juan J. 1985. "From Primordialism to Nationalism." Pp. 203-253 in *New Nationalisms of the Developed West*, ed. Edward A. Tiryakian and Ronald Rogowski. Boston: Allen and Unwin.

Lipset, Seymour Martin. 1979. "Approaches to Social Stratification." Pp. 29-58 in *Social Stratification: Canada*, 2d ed., ed. James E. Curtis and William G. Scott. Scarborough, Ont: Prentice-Hall.

Lipset, Seymour Martin, and Stein Rokkan, eds. 1967. *Party Systems and Voter Alignments*. New York: Free Press.

Lubin, Martin. 1982. "Quebec Nonfrancophones and the United States." in *Problems and Opportunities in U.S.-Quebec Relations*, ed. Alfred O. Hero, Jr. and Marcel Daneau. Boulder: Westview Press.

MacLennan, Hugh. 1945. *Two Solitudes*. New York: Popular Library.

Makabe, Tomoko. 1979. "Ethnic Identity Scale and Social Mobility: the Case of Nisei in Toronto." *Canadian Review of Sociology and Anthropology* 16(2):136-146.

Marx, Karl. 1868. *Manifesto of the Communist Party*. Sections reprinted in *The Marxists*, ed. C. Wright Mills. New York: Dell.

Mason, Philip. 1970. *Race Relations*. London: Oxford University Press.

Mauzy, Diane. 1993. "Malaysia: Malay Political Hegemony and 'Coercive Consociationalism'." Pp. 106-127 in *The Politics of Ethnic Conflict Regulation*, ed. John McGarry and Brendan O'Leary. New York: Routledge.

McNeill, William H. 1986. *Polyethnicity and National Unity in World History*. Toronto: University of Toronto Press.

McRae, Kenneth. 1973. "Consociationalism and the Canadian Political System." Pp. 238-261 in *Consociational Democracy: Political Accommodation in Segmented Societies*, ed. Kenneth McRae. Toronto: McClelland and Stewart.

———. 1983. *Conflict and Compromise in Multilingual Societies*. Vol. 1, *Switzerland*. Waterloo, Ont.: Wilfrid Laurier University Press.

———. 1986. *Conflict and Compromise in Multilingual Societies*. Vol. 2, *Belgium*. Waterloo, Ont.: Wilfrid Laurier University Press.

McRoberts, Hugh, John Porter, Monica Boyd, John Goyder, Frank Jones, and Peter Pineo. 1976. "Différences dans la mobilité professionnelle des francophones et des anglophones." *Sociologie et Sociétés* 8(2):61-79.

McRoberts, Kenneth. 1979. "Internal Colonialism: The Case of Quebec." *Ethnic and Racial Studies* 2(3):293-318.

———. 1988. *Quebec: Social Change and Political Crisis*, 3d ed. Toronto: McClelland and Stewart.

Meisel, John, and Vincent Lemieux. 1972. *Ethnic Relations in Canadian Voluntary Associations*. Document 13 of the Royal Commission on Bilingualism and Biculturalism. Ottawa: Information Canada

Melson, R., and H. Wolpe. 1970. "Modernization and the Politics of Communalism: A Theoretical Perspective." *American Political Science Review* 64:1109-1121.

Memmi, Albert. 1972. *The Colonizer and the Colonized*. Boston: Beacon Press.

Meyer, John W., John Boli-Bennett, and Christopher Chase-Dunn. 1975. "Convergence and Divergence in Development." *Annual Review of Sociology* 1:223-246.

Meyer, John W. 1980. "The World Polity and the Authority of the Nation-State." Pp. 109-137 in *Studies of the Modern World System*, ed. Albert Bergesen. New York: Academic Press.

Middleton, Russell. 1963. "Alienation, Race and Education." *American Sociological Review* 28(6):973-977.

Migué, Jean-Luc. 1970. "Le nationalisme, l'unité nationale et la théorie économique de l'information." *Revue canadienne d'économique* 3:183-198.

Milne, R. S. 1981. *Politics in Ethnically Bipolar States*. Vancouver: University of British Columbia Press.

Milner, Henry. 1978. *Politics in the New Quebec*. Toronto: McClelland and Stewart.

Milner, Sheilagh Hodgins, and Henry Milner. 1973. *The Decolonization of Quebec*. Toronto: McClelland and Stewart.

Monière, Denis. 1977. *Le développement des idéologies au Québec*. Montréal: Québec-Amérique.

Montcalm, Mary-Beth. 1984. "Quebec Separatism in a Comparative Perspective." Pp. 45-58 in *Quebec: State and Society*, ed. Alain-G. Gagnon. Toronto: Methuen.

Moore, William Henry. 1919. *The Clash! A Study in Nationalities*. Toronto: J. M. Dent & Sons.

Moreau, François. 1992. "La résistible ascension de la bourgeoisie québécoise." Pp. 335-353 in *Le Québec en jeu: comprendre les grands débats*, ed. G. Daigle. Montreal: Presses de l'Université de Montréal.

Murphy, Raymond. 1979. *Sociological Theories of Education*. Toronto: McGraw-Hill Ryerson.

———. 1981. "Teachers and the Evolving Structural Context of Economic and Political Attitudes in Quebec Society." *Canadian Review of Sociology and Anthropology* 18(2):157-182.

———. 1988. *Social Closure: The Theory of Monopolization and Exclusion*. Oxford: Clarendon Press.

Myrdal, Gunnar. 1944. *An American Dilemma*. New York: Harper and Bros.

Nagel, Joanne, and Susan Olzak. 1982. "Ethnic Mobilization in Old and New States: An Extension of the Competition Model." *Social Problems* 30 (December):127-143.

Neatby, Hilda. 1972. *The Quebec Act: Protest and Policy*. Scarborough, Ont.: Prentice-Hall.

Nielsen, François. 1980. "The Flemish Movement in Belgium after World War II: A Dynamic Analysis." *American Sociological Review* 45(1):76-94.

Niosi, Jorge. 1980. *La bourgeoisie canadienne: Le développement et la croissance d'une classe dominante*. Montréal: Québec-Amérique.

Noel, Alain. 1993. "Politics in a High Unemployment Society." Pp. 422-449 in *Québec: State and Society*, 2d ed., ed. Alain-G. Gagnon. Scarborough, Ont.: Nelson Canada.

Olzak, Susan. 1982. "Ethnic Mobilization in Quebec." *Ethnic and Racial Studies* 5(3):253-285.

Ouellet, Fernand. 1980. *Lower Canada 1791-1840: Social Change and Nationalism*. Toronto: McClelland and Stewart.

Park, Robert E. 1950. *Race and Culture*. New York: Free Press of Glencoe.

Parkin, Frank. 1979. *Marxism and Class Theory: A Bourgeois Critique*. London: Tavistock.

Parsons, Talcott. 1951. *The Social System*. New York: Free Press.

———. 1965. "Full Citizenship for the Negro American? A Sociological Problem." *Daedalus* 94(4):1009-1054.

Pinard, Maurice. 1975. "La dualité des loyautés et les options constitutionnelles des Québécois francophones." in *Le nationalisme québécois à la croisée des chemins*, ed. Albert Legault and Alfred O. Hero, Jr. Quebec: Centre québécois de relations internationales, Université Laval.

———. 1976. "Pluralisme social et partis politiques: Quelques éléments d'une théorie." Pp. 37-52 in *Partis politiques au Québec*, ed. Réjean Pelletier. Montreal: Hurtubise HMH.

Pineo, Peter. 1977. "The Social Standing of Ethnic and Racial Groupings in Canada." *Canadian Review of Sociology and Anthropology* 14(2):147-57.

Ponting, J. Rick. 1987. "Canadian Public Opinion on Native Issues, 1976-1986: An Overview." Paper presented at the Ninth Biennial Conference of the Canadian Ethnic Studies Association. Halifax, Nova Scotia, 16 October.

Ponting, J. Rick, and Roger Gibbins. 1980. *Out of Irrelevance: A Socio-Political Introduction to Indian Affairs in Canada.* Toronto: Butterworths.

Ponting, J. Rick, and Roger Gibbins. 1981. "The Reactions of English Canadians and French Québécois to Native Indian Protest." *Canadian Review of Sociology and Anthropology* 18(2):222-238.

Pool, Jonathan. 1969. "National Development and Language Diversity." *Monda Lingvo-Problemo* 1:140-156.

Porter, John. 1965. *The Vertical Mosaic: An Analysis of Social Class and Power in Canada.* Toronto: University of Toronto Press.

Porter, John. 1975. "Ethnic Pluralism in Canadian Perspective." in Nathan Glazer and Daniel P. Moynihan (eds.), *Ethnicity: Theory and Experience.* Cambridge: Harvard University Press.

Ragin, Charles. 1977. "Class, Status, and 'Reactive Ethnic Cleavages': the Social Bases of Political Regionalism." *American Sociological Review* 42(4):438-450.

Raynauld, André, Gérald Marion, and Richard Béland. 1965. "La répartition des revenus selon les groupes ethniques au Canada." Research report submitted to the Royal Commission on Bilingualism and Biculturalism. Ottawa: Queen's Printer.

Reader's Digest. 1991. *Eurodata.* Paris: Reader's Digest International.

Redfield, Robert, Ralph Linton, and Melville Herskovits. 1936. "Outline for the Study of Acculturation." *American Anthropologist* 38:149-152

Reed, John Shelton. 1972. *The Enduring South: Subcultural Persistence in Mass Society.* Toronto and London: D. C. Heath.

Reid, Angus. 1991. *Multiculturalism and Canadians: National Attitude Survey,* report submitted to Multiculturalism and Citizenship Canada. Toronto: Angus Reid Group.

Reid, Angus. 1993. *Reid Report.* Toronto: Angus Reid Group.

Rocher, Guy. 1973. *Le Québec en mutation.* Montreal: Hurtubise HMH.

———. 1992. "Autour de la langue: crises et débats, espoirs et tremblements." in *Le Québec en jeu: comprendre les grands défis,* ed. G. Daigle. Montreal: Les Presses de l'Université de Montréal.

Rokkan, Stein. 1970. *Citizens, Elections, Parties: Approaches to the Comparative Study of the Processes of Development.* Oslo: Universitets-forlaget.

Roseborough, Howard, and Raymond Breton. 1971. "Perceptions of the Relative Economic and Political Advantages of Ethnic Groups in Canada." Pp. 401-425 in *Canadian Society: Sociological Perspectives.* 3d ed., abridged, ed. Bernard R.

Blishen, Frank E. Jones, Kaspar D. Naegele, and John Porter. Toronto: Macmillan.

Rosenberg, M. Michael, and Jack Jedwab. 1992. "Institutional Completeness, Ethnic Organizational Style and the Role of the State: the Jewish, Italian and Greek Communities of Montreal." *Canadian Review of Sociology and Anthropology* 29 (3):266-287.

Rosenberg, Morris, and Roberta G. Simmons. 1972. *Black and White Self-Esteem: The Urban School Child.* Washington: American Sociological Association.

Royal Commission on Biculturalism and Bilingualism. 1969. *Report.* Vol. 3. *The Work World.* Ottawa: Queen's Printer.

Rudin, Ronald. 1985. *The Forgotten Quebecers: A History of English-Speaking Quebec 1759-1980.* Quebec: Institut québécois de recherche sur la culture.

———. 1993. "English-speaking Quebec: The Emergence of a Disillusioned Minority." in *Quebec: State and Society,* 2d ed., ed. Alain-G. Gagnon. Scarborough, Ont.: Nelson Canada.

Rueschemeyer, Dietrich, Evelyn H. Stephens, and John D. Stephens. 1992. *Capitalist Development and Democracy.* Chicago: University of Chicago Press.

Ryder, Norman. 1955. "The Interpretation of Origin Statistics." *Canadian Journal of Economics and Political Science* 21(4):466-479.

Ryerson, Stanley B. 1945. *Unequal Union.* Toronto: Progress Books.

Salée, Daniel. 1992. "Autodétermination autochtone, souveraineté du Québec et fédéralisme canadien." Pp. 372-401 in *Bilan québécois du fédéralisme canadien,* ed. Francois Rocher. Montreal: VLB éditeur.

Sales, Arnaud. 1979. *La bourgeoisie industrielle au Québec.* Montreal: Les Presses de l'Université de Montréal.

Sales, Arnaud, and Noel Bélanger. 1985. *Décideurs et gestionnaires: Etude sur la direction et l'encadrement des secteurs privé et public.* Quebec: Editeur officiel du Québec.

Schermerhorn, R. A. 1978. *Comparative Ethnic Relations.* Chicago: University of Chicago Press, Phoenix Edition.

Schmid, Carol L. 1981. *Conflict and Consensus in Switzerland.* Berkeley and Los Angeles: University of California Press.

Schnurmacher, Thomas. 1994. "Bronfman Tops Magazine's List of Quebec's Rich and Famous." *Montreal Gazette,* 20 July.

Shibutani, Tamotsu, and Kian M. Kwan. 1965. *Ethnic Stratification.* New York: Macmillan.

Skocpol, Theda. 1979. *States and Social Revolutions: A Comparative Analysis of France, Russia and China.* Cambridge: Cambridge University Press.

Smelser, Neil. 1964. "Toward a Theory of Modernization." in *Social Change: Sources, Patterns, and Consequences,* ed. Amitai Etzioni and Eva Etzioni. New York: Basic Books.

———. 1976. *Comparative Methods in the Social Sciences.* Englewood Cliffs, N.J.: Prentice-Hall.

Smith, Anthony D. 1971. *Theories of Nationalism.* New York: Harper and Row.

———. 1978. "The Diffusion of Nationalism: Some Historical and Sociological Perspectives." *British Journal of Sociology* 29(2):235-248.

Smith, Anthony D. 1986. "State-Making and Nation-Building." in *States in History,* ed. John A. Hall. Oxford: Basil Blackwell.

Smith, Michael R. 1994. "L'impact de Québec, Inc., répartition des revenus et efficacité économique." *Sociologie et Sociétés* 26(2):91-110.

Smooha, Sammy. 1978. *Israel: Pluralism and Conflict.* London: Routledge Kegan Paul.

Taddeo, Donat, and Raymond Taras. 1987. *Le débat linguistique au Québec.* Montreal: Presses de l'Université de Montréal.

Taylor, Charles. 1965. "Nationalism and the Political Intelligentsia: A Case Study." Queen's Quarterly 72 (spring). Reprinted in *Social and Cultural Change in Canada,* vol. 1, ed. W. E. Mann. Toronto: Copp Clark, 1970.

Taylor, Charles L. and Michael C. Hudson. *World Handbook of Political and Social Indicators.* 2d ed. New Haven, CT.: Yale University Press.

Taylor, Donald L., David J. McKirnan, John Christian, and Luc Lamarche. 1979. "Cultural Insecurity and Attitudes toward Multiculturalism and Ethnic Groups in Canada." *Canadian Ethnic Studies* 11 (2).

Trofimenkoff, Susan Mann. 1983. *The Dream of Nation: A Social and Intellectual History of Quebec.* Toronto: Gage.

Turner, Jonathan. 1974. *The Structure of Sociological Theory.* Homewood, Ill.: Dorsey Press.

Vaillancourt, François. 1992. "An Economic Perspective on Language and Public Policy in Canada and the United States." in *Immigration, Language, and Ethnicity: Canada and the United States,* ed. Barry R. Chiswick. Washington, D.C.: AEI Press.

Vaillancourt, François. 1993. "The Economic Status of the French Language and Francophones in Quebec." in *Quebec: State and Society,* 2d ed., ed. Alain-G. Gagnon. Scarborough Ont.: Nelson Canada.

Van den Berghe, Pierre L. 1967. *Race and Racism: A Comparative Perspective.* New York: Wiley.

Van den Berghe, Pierre L. 1972. "Paternalistic vs. Competitive Race Relations." in *Racial and Ethnic Relations,* 2d ed., ed. Bernard Segal. New York: Crowell Collier.

Van den Berghe, Pierre L. 1973. "Pluralism." in *Handbook of Social and Cultural Anthropology,* ed. John J. Honigmann. Chicago: Rand McNally.

Verdery, Katherine. 1979. "Internal Colonialism in Austria-Hungary." *Ethnic and Racial Studies* 2(3):379-399.

Vincent, Sylvie. 1992. "La révélation d'une force politique: les Autochtones." Pp. 749-790 in *Le Québec en jeu: Comprendre les grands défis*, ed. G. Daigle. Montreal: Les Presses de l'Université de Montréal.

Wallerstein, Immanuel. 1979. *The Capitalist World-Economy*. Cambridge: Cambridge University Press.

Weber, Max. 1978. *Economy and Society: An Outline of Interpretive Sociology*. Rev. ed., ed. Gunther Roth and Claus Wittich. Berkeley: University of California Press.

Weiner, Myron. 1978. *Sons of the Soil: Migration and Ethnic Conflict in India*. Princeton: Princeton University Press.

Weinfeld, Morton. 1985. "Myth and Reality in the Canadian Mosaic: 'Affective Ethnicity'." Pp. 65-86 in *Ethnicity and Ethnic Relations in Canada*, 2d ed., ed. Rita M. Bienvenue and Jay E. Goldstein. Toronto: Butterworths.

Wirth, Louis. 1945. "The Problem of Minority Groups." in *The Science of Man in the World Crisis*, ed. Ralph Linton. New York: Columbia University Press. Reprinted in *Minority Responses: Comparative Views of Reactions to Subordination*, ed. Minako Kurokawa. New York: Random House, 1970.

———. 1964. *On Cities and Social Life*. Chicago: University of Chicago Press.

Young, Crawford. 1976. *The Politics of Cultural Pluralism*. Madison: University of Wisconsin Press.

Zeitlin, Irving. 1973. *Rethinking Sociology*. Englewood Cliffs, N.J.: Prentice-Hall.

Zolberg, Aristide. 1975. "Les nationalismes et le nationalisme québécois," in *Le nationalisme québécois à la croisée des chemins*, ed. Albert Legault and Alfred O. Hero, Jr. Quebec: Centre québécois de relations internationales, Université Laval.

INDEX

ABOUT THE AUTHOR

LESLIE S. LACZKO was born in Hungary and moved to Quebec as a child with his parents. He holds degrees from the University of California, Berkeley, and McGill University and is an associate professor of sociology at the University of Ottawa.